Scarecrows

Four seeds you have to sow.
One for the rook and one for the crow,
One to die and one to grow.

An old country rhyme

Scarecrows

Gregory Holyoake

UNICORN PRESS

For radio presenter

BARBARA STURGEON

a country girl at heart.

Unicorn Press
76 Great Suffolk Street
London SE1 0BL

www.unicornpress.org
email: unicornpress@btinternet.com

First published by Unicorn Press 2006

ISBN 0 906290 83 X

Designed by Mick Keates
Printed in China for Compass Press Limited

Half-title: Traditional scarecrow in Tony Cruse's garden, Wiltshire.
Title pages: Gary waves the flag for Britain on an allotment in Ashford

CONTENTS

INTRODUCTION

"As the crow flies..."

SCARECROWS are making a reappearance in our fields to liven up a leisurely stroll, country drive or train journey. Dressed in cast-off clothes and draped over crossed sticks these quaint, ragged figures with their wide open arms seem to welcome us to the countryside.

Today scarecrows can be found in a variety of places keeping vigil over farms, allotments, small holdings and garden centres. They appear in the early spring to protect winter corn and oilseed rape but latecomers arrive to guard summer fruits.

Examples have been spotted perched in trees protecting cherries, watching over vegetable plots in back gardens and even guarding the coastline to prevent seagulls from stealing food when driven inland by wintry weather. They scare not only crows but rooks, sparrows, starlings and particularly pigeons, those persistent pests who display a voracious appetite for succulent peas.

Farmers have experimented in recent decades with a variety of devices including gas guns, kites, balloons and chemicals to discourage wild birds from devouring their valuable seeds, shoots and crops. The best of these inventions combine sight with sound and are undoubtedly effective in the short term. Yet there are drawbacks: they may be prone to vandalism, they sometimes develop a mechanical fault or their use has been restricted by increasingly tight controls over noise pollution.

Most farmers agree that there is no true substitute for a workman, preferably armed with a shotgun, patrolling their fields. In times past this was perfectly feasible when village boys or retired farmhands were employed to chase away birds but nowadays labour costs are too prohibitive. Hence the return to the tradition of placing a substitute for the human race – stuffed and static – in the fields.

All scarecrows have the same basic shape – an upright figure supported by crossed sticks and packed with rags, straw or paper – but dressing them presents a challenge. Their frame allows an ideal opportunity for recycling and body parts can be formed from a variety of discarded materials. A few figures sport formal attire such as an old three-piece suit or morning coat complete with top hat and silk scarf but most wear casual clothing: jeans, dungarees, corduroys and raincoats. Accoutrements may include an umbrella, shooting stick or even an imitation blunderbuss!

opposite: Charlie Chalk, Dover.

Heads are ingeniously formed from flowerpots, footballs, upturned buckets, hessian sacks, carved timber, pillow cases, turnips, swedes and pumpkins. Hats, often set at a rakish angle, appear in profusion – deerstalkers, sou'westers, school caps, sun hats, bowlers, trilbies, panamas, homburgs. Fashion accessories number belts, bags, gloves and headscarves. But farmers be warned: tramps have been known to strip scarecrows of their better clothing while stray horses may munch on the straw stuffing.

Scarecrows exert their influence for only a limited period of time until the birds perceive that these silent figures can render them no actual harm. Their effectiveness depends largely upon movement so various devices have been devised to fool wily birds. Paper streamers, coloured ribbons or strings of silver foil dangle from the arms; tin cans, broken mirrors and computer discs tied to the cross bar tinkle in the wind while long sticks looking from a distance like barrels of a shotgun sway alarmingly.

A recent innovation has been the female scarecrow. Indeed, activists in the feminist movement held aloft a dressmaker's dummy fixed to crossed sticks on which were draped a bra and handbag on their protest march through London in the early 1970s. It looked for all the world like a militant scarecrow! Normally, these are more conventionally garbed. They are either dressed in country tweeds, casually parading in summer frocks or elegantly draped in designer gowns with shoes, handbags and hats worthy of Ascot. Their arrival in the fields may not be due entirely to the effectiveness of Women's Lib. Farmers simply recognise that ladies' flapping dresses and rippling hair can be formidable deterrents against marauders.

Occasionally, scarecrows are arranged in groups to form a striking tableau. They have been observed playing in a pop band, attending a bridal party, driving tractors, climbing trees, placed in stocks and – shamelessly – sitting on a loo! They have been reported rising from hedgerows like a ghost, slumped against a telegraph pole like a drunkard and wrapped in plastic bin liners to imitate punk rockers. Once an entire suit of armour was reassembled as a scarecrow in the early 19th century.

Masks enable scarecrows to resemble national celebrities such as pop stars, politicians and even members of the royal family. Thus Prince Charles, Princess Diana, Camilla, Margaret Thatcher, John Major and Tony Blair have all been spotted in spare moments guarding crops and vegetables in the heart of the countryside. Curiously, scarecrows, like waiters, are often dressed a decade behind in terms of fashion and unwittingly preserve a touch of history. One character dressed in the uniform of a British Rail guard was spotted beside the railway line at Dover while a representative of the National Coal Board was noticed in cabbage fields at Ramsgate near the redundant collieries of East Kent.

The image of a scarecrow has inspired everything from cake decoration to tattoos, from key rings to costume jewellery. Brittains, the famous toy manufacturer, added a lead scarecrow dressed in a top coat and bowler hat to their Home Farm lead farmyard in 1924 and Mattel Toys marketed Barbie Dolls in a 'Wizard

opposite: Lyme Regis lady.

of Oz' collection for their 'Hollywood Legends' including Ken dressed as the Scarecrow in 1996. Lilliput Lane miniatures placed a tiny scarecrow in the allotment of their Collectors' Club Special, 'Gardener's Cottage', while a novelty teapot in the form of a scarecrow has been produced by the Teapottery, Keswick. And a cheerful scarecrow appeared on an Iranian stamp to celebrate Children's Week in 1974.

Scarecrows are sometimes regarded by their makers as a firm friend and once or twice they are even brought into their owner's homes. "When we gave a dinner party at our house for a party of arty folk from the village we found we were thirteen to dinner," revealed Carolyn Stone from Lower Buckton, Leintwardine, Shropshire. "Not wanting to tempt fate, we borrowed a scarecrow from a neighbouring farm and laid a place for him at the head of the table. We kept replenishing his glass, which I obligingly drank as I went round serving courses. It was odd to see him sitting nonchalantly between a county judge and a Q.C. The scarecrow looked aghast as the judge's wife sat on his lap and we all ended up dancing with him on the dining room table!"

Sue Underwood, an holistic therapist from Deal in Kent, was pursuaded by her business partner to rent an allotment one spring. Her two children, Daniel and Becky, made her the perfect birthday gift of a scarecrow to oversee the new plot. "He was beautifully dressed with fabulous features like glasses, nose and moustache," she recalls. "I named him Russ after my favourite actor, Russell (would-you-believe-it?) Crowe, star of cult film, 'The Gladiator.'

"Trouble was I was expelled from the allotments soon after," Sue winces. "I'd paid someone to dig it over and then I stuck in lots of sticks pretending I'd planted seeds. I thought I'd just turn up on a sunny afternoon with my glass of wine and expect the other gardeners to take pity on me and hand over some of their vegetables. The manager told me firmly that this was not quite the spirit and asked me, politely but firmly, to leave."

Sue brought her scarecrow home and placed him in the bay window of her seafront home. He became a permanent feature so she dressed him in clothes to match the seasons. At Christmas Sue decorated Russ with flashing lights, baubles and a plastic star. "Friends were envious of my novel Christmas tree and thought it the most unusual they'd ever seen."

At the end of the season, though, most hardworking scarecrows will inevitably be thrown on the rubbish tip or dumped upon a bonfire – a miserable reward for standing solitary in the fields in all weathers, rain or shine, from dawn to dusk. Its only friends will have been a stray pheasant, perhaps, or a foraging fox sheltering from a storm beneath its overcoat. Then, again, a field mouse might breed in one of its pockets or a family of robins nest inside its battered hat. Luckier scarecrows will be stored in a barn for the winter and redressed ready to be returned to the fields the following spring.

opposite: Football head, Kent.

1. SCARECROWS IN HISTORY

THE ORIGIN OF SCARECROWS is cloaked in paradox and mystery. Their outstretched arms nailed to crossed sticks suggest crucified victims staked out on desolate fields. They shock predators and trespassers alike, haunting remote farmland from dawn to dusk. And yet on closer inspection their comical features and artistic touches often reveal an imaginative creator intent on bringing humour to our bleak countryside in early spring.

Scarecrows may be hastily made by vexed commercial farmers who dress them in second hand clothes to do a real job of work keeping pestilent birds from valuable crops or they may be painstakingly constructed by refined weekend gardeners from natural materials to adorn organic allotments. Whatever their purpose, their fate is to be reduced by the elements to torn rags on jagged sticks, bowing humbly to the wind.

Today they are regarded as being more ornamental than ominous. Indeed, they have influenced both fashion and commerce in modern times. The 'Scarecrow Look' of the late 1980s briefly brought country casuals to the city while designer scarecrows often appear in the media to lure customers into purchasing a vast array of consumer goods.

GREEK GOD

Britain's humble scarecrow may have derived from a Greek god of fertility named 'Priapus' (or 'Priapos') Originally, Priapus was worshipped in the region of the ancient Hellespont – now the Dardanelles – of Turkey. His cult was adopted by the Greeks after Alexander the Great (356–323 B.C.) encouraged interchange of religious and cultural ideas between East and West. It flourished in influential Hellenistic cities such as the Egyptian port of Alexandria but it also spread to Italy where it became popular in Rome. Worship of Priapus thrived throughout the third century although it was never taken seriously as he was treated, apparently, with affectionate disrespect.

opposite: Tweezle.

According to Greek mythology, Priapus was the illegitimate son of Aphrodite and Zeus (although his father is given variously as Adonis, Dionysus, Hermes and Pan) Their child was represented as an ugly, bearded dwarf with a red face and gigantic phallus. A legend tells how Zeus' jealous wife, Hera, ensured the infant was born with this rude deformity to mock the lovers' deceitful affair. Aphrodite heartlessly abandoned Priapus in the mountains but he was found by nomadic shepherds who raised him since they found the misshapen youth useful in guarding their flocks and scaring off trespassers.

Priapus was regarded as the protector of farmers, shepherds, fishermen, vine growers, bee keepers and goatherds. His emblems were the cornucopia, pruning knife and a phallus, and he received first fruits with libations of milk and honey. Further, he was adopted as the guardian of orchards, gardens and vineyards where his crude statues, painted bright red, were erected to ward off thieves. Donkeys, asses and pigs were his sacrificial animals, reflecting his animal lust, and there is extant a collection of 'priapeia', anonymous, obscene Latin verses. *The Oxford Classical Dictionary* underlines this dual role of Priapus: "He was adopted as a god of gardens, where his statue was a sort of combined scarecrow and guardian deity."

The Romans copied the Greek custom of carving wooden statues of Priapus to ward off birds from their fruit and crops. Columella, a Spanish gardener cum Roman soldier who lived in the first century A.D., cultivated vast acres of land in Central Italy. He recommended that Priapic statues should ideally be hewn out of an old tree stump in his treatise on agriculture, 'De Re Rustica' (*c*.65 A.D.). Roman gardeners daubed figures of this rustic satyr purple and gave him a club in one hand, to make him appear more dangerous, plus a sickle in the other to ensure an abundant harvest.

Male mannequin on a misty morning at Penshurst.

Gradually, the Romans adopted this rude hermes as a household god where he was credited with bringing fertility and prosperity to the inhabitants. Roman citizens placed fountain statues of Priapus spurting jets of water from his penis in their courtyards and wall paintings of him surrounded with baskets of fruit and garlands of greenery in the villas. Replicas of Priapus' phallus were hung adorned with bells on the threshold of houses to ward off evil spirits and bring good luck to the occupants. A painting of Priapus weighing his huge member graced a prominent wall of the House of Vettii in Pompeii. It was abruptly buried by the eruption of Mount Vesuvius in 79 A.D. but today the restored panel, which miraculously survived, is on display.

When Roman armies ventured into Gaul (this region encompassed France, parts of Belgium, southern Holland, western Germany and northern Italy) they introduced the conquered races to scarecrows in the form of Priapus who was guaranteed to protect their newly-planted crops and vineyards. His cult was eventually introduced into Britain during the Roman occupation (43–400 A.D.) where he became a feature of villas and vineyards. Images of the deity were also placed in the centre of ornamental gardens, especially near beehives, where he wielded a reaping hook. Alas, there is only one solitary trace of his ancient cult to survive. A relief depicting a horned god with a Latin inscription which translates, "the phallus of Priapus", was located at the front of 'Birrens' to the north-west of Hadrian's Wall. Perhaps it was displayed as an ornament to a garden wall?

The arrival in Kent of St Augustine and his monks in 597 A.D. ensured that the worship of Priapus, however lightly honoured, diminished since it represented obscenities that were deeply offensive to Christians. European farmers, nonetheless, have over the centuries unwittingly perpetuated this dubious connection between a bountiful harvest and a Greek god famed for his licentiousness. Even today, scarecrows, which are generally male, emulate Priapus' comical – and frequently vulgar – stance poking fun at and frightening off trespassers.

PAGAN SACRIFICES

An alternative – and far more gruesome – possibility is that scarecrows evolved from human sacrifices to the gods of nature by primitive tribes to ensure the survival of their crops. Victims, who were mainly, although not exclusively, male were sacrificed so that their seed would fertilise the virgin earth.

The Druids, who formed the influential priesthood of the Celtic tribes at the time of the Roman invasions of Britain, officiated at human sacrifices after successful battles as a thank offering to powerful spirits. Strabo (c.63 B.C.–24 A.D.) the Greek historian, geographer and philosopher, chronicled the barbaric practices of the Gallic Celts whose territory stretched from Northern Italy to Southern Britain: "We are told of still other kinds of sacrifices; for example, they would shoot victims to death with arrows, or impale them in temples, or, having built a colossus of straw and wood, throw in cattle and animals of all sorts and human beings, and then make a burnt offering of the whole thing."

Julius Caesar (*c.*100 B.C.–44 B.C.) the Roman General who conquered almost the entire Celtic world, was determined to stamp out such barbaric practices. He expressed revulsion in his *Commentaries* that Celts immolated human beings, generally criminals, and employed Druids to oversee these cruel ceremonies. Caesar was horrified that the Celts of Gaul "make use of colossal figures composed of twigs which they fill with living men and set on fire." (Gallic War VI 2.16). Modern scholars warn that both Strabo and Caesar are biased in their comments and rely heavily on the observations of a Greek explorer, Posidonious (*c.*135–50 B.C.) whose original histories of the ancient world have perished.

Peter Berresford Ellis includes a visualisation of one towering 'Wicker Man' in his authorative, *A Brief History of the Druids* (2002) but he, also, cautions that both Caesar and Strabo's views may be pure propaganda written at a time when the Romans were contemplating their expeditions to Britain. Archaeological excavations of the Celtic hill fort at Danebury in Wiltshire, however, revealed the wholesale burial of human and animal sacrifices in deep pits where grain was stored which experts have interpreted as either a thank offering to the underground gods for preserving the grain or as a propitiation in the hope of a good harvest. Further, Drs Ross and Robins, after studying the strangled body in the bog known as 'Lindow Man' found at Wilmslow, near Manchester, in 1984, affirm British Celts practised capital punishment but turned it into a religious act. "Human beings were sacrificed," they conclude, "in order to propitiate the gods of blight and crop failure."

Sir James Frazer (1854–1941) in *The Golden Bough*, a study of magic and religion in twelve volumes, catalogued the savagery of ritual sacrifice in the ancient world – from Africa to Egypt, from Sweden to Greece – which fascinated anthropological scholars of Victorian and Edwardian Britain. He rehearsed in repulsive detail the methods of human sacrifice by primitive tribes to ensure the survival of their crops or to thank pagan gods for a plentiful harvest.

Ancient Mexicans, for instance, conceived the maize as a personal being who experienced the whole human life cycle. They offered victims at certain times of the year to coincide with the age of their crops. Therefore, they sacrificed new-born babies when the maize was sown; older children when it sprouted and mature men when it was fully ripened. At Lagos, in Nigeria, it was the custom annually for fetishmen to impale a young girl alive, alongside sheep and goats, yams and maize, soon after the spring equinox. Often the ritual of the killing reflected the method of harvesting the crops. Thus, African tribesmen bludgeoned their victims with spades and hoes while Mexican natives ground them, like corn, between two stones.

Pawnee Indians first fattened their victim (mercifully kept in ignorance of his fate) before dressing him in gaudy clothes and tying him to a stake where he was pierced by arrows and beheaded by a tomahawk. Philippine Islanders, who were passionate head hunters, decapitated at least one luckless human on every farm, hanging them on a sacred tree for the benefit of their rice crops. Horrifically, Frazer recorded in the abridged edition of his work published in 1922: "These sacrifices have been offered by men now living..."

Frazer also delved into ancient mythology to account for the sacrifice of human victims when they were regarded as substitutes for the primitive harvest deities. Artemis, Greek Goddess of Nature, was suspended in effigy above her sacred grove among the Arcadian Hills where she was known as the 'Hanged One.' Osiris, the Egyptian Corn God, was also represented by an image moulded of earth and corn which was buried with funereal rites in order that, dying, he might come to life and enrich new crops. Such strange customs are examples of harmless charms and sympathetic magic yet Frazer warns that there is evidence that at one time "the slain corn-spirit was represented by a human victim."

Wicker Man

Kings who grandly presented themselves to their tribes as gods were themselves sacrificed for the fruitfulness of the earth. Legends in places as diverse as Norway and British New Guinea point to the gruesome practice of dismembering the body of a king, priest or magician and burying their flesh in different parts of the country in order to ensure the fertility of the soil and the fecundity of man and beast. A belief commonly held among primitive tribes was that their king controlled the elements and that he must be held responsible for the failure of their crops owing to the inclemency of the weather. Inevitably, kings, who demanded to be worshipped as gods, found it was their ill luck to be sacrificed to ensure fertility until they hit upon the idea of substituting a deputy in their stead! At first it was thought appropriate that the king's son should die in his place, although he, too, was replaced by the sacrifice of animals and, later still, effigies which may be the forerunner of our scarecrows.

Frazer further considered that the sacrificial rites of the Gallic Celts on which the fertility of the land was thought to depend could be traced in the ubiquitous fire festivals which he witnessed in nineteenth-century Europe. Grotesque wicker-work giants, often concealing men who artfully manipulated them, were dragged on rollers through the city streets and set alight to the amusement of the populace each summer. Fire festivals were held formerly in parts of England including Coventry, Chester and Salisbury.

Frazer quotes an anonymous sixteenth-century writer who watched "uglie giants, marching as if they were alive, and armed at all points, but within they are stuffed full of browne paper and tow", burned publicly as the climax to one Midsummer pageant. Again, the author noted that the most clear and unequivocal traces of human sacrifices yet lingered in the Beltane fires which were lit each May Day in the Central Highlands of Scotland among a Celtic people, who situated in a remote corner of Britain and almost completely isolated from foreign influence, "had till then conserved their old heathenism better than any other people of Eastern Europe."

All these festivals, unlike the Druid ceremonies, took place without expenditure of human life. Yet Frazer in *The Golden Bough* also catalogues horrific annual bonfires in past centuries where small animals, particularly cats, were burned alive in wicker cages or baskets throughout Europe. These, he concluded, were considered to be "familiars" that were killed to exorcise their evil spirits intent on blighting farmers' crops. He further reminded his readers of the habit of burning witches in Britain during the sixteenth and seventeenth centuries and he suggested that: "The execution of these wretches is really calculated to ensure an abundant harvest by removing one of the principal causes which paralyse the efforts and blasts the hopes of the husbandmen."

Barbara Walker's *A Woman's Dictionary of Symbols and Sacred Objects* (1988) summarises this theory that scarecrows are the substitute for human sacrifice: ". . . the custom of setting up a man on a wooden cross, as a magical protection for fields, has been practised from remote antiquity. The original scarecrow seems to have been an actual sacrifice in prehistoric times. Later, the sacrificial god-man was dismembered, like Osiris, and pieces of his flesh or blood were distributed to all the fields of the land to encourage crops."

Christians believe that Jesus, who was both human and divine, made the supreme sacrifice by dying on a cross to reconcile Man with God. His death, they contend, was for the benefit of all mankind rather than a ritual slaughter to ensure the survival of crops. Christianity has spread over two thousand years to influence civilisation of the entire Western World. Nonetheless, pagan customs linger and have become confused with Christian ideas across modern Europe.

In Northern France, where Druidic rites were once prevalent, an effigy of Christ on the cross is set amidst the corn each spring. In Germany, a straw figure of Judas who betrayed Christ is burned in churchyards and the charred stake planted in the fields to preserve the wheat from blight on May Day. In Finland, the sacrificial spirit supposed to protect crops is still known as 'Pellon Pekko' ('Little Peter of the Fields') This refers to the tradition that St Peter the Apostle was crucified for his faith on an inverted cross and that an upturned stake among the corn will allow the "petra", or phallic spirit, to pass into the ground to fertilise Mother Earth. And in Britain, it is surely a remarkable coincidence that scarecrows with their distorted bodies that appear to imitate a crucifixion are placed in the fields at Eastertide.

Claudia de Lys suggests in her *Book of Superstitions* (1979) that the Christian cross was regarded by farmers as a charm to ward off harmful spirits. "Originally it was the cross symbol in the guise of a man, that was placed outdoors as a protective power to keep away robber-birds and other intruders. The scarecrow is a ridiculous object today but once, with its suggestion of a human cross, it was intended to keep at a distance all evil influences and to terrify without inflicting injury."

The practice of strapping the bodies of sacrificial victims to crosses in fields to appease the gods of fertility and fecundity would have had an undesirable side effect. Gruesome corpses may have kept wild birds away initially but they would eventually have attracted carrion crows who seized the opportunity to feed off the rotten flesh. When it was realised they had little influence in appeasing the gods – the weather in Britain being notoriously fickle – folklorists believe that human sacrifices were replaced with wooden or straw effigies.

It is plainly evident that the horrific ritual of staking out a sacrificial victim – arms outstretched and head bowed in agonising death throes – resembles the stance of the scarecrow. Possibly, these grotesque creatures in our rural landscape are the linear descendants of pagan sacrifices – gods or men – now offered in effigy and, although no longer thought of by farmers as offerings to a deity to ensure an abundant harvest, scarecrows still fulfil the role of guardians of the fields.

ROOK AND CROW

Cultivation of the fields for the production of wheat and barley was a most fundamentally important activity of medieval England. It provided for the two essential ingredients of daily life: bread and ale. The method of sowing was for a man with a wicker basket to broadcast seeds by hand. He would be closely followed by a heavy horse pulling a harrow to cover the seeds in the furrow. This primitive style of sowing was an open invitation for birds to scavenge and the problem is highlighted by two illuminated paintings in the *Luttrell Psalter.*

The Psalter, which was commissioned by Sir Geoffrey Luttrell (1276–1345) of Irnham, Lincolnshire, is now in the British Library. Psalters containing a calendar, psalms, collects, canticles and a litany in Latin were a grander version of the Continental 'Books of Hours.' Such lavishly decorated personal prayer books were prized by the English nobility. *The Luttrell Psalter* was written and illuminated on quality vellum in the neighbourhood of East Anglia around 1340. The text is presented in large, square, liturgical script and was obviously designed to be read at a short distance. This Psalter is famous for its sequence of richly-detailed scenes of fourteenth-century life, literally spanning the cradle to the grave.

Most valued are the agricultural scenes. The anonymous artist depicts the activity, 'Sowing', by painting a farmer scattering grain from a rectangular box with wattled sides which he carries slung around his neck. He includes an amusing detail of a fat crow dipping into the sower's seedbag while his dog chases a second bird off the newly-sown field. A companion painting, 'Harrowing', presents another action picture where a slinger attempts to hit a pair of thieving birds but one of his shots passes midway between them. (A third vignette shows a patient clerk catching a bird in a snare, which consists of a net attached to a rope on a long pole, presumably for food.)

In medieval times crows were one of the few protected birds. They were enticed into towns and cities to feed upon offal thrown overnight onto the streets. There, acting as scavengers, they also fed upon exposed flesh of traitors whose heads were spiked on poles and whose bodies were hung on gibbets for crimes against their sovereign. By pecking at eyes, these birds were thought to develop supernatural vision so that they could

'Sowing' from the *Luttrell Psalter* of Irnham, Lincolnshire
British Library, London/The Bridgeman Art Library

see into the future. Countrymen believed that if several crows fluttered over a man's head he was marked for death and that if they forsook a wood in unison, poverty and famine were sure to follow. Witches favoured crows as their familiars for divination and they often appeared in paintings as the epitome of evil.

Superstition may also account in part for the late appearance of scarecrows in the countryside of Britain. (All black birds were termed 'crows' at one time which might be the reason why the standing figure in the field acquired the blanket term, 'Scarecrow'.) Country folk, steeped in myth and legend, firmly believed in the power of witchcraft. They thought that discarded clothes could still be used to exert control over the original owner – for good or evil – even from a distance. Naturally, they were reluctant to lend any clothing, particularly intimate items such as a hat, a scarf or a glove, that might be used for casting harmful spells.

Successive monarchs gradually became convinced that certain wild birds brought devastation to crops and caused economic damage. James I of Scotland (1406–1437) ordered the destruction of rooks in 1424. His law was ratified in 1533 when an Act was passed "to destroy choughs, crows and rooks" because of alleged harm they did to corn. Parishes were required to set nets to capture the birds or, failing that, pay a daily fine of ten shillings.

Henry VIII also recognised that these same birds were causing problems to farmers in England and he commanded that every labourer should actively destroy them. Parishes of at least ten households were directed to provide nets and facilities for catching pestilent birds. Elizabeth I reinforced her father's edict to eliminate "noyfull fowls" including the corvids, buzzard, cormorant, kite, osprey, harrier, shag, woodpecker, kingfisher, cormorant and bullfinch. Churchwardens were given authority to pay a bonus for their destruction and funds were raised by increasing taxes.

Farming flourished so that young children and mature men gained plentiful employment as human birdscarers. They patrolled the fields waving their arms and crying wildly but sometimes they were armed with either a catapult and a bag of stones or, for the more skilful, a crossbow. There are several references to these valiant "shooers" or "scarers" in early literature.

Thomas Tusser (1524–1580) was a musician who also penned a practical guide to farming, *Five Hundred Good Points of Husbandrie* (1557) He owned land at Cattawade in Suffolk where he cultivated fields close to those which would later be worked by John Constable's family in the eighteenth century. Tusser's book, published in the year that Elizabeth I ascended the throne, is the source for a great number of rural proverbs, saws and platitudes. A few of these refer to scaring birds away with weapons:

> With sling or bowe,
> Keep corn from Crowe.
>
> *September's Abstract*

> No sooner sowing, but out by and by,
> with mother or boy, that Alarum can cry:
> and let them be armed with sling or bowe,
> to skare away piggen, the rooks and the crowe.
>
> *September's Husbandry*

Interestingly, a footnote in the *New Edition* (1812) asserts:

> "The rook and the crow are no doubt injurious at seed-time and harvest; but as they are
> rather insectivorous than granivorous birds, they amply compensate at other seasons for
> any temporary depredations, if properly watched. Their numbers unquestionably should
> be kept within bounds, but to exterminate them would be to leave the earth a prey to
> grubs and worms. Pigeons, however, are at all times destructive. It is calculated that a pair
> of them would eat a quarter of corn a year. The returns from them, in every possible way,
> can be no equivalent for this."

Earliest mention of farm boys employed as scarecrows in print occurs in *The Arte of Rhetorique* (1553) written by the courtier, statesman and author, Thomas Wilson (1525–1581). Wilson was born in Lincolnshire, although he spurned his fellow countrymen for their dullness and rusticity when he sought the intellectual stimulus of London life. He was educated at King's College, Cambridge, before travelling widely abroad and settling in Rome where his writing was regarded as heretical. At one time Wilson was implicated in an intrigue at the Papal Court against Cardinal Pole and he was arrested by the Inquisition. He was tortured but escaped with his life after a timely insurrection in the city. Wilson returned to England during the last year of the reign of catholic Mary and continued to write under the patronage of protestant Elizabeth.

Wilson's *Arte of Rhetorique* was a popular tome often reprinted until its demand dwindled around the time of the Spanish Armada. It was read avidly by seekers after eloquence and literary skill and is regarded by some as "the first work of criticism in the English language." The author compares, in his archaic country style, public speakers, who give their opinions without prior thought or due consideration, to boys employed as vociferous bird scarers:

> "But they that take vppon them to talke in open audience, and make not their accompt
> before, what they will fpeake after: fhall neither be well liked for their inuention, nor
> allowed for their wit, nor efteemed for their learning. For what other thing doe they, that
> boult out their wordes in fuch fort, and without all aduefement vtter out matter: but fhew
> themfelues to play as yong boys or fcarre Crowes doe, which fhout in the open and plaine
> fields at all aduentures hittie miffie."

During times of war and pestilence there was inevitably a reduced manpower on the land. In 1348, when the Great Plague struck Britain and killed half the population, landowners were forced to find other means of protecting their crops. Scarecrows, which are humans in effigy, may then have begun to take the place of the humble farm labourers although they were never as effective as the roving birdscarer. The poet, Robert Bloomfield (1766–1823) alludes to the substitution of static scarecrows for men armed with rifles in 'The Farmer's Boy' (1798). He implies that their effect is as limited as the gruesome practice of stringing up shot birds as a deterrent to other pests:

> But still unsafe the big swoln grain below,
> A fav'rite morsel with the Rook and Crow;
> From field to field the flock increasing goes;
> To level crops most formidable foes:
> Their danger well the wary plunders know,
> And place a watch on some conspicuous bough;
> Yet oft the sculking gunner by surprise
> Will scatter death amongst them as they rise.
> These, hung in triumph round the spacious field,
> At best will but a short-lived terror yield:
> Nor guards of property: (not penal law,
> But harmless riflemen of rags and straw);
> Familiariz'd to these, they boldly rove,
> Nor heed such centinels that never move.

FIELD POLICE

For centuries, elderly people and young children were employed in scaring birds away from growing corn by unscrupulous farmers who treated them badly and made them poor recompense. These "Crusoes of the lonely field" were armed with homemade devices such as an old pail and stick which they beat or a tin can filled with pebbles which they repeatedly shook. Alternatively, they were provided with catapults and a bag of stones to aim at individual birds or sometimes they were handed a firearm which they perilously fired in order to drive off persistent offenders. As a last resort they shouted, at least for part of the time, which brought its own benefits since the bird scarer could at least hear a human voice, albeit his own. Young Joseph Ashby of Tysoe gave another reason to a sympathetic enquirer, "You couldn't cry when you shouted!"

'Rook starving', as bird scaring was termed, was one of the most hated tasks on a country farm.

Misericord of bird scarers,
St Mary's Church, Ripple

It was such a lonesome occupation because one scarer was sufficient to patrol several acres. Cold and hungry, the unfortunate labourer had to keep constantly on the move and anyone caught taking a break received a sharp reprimand from the farmer who in most instances did not hesitate to wield his stick. One old lady in Blaxhall, East Suffolk, was employed to scare crows for the whole of the harvest holidays for the princely sum of six shillings in Queen Victoria's reign. The poor woman was required to shake a wooden clapper all day long and whenever she fell silent the farmer would look out from the comfort of his house or send his bailiff to investigate.

St Mary's Church at Ripple, Hereford and Worcester, possesses a series of fifteenth-century pictorial carved misericords (hinged seats for clergy) in the chancel depicting the monthly tasks of the medieval farmer. April is suitably represented by a pair of human birdscarers dressed in tunics with impossibly wide sleeves. Their arms are raised and their mouths wide open as they scamper across the fields to shoo away the birds. One man wields a club while his partner carries a rattle (sometimes mistaken for a flag) This primitive instrument probably involved a lantern wheel fixed to the handle which caused the clapper to click on each of its staves as the body was rotated with each flick of the wrist. This is the earliest known example of a medieval rattle with its clever application of a miniature lantern wheel, commonly found in postmills.

Three types of scarers evolved intended to complement a person's voice. The simplest were homemade wooden shingles tied in pairs to a flat handle so that they made a tremendous din when shaken. An alternative was the iron rattle composed of discs threaded on a spindle. The most effective tool, however, was the rattle with its toothed wheel that clicked upon springy strips of beech. Improvisation was commonplace in the country, though, and there is one account of a perfectly effective birdscarer formed from the busk of a grandmother's stays!

The development of firearms provided farmers with deadly weapons to combat the problem of crows. The medieval crossbow, which fired iron bolts, was replaced by the shotgun to stalk nuisance birds in the Stuart period. Shooting wildlife became more accurate with the invention of breech loading guns, double-barrelled shotguns and the indiscriminate blunderbusses. Parties on country estates throughout the following centuries enjoyed the ruthless slaughter of any predatory bird although their sport, admittedly, focused mainly on acquiring prodigious bags of game. More humanely, the agriculturist, William Cobbett (1763–1835) recommends shooting at birds with powder which "will alarm them so that they will quit the spot" in *The English Gardener* (1829).

The Agricultural Revolution in the countryside between 1700 and 1850 coincided with the expansion of the population of Britain which trebled in size. Tenant farmers with capital and expertise seized the opportunity to extend their farmland deep into previously uncultivated territory. Corn and wheat were required to feed the population during the protracted French and American Wars when imported food was prohibited. Modern inventions such as mechanised seed drills completely revolutionised farming and new crops were introduced such as turnips which fed both men and animals. (A few served as heads for scarecrows).

Children were widely employed on farms in those dark times with such unenviable tasks as "mushroom watching" or "muck knocking." The season began in early spring when they were engaged in a range of tedious tasks including weeding allotments, setting potatoes, wood chopping, collecting acorns, minding cows, rat catching and stone picking which enabled the farmer to plough his fields unhindered. (Stones were utilised for making walls and paths.) Children worked in groups with their family or under the supervision of an experienced labourer. Bird scaring, however, was universally hated by youngsters because they were required to venture out into the desolate fields at first light and remain there until the birds had gone to roost. They operated in the rawest winter months when the seeds were

Bird scaring was a major occupation for country boys in the early and mid-Victorian years. (*Punch* 1852)

sown and later in the full summer heat as the corn began to ripen. Further, they worked seven days a week although it was customary not to pay children for working on the Sabbath. Yet this work was a healthier alternative to labouring in factories or down the mines which opened up during the Industrial Revolution that swept towns and cities in the late-eighteenth and early-nineteenth centuries.

Mothers, particularly, welcomed the opportunity to send their offspring into the fields since the money they earned aided the modest family income. Elizabeth Wilson, a labourer's wife from Exning, in Suffolk, recorded in the 1860s that her son earned "5d a day for six days, or 2s and 6d a week" but "nothing for Sundays." Despite the long hours, bird scaring provided plentiful opportunities for employment throughout the farming year. "The chief times are when the corn is sown and when it is getting ripe, but sometimes birds are kept from the stacks too," Mrs Wilson explained to a social worker. "One of my boys had to do this all through the winter. The crows come and pull the straws out and litter them all over the field, so that they have to be picked up."

A team of boys could often prove a nuisance in the village. One annoying trick they might play was to rattle their clackers outside doors and windows demanding food. Robert Chambers in his *Book of Days* (1866) confirms this practice: "Boys used to go about clacking at doors, to get eggs or bits of bacon wherewith to make up a feast among themselves; and when refused, would stop the keyhole with dirt, and depart with a rhymed denunciation."

Indeed an old rhyme recognised that boys worked best in isolation:

> One boy is a boy,
> Two boys is half a boy,
> Three boys are no boys at all.

There were traditional forms of shouting and countless rhymes to acompany bird scaring in certain districts. This example was recorded in Suffolk:

We've ploughed our land,
We've sown our seed,
We've made all neat and gay;
So take a bit and leave a bit:
Away, birds, Away!

Boy scarer: Billy 'Dan' Boldero with crow scaring clappers. From *Pictures from a village*, courtesy of Boydell Press.

And this old song from Somerset, 'The Clapper Boy's Call', highlights the plight of these lads in wintertime:

He hi ho hi, here I go
Up to my knees in snow.
Girt bird, little bird, take enough, peck enough!
My maester's got enough home to barley mow.

From the mid to late nineteenth century the government became increasingly concerned by the exploitation of children working on farms. Various Education Acts passed between 1870 and 1880 enforcing the attendance at school of every child between the ages of five to fourteen nationwide were fiercely resisted by farmers who wanted cheap labour and parents who needed the money. Further Acts of Parliament prohibiting the employment of children below the age of eight in agriculture (1875) and abolishing school fees (1891) greatly improved school attendance in rural areas. Yet even by the turn of the century the laws regarding child labour were imperfectly applied and, indeed, late into the 1950s children might be legally excused school for seasonal fruit, vegetable or hop picking. Admittedly, long before this time compulsory education had been implemented and the army of juvenile 'field police' had been replaced by static scarecrows across Britain.

Great men, it seems, never forgot their humble origins employed as bird scarers in the fields of Britain. One such was William Cobbett (1763–1835) M.P. for Oldham, who toured England on horseback and published an account of his journeys under the title, *Rural Rides* (1830). Cobbett was born in Farnham, Surrey, the son of a humble farmer and could therefore claim to be a true countryman. After running away to sea, he enlisted as a soldier and rose to the rank of sergeant.

Later, he toured France and America before embarking on a political career, writing caustic pamphlets under the apt pseudonym, 'Peter Porcupine.' Finally, he returned to rural life when he purchased a farm at Botley, Hampshire, which served as his base from which he travelled to explore the countryside of Georgian England.

Cobbett, who achieved fame as a political reformer, farmer and nurseryman, vividly recalled the misery of his childhood in his autobiographical sketch, *The Progress of a Ploughboy to a Seat in Parliament* (1835): "I do not remember the time when I did not earn my living. My first ocupation was driving the small birds from the turnip seed, and the rooks from the peas. When I trudged afield, with my wooden bottle and my satchel over my shoulders, I was hardly able to climb the gates and stiles, and at the close of day, to reach home was a task of infinite labour." During one of his *Rural Rides*, Cobbett strayed into the abundant fruit orchards of Buckinghamshire and his thoughts raced back to the trauma of his youth: "I saw the little boys, in many places, set to keep the birds off the cherries, which reminded me of the time when I followed the same occupation, and also the toll that I used to take in payment." (24 June 1822)

Blossoming cherry trees were until recently a beautiful sight in the fields of North Kent. John Aubrey (1626–1697) antiquary and biographer, catalogues their history in his *Brief Lives*: "Cherries were first brought into Kent in the reign of Henry VIII, the king, being in Flanders and liking the cherries, ordered his gardener, Richard Harris, who brought them hence and propagated them in England." A modern author, Alan Major, whose family were themselves cherry pickers, has also chronicled the history of this seasonal fruit in his book, *Cherries in the Rise* (1981) There he complains that the major natural hazard to their cultivation is wild birds – jays, blackbirds, thrushes, wood pigeons but mainly starlings that wreak havoc on the entire crop as they flock in their thousands.

Alan Major recalls the methods which farmers adopted in the past for warding off these troublesome birds. One tactic which survived until the early years of the twentieth century was to despatch a lad, often as his first farm job, to run around the cherry orchards shouting and whirring wooden clappers or hand rattles, shaking stones in a tin or banging two metal objects together to create a sudden din. Alternatively, an elderly man armed with a double-barrelled shotgun, loaded with black powder scare cartridges, moved around the orchards periodically firing at the offending flock. One further ruse was to make junk metal mobiles from kitchen utensils and hang them from ropes next to sheets of corrugated iron nailed to trees. A labourer would spasmodically pull the pots and pans away from the corrugated iron and then let them fall back onto it with an almighty crash to frighten marauders.

Cherry growing, which had been in decline for decades, prospers once more in Kent. This is largely due to the cultivation of dwarf trees which are not only easy to propagate but can be covered with nets to protect them against bird predation. As a further precaution the practice of employing humans to scare birds from cherry gardens has been revived in recent years. A Kentish farmer, Eddie Waltham, advertised for unemployed youngsters to protect his prize-winning cherries at Buckhole Farm, near Rochester, in Kent, in 1985. Eddie's fruit farm was poorly sited since it was bounded on three sides by High Halstow Bird Sanctuary. "Starlings and finches would strip my entire stock in just one day," complained Eddie, "and I would lose about 20,000." Eight athletic youths were selected from over one hundred applicants and they were required to work in two shifts from dawn until dusk. Those that lasted a whole month were football fans used to wielding rattles and shouting slogans on the terraces of Birmingham City Stadium.

VICTORIAN SCARECROWS

Heyday of the scarecrow was undoubtedly the mid-to-late Victorian period when stuffed figures completely replaced the pitiful, reluctant characters – young or old – that had haunted the isolated fields of Britain. There were soon complaints, however, that the quality of these substitute figures was short-lived and that farmers scrimped and saved when it came to creating realistic representatives of the indefatigable race of bird scarers on their farms.

Sir Henry Rider Haggard (1856–1925) the popular writer of adventure fiction whose novels include *King Solomon's Mines* and *She*, was also a dedicated countryman. He visited South Africa in early life but at the age of twenty-four returned to East Anglia where he settled down as a gentleman farmer. He owned two small farms – Bedingham and Ditchingham – on the Norfolk/Suffolk border where he actively campaigned on behalf of better conditions for farm labourers. In his factual book, *A Farmer's Year* (1898) he accurately recorded the daily round of a farmer in the late Victorian period. Sir Henry "mirrors faithfully" the great agricultural depression at the end of the nineteenth century and at one point even lamented the decline of traditional scarecrows (which he refers to as 'mawkins') that he required his bailiff, Hood, to erect in early February:

> "In walking round the farm this afternoon I noticed that the rooks are playing havoc on
> the three acres of mixed grain which we drilled a few days ago for sheep food. They are
> congregated there literally by scores, and if you shout at them to frighten them away, they
> satisfy themselves by retiring to some trees near at hand and awaiting your departure to
> renew their operations. The beans attract them most, and their method of reducing these

into possession is to walk down the lines of the drill until (as I suppose) they smell a bean underneath. Then they bore down with their strong beaks and extract it, leaving a neat little hole to show that they have been there. Maize they love even better than beans; indeed it is difficult to keep them off a field sown with that crop.

Hood promises to set up some mawkins to frighten them, but the mawkin nowadays is a poor creature compared with what he used to be, and it is a wonder that any experienced rook consents to be scared by him. Thirty years or so ago he was really a work of art, with a hat, a coat, a stick, and sometimes a painted face, ferocious enough to frighten a little boy in the twilight let alone a bird. Now a rag or two and a jumblesale cloth cap are considered sufficient, backed up generally by the argument, which may prove effective, of a dead rook tied up by the leg to a stick."

William Coles Finch (1860–1940) who explored the countryside in the early years of the nineteenth century, considered that the scarecrow still retained its pride of place in Kent. (*Life in Rural England*, 1928)

"Apparently the only rural occupant of the fields who has not changed with the years is the dummy scarecrow. In both form and attire he is the same as of old, and may frequently be seen standing, gaunt and lonely, in the centre of the corn fields; his fleshless hop-pole arms and legs protruding through what were probably the discarded coat and trousers of some farm worker. These, for want of a fuller interior, flap wildly in the breeze, while the big round wurzel head or one of a cruder form, supports an old slush hat, and often a dirty old short clay pipe breaks the monotony of the wurzel of turnip face.

"Braving the elements there stands our persisitent friend; but with the progress of the seasons come his gradual dissolution, his sudden reappearance and again dissolution. His turnip head, now soft and shapeless, *sans* hat, *sans* pipe; the gaunt wooden stakes *sans* everything, they stand in unabashed nudity, absolutely ignored by the once frightened birds. Some actually perch upon these remains of the anatomy of the poor scarecrow. His wooden limbs later make their final sacrifice to utility on the hearth of the waggoner's mate."

REGIONAL NAMES

The Oxford English Dictionary gives numerous definitions for the word 'scarecrow': "1. A person employed in scaring birds; 2. a device for frightening birds from growing crops, usually a figure of a man dressed in old and ragged clothes; 3. a person whose appearance causes ridicule; a lean, gaunt figure; one who resembles a scarecrow in his dress; a guy." Various spellings are also recorded most of which are obsolete: scarrecrowe, skar-crowe, scarrecrow, scarcrowe, skarcrow and scarecrow (formerly written with a hyphen) In addition there are a host of regional names for scarecrows some of which are extant.

'Bo Boy' is the colloquial name for a scarecrow in Kent. Perhaps this derives from the game where one person hides and jumps out on an unsuspecting victim and shouts, "Boo", to administer a mild shock? Since the intention of the scarecrow is to surprise this explanation would seem perfectly feasible. 'Tatterdemalion' was an alternative Kentish word for scarecrow although more usually this referred to an old man with his clothes in tatters.

Another name for a scarecrow is 'shoyhoy' which was "imitative of the cry used for scaring birds" according to the *Oxford English Dictionary*. The dictionary also defines shoyhoy as a person who "scares away birds from a sown field." William Cobbett constantly refers to scarecrows as shoyhoys: "A fellow, who has had the stocks under his eye all his lifetime, and has never seen a pair of feet peeping through them, will stand no more in awe of the stocks than rooks do of an old shoyhoy," he opined in his *Rural Rides*.

The English Dialect Dictionary provides this definition for the word 'mawkin' ('maukin' or 'malkin') which is common throughout East Anglia: "A scarecrow, an effigy of a man or woman, made of old clothes stuffed with straw, put up in fields to scare birds." Alternative meanings are "a half-grown girl; especially one to do light house-work; a slattern, an untidy person; a showily or eccentrically dressed person; a term of abuse or contempt for anyone; a mop; a bundle of rags fastened to a pole; especially used to clean out the hot embers from a brick oven before the bread is put in." The *Oxford English Dictionary* simplifies these meanings: "A scarecrow; a ragged puppet or grotesque effigy; a guy."

The English Dialect Dictionary also gives several meanings for the word 'hodmandod' (variations are hodmedod, homadod, hodmandon) in addition to the simple name for a scarecrow: "An ill shaped, deformed person; an overgrown stupid boy, a simpleton; a mean, stingy person; old or very poor clothes, rags; empty snail shells." (This latter definition is illustrated by a reference to the custom of country folk suspending a number of snails in their shells by string to the chimney in the belief that, as they dried, it would cure whooping cough.)

Again, *The English Dialect Dictionary* gives various meanings for 'mommet' (variations are mammet, mawmet and murmet) which is the word for a scarecrow found mainly in the north of England: "An

image, an effigy; a puppet, an odd figure; frequently used as a term of abuse." There are oblique references to the word in John Raymond's novel, *Love and a Quiet Life* (1894) and R.D. Blackmore's, *Christowell* (1881)

'Tattiebogle' is the Scottish name for a scarecrow standing in a field of potatoes. Tattie, tatie or tawtie are all Scottish words for potato while bogie, boggle or bogill refers to a ghost or phantom. *Chamber's Concise Scots Dictionary* gives several interesting definitions for 'tatiebogle': "1. a scarecrow, especially one in a potato field; 2. a ragged, unkempt or grotesquely dressed person; 3. a large raw potato with matchsticks stuck in it as a toy; 4. a turnip-lantern used at Hallowe'en." Frequently, the heads of Scottish scarecrows are formed from purple winter turnips (equivalent to the English swedes)

The most popular name for a scarecrow throughout the centuries is 'Jack-a-Lent.' 'Jack' is a synonym for a rogue (and in this context it was once a common term for the lowest of the court cards) whose application invariably implies knavish intent. Examples include Jack Tar (an ordinary sailor) Jack Frost (the personification of wintry weather) and Jack Ketch (a hangman). Variations of the word are cheapjack (a dubious market trader), jumping jack (a startling firework) and jackdaw (a small thieving crow noted for its loquacity). Further, there is Jack-in-the-Green (an impish face peering through greenery which traditionally accompanies May Day celebrations), Jack-in-the-Box (a toy that springs a surprise), Jack-of-all-Trades (generally considered to be a Master-of-None) and Jack-o'-Lantern (an eerie face carved out of a hollow pumpkin illuminated from inside by a candle at Hallowe'en).

Lent is the period from Ash Wednesday until Maundy Thursday consisting of forty weekdays which devout churchmen devote to fasting and penitence in commemoration of Christ's sojourn in the wilderness. This season coincides with the time farmers place scarecrows in their fields to protect growing crops. Ironically, the posture of the scarecrow with its outstretched arms corresponds with the agonised image of Christ on the cross at Easter.

The *Oxford English Dictionary* defines 'Jack-a-Lent' not only as "a puppet, an insignificant or contemptible person" but also "a figure of a man set up to be pelted; and ancient form of the sport, 'Aunt Sally', practised during Lent." An old rhyme confirms the short duration of this curious activity:

"Ever upon Easter Day, All Jack-a-Lents were cast away.

Throwing missiles at live cockerels was an alternative entertainment found at country fairs (presumably the ones you killed you kept to eat) and this was one of the novel attractions advertised to tempt patrons onto the frozen ice during the famous Frost Fair on the River Thames in 1684.

A more detailed account appears in Robert Chambers' *The Book of Days* (1866) under the heading, 'Ash Wednesday':

> "The popular observances on Ash Wednesday are not of much account. The cocks being now despatched, a thin scare-crow like figure or puppet was set up, and shied at with sticks, in imitation of one of the sports of the preceding day. The figure was called a Jack-a-Lent, a term which is often met with in old literature, as expressive of a small and insignificant person."

INSULTS

The Dictionary of Slang and Unconventional English reveals that 'Scarecrow' was underworld jargon for an apprentice thief who has become well known to the police. Thereafter, the young criminal, his cover blown, was so closely watched by enforcers of the law that "he may as well stay at home as go out." It is not surprising, therefore, to learn that to refer to a person as a 'scarecrow' is a supreme insult.

William Cobbett rants about ineffective Members of Parliament in his *Weekly Political Register*. He names and shames several of them in his columns and likens them to scarecrows (or "shoy-hoys", which was their colloquial name in Hampshire) He had observed how familiarity bred contempt among the sparrows for a particular scarecrow positioned in his neighbour's garden at Botley. Similarly, representatives of the landed gentry promised much before they were elected to Parliament but proved their incompetence once they actually took their seat in the House of Commons. They were adept, in his opinion, at avoiding fighting issues of real concern to the countryside.

First dipping his quill in vitriol, Cobbett completes his character assassination: "Look at the conduct of these shoy-hoys during the present session; and then say, whether it would not have been as well to put in their seats so many old coats, stuffed with straw, having, for a head, a large turnip on a stake, with the latter to support the body erect." After several columns of invective, he bitterly concludes: "The object of these remarks on the shoy-hoys, is to convince all those who read, that we have no dependence on any body now in Parliament; and that, therefore we must rely upon ourselves." (14 August 1819).

Sir Walter Thornbury (1828–1876) a prolific writer on country matters, was pursuaded by Charles Dickens to contribute articles to his journal, *All The Year Round*. He embarked on a series of journeys from London across the country "as the crow flies" and recorded his impressions whenever he passed a particularly beautiful or memorable place. The title page of his collected essays, *A Tour Round England* (1870) bears an inspired illustration that replaces a crow for the weather cock on a church steeple.

Thornbury made a fleeting visit to Reading ('First Flight – Due West') where he first toured the historic Abbey before investigating the parish church of St. Lawrence. There, he reveals, Queen Elizabeth I attended divine service. Her Majesty was safely ensconced in the canopied pew of the Knollys family where she keenly followed the sermon while shielded from public gaze. "What a scarecrow to a blushing curate that stiff old lady in the ruff and jewelled stomacher must have been," Thornbury surmises, "glowering at him from under the bushy pyramid of her auburn hair."

Thornbury was an eccentric gentleman who lived for most of his life on a farm in Shropshire. He placed five scarecrows on his land – three men and two women – who were dressed annually in new suits of clothes. This may be accounted for by the fact that, according to one story, passing tramps helped themselves to their clothes and left their own cast-offs in return. Thornbury was a great champion of scarecrows which he regarded as "a symbol of the passing seasons and, made in man's image, stand in our stead as silent observers of the glory of nature at work."

Queen Victoria proposed one evening that her honoured guests should participate in a country dance at Windsor Castle. "The obedience was like the effect of a magical horn," Lady Lyttleton, Her Majesty's waspish lady-in-waiting, confided in her diary. "Lord Aberdeen (Prime Minister Robert Peel's Foreign Secretary) looked more like a scarecrow than ever," she scoffed, "quite as stiff as timber."

RUMOURS OF WAR

There are unconfirmed reports that a British spy involved in tracking down enemy agents broadcasting messages to Germany bore the codename, 'Scarecrow', during World War I while officers of the Home Guard were rumoured to have disguised themselves as scarecrows to keep watch for an invasion across the English Channel during World War II. Authentic scarecrows must have been sparsely dressed since there was a paucity of clothing for ordinary folk to keep themselves warm in these perilous times.

A typical wartime scarecrow is described in *The Story of a Norfolk Farm* by Henry Williamson (1895–1977). This autobiographical account of an amateur farmer was written between the spring of 1937 and the summer of 1939 and published in 1941. Williamson was a true nature writer whose most enduring book was *Tarka the Otter* but he also wrote a host of romantic novels set in Devon. At the advent of the Second World War he had become disillusioned with life and felt he needed a fresh challenge. He risked all his finances on the purchase of 'Old Castle Farm', near Durston, in Norfolk. This proved to be a daunting venture. Not only did this inexperienced farmer have to face the deprivations of working the land during the early years of the war but inevitably he aroused the suspicions of the local community who did not, at that unsettling time, welcome a stranger in their midst. Moreover, Williamson was a supporter of Mosley and an admirer of Hitler which unpopular alliances led to his eventual internment.

Williamson's lifelike scarecrow, or 'malkin', which his farmhand, Jimmy, had pursuaded him to place on the windy nook, 'Hang High', to protect barley seed, brought back horrific reminders of fighting in the trenches during the Great War. At the age of seventeen, he had joined the Army and saw action on the Western Front, an experience that left him psychologically scarred. The bloated figure of his scarecrow seemed to him to be a portent of the fate that awaited thousands of young soldiers who risked death and mutilation during the impending conflict with Germany.

> "It was a most realistic figure of a man, bringing back memories of the chalky cornfields of Picardy – although we never thought of them as cornfields – above the Somme. Jimmy had made the malkin of an old faded coat and a pair of grey flannel trousers, stuffed with straw. Its paper face was bleached with the sun: and whenever I had seen it, suddenly, as I had been rolling the 'Hang High' field, it had given me a start. The legs were rounded as though swelled. It looked like something that had died in that position, in a warning attitude, its arms spread out, its shattered head thrown back. Jimmy had been too realistic. The malkin should have conveyed a sense of the comic. Its clothes should have flapped on it. It should have grinned, with a mangold for a face, a pipe, and an old shapeless hat, with hair of hay or straw. It was not a scarecrow: it was a reminder of things that had been forgotten, and were likely to happen again, unless men began to think differently, with the clarity and logic of genius."

Private 10061 Thomas James Highgate – aged just nineteen – was the first British soldier to be executed for desertion in World War One. This Kentish teenager was born in Gravesend but later moved to Shoreham where he worked as a farm labourer. He enlisted in the Army and served with B. Company, 1st Battalion of the Royal West Kent Regiment in Dublin. Mobilisation was ordered immediately war started and Tom promptly sailed with 80,000 men who formed the British Expeditionary Force to France. He was sent to fight the Germans at the Battle of Mons where almost eight thousand British troops were slaughtered. His comrades fought tenaciously but, facing double their number in enemy soldiers and artillery, were in clear and present danger and forced to retreat.

The West Kents fell back, as ordered, but some time later, and while not under fire, Tom became separated from his battalion. He was found in a barn having discarded his uniform, rifle and ammunition and wearing civilian clothing taken from a scarecrow. He was court martialled, found guilty and shot at dawn in front of a company of marching men from the Dorset Regiment and the Cheshire Regiment. His execution was carried out "as publicly as possible" and his fate was broadcast to the entire Army. Tom was the first of 306 soldiers summarily executed by British Military Authorities for alleged cowardice, disobedience or desertion.

At the commencement of World War II, 'Scarecrow Patrols' were initiated by flights of Tiger Moths based around the coast of Britain. "Their specific aim was to observe enemy submarines which was an extremely dangerous and frustrating operation," reveals Stuart McKay in his history of the de Havilland Tiger Moth. Tiger Moths, later supported by a limited number of Hornet Moths, performed their heroic task between December 1939 and May 1940. At that time RAF Coastal Command possessed few aircraft suitable for anti-submarine patrols within reach of Britain's vital and vulnerable ports.

RAF Coastal Command worked on the theory that regular, visible patrols of individual aircraft would keep prowling submarines below persicope depth and thus render them blind and relatively harmless to shipping. It was rightly assumed that commanders of submarines would tactfully submerge at the sight or sound of an approaching aircraft. Two or three sweeps were made each day although it was normally during the dawn and dusk patrols that submarines were to be found on the surface. (A tell-tale tiny white feather in the water indicated that a periscope was pushing through the calm sea.) Pilots always hunted in pairs, within sight of each other, zigzagging about below a thousand feet to give any U-boat commander the false impression that the aircraft were about to attack. Appropriately, these bizarre random patrols intended to harry or scare enemy submarines were termed, 'Scarecrow.'

One pilot, David Masters, summed up these Coastal Patrol Flights in his book, *So Few* (1942) "There was nothing spectacular about the Scarecrow Patrols, nothing to win high honours. Of the six pilots who formed the first flight, three alas are no more. But the amateur pilots who joyfully risked their lives without question for day after day flying far out to sea, sitting in open cockpits exposed to all the rigours of a terrible winter, until fully-armed aircraft were manufactured to take up the task, won, by their quiet confidence and their physical endurance, a worthy place in British history."

Traditional scarecrows also did their bit for the War Effort and obligingly posed for several Ministry of Information propaganda posters during World War II. Perhaps the most effective encouraged patriots to 'Save Waste for War Weapons.' A scarecrow dressed in a top hat, gloves and overcoat rises from a rubbish dump consisting of a cartwheel, rake, pail, tyres and petrol can with the legend printed in red and black ink: 'RAGS make uniforms, METAL makes tanks, PAPER makes bullets.'

POLITICAL CARTOONS

World leaders from Hitler to Mao Tse-tung have been ridiculed as scarecrows in sketches and cartoons. Scarecrows have also been featured by artists in prints and engravings commenting on national events from the Napoleonic Wars to World War II.

The Print Room of the British Museum contains a couple of clever political cartoons featuring scarecrows. The first is by Isaac Cruikshank (1756–1811) called 'The Scarecrows' Arrival, or Honest Pat giving them an Irish welcome' (10 June 1803). It is a hand coloured engraving published by S.W. Fores of 50, Piccadilly, London, and dates from the Napoleonic Wars. A brawny Irish peasant stands on the seashore flinging dung from his shovel at French invaders headed by Napoleon Bonaparte. All the Frenchmen are depicted as skeletons wading through deep water still wielding their weapons and flying the tricolour.

Napoleon steps out of the foam wearing an outsize tricorn hat with a feather and flourishing his sabre. "Now my boys," Boney postures, "halloo, away – vil frighten Mr. Bull out of his wits, we vil make him quake like the Dutch, the Italian, the Swiss and the rest of our friends." Pat retaliates, "Och it is your own pratty figure it is, Master Bonny, d'ye think that Pat was to be blarney'd by such Scare Crows – no – no – Bother, the time is gone by, Pat's eyes are wide open and look ye, if you don't immediately jump into the sea to save your lives, I will shovel you all there to save mine." Behind him is a low stone fortification on which cannon are mounted with a terse notice: 'Man Trap and Spring Guns. Beware." The point of the cartoon was to represent a united front between England and Ireland at a time when an invasion by Napoleon Bonaparte was thought to be imminent.

The second is an anonymous monochrome engraving called, 'Scarecrows in Ireland' (3 May 1824). This was published by John Fairburn of Broadway, Ludgate Hill, for one shilling and highlights a scandal involving the 10th Hussars. It shows a scene outside a country alehouse whose sign is an empty bottle displayed on a pole projecting from a gable beneath a thatched roof with a smoking chimney. A notice over the door reads: 'Dry Lodging For Man and Horse by Pat Quigly.' Pat, himself, stands burly and bare legged, peering at three scarecrows in a field of barley beyond a stone wall. These consist of Hussar officers flourishing their sabres and sabretaches while pinioned with arms and legs akimbo. The air is thick with startled birds.

Irish Pat leans on his spade and points to the impaled Hussars. "To be sure haven't I put them to a good use at last, Judy – the devil fire the crow or magpie will come near the barley now and I'll stick up more of them in the paraty (sic) field, honey." His wife, Judy, replies, "Arrah, Pat, my Jewel, but your (sic) a darling for finding out scare-crows – They're better than the ould Wig that was up there before." A fat pig looks bemused from his lean-to sty on which a boy climbs for a better view of the scarecrow while a young girl also peers from a casement window. The cartoon served as a folding frontispiece to accompany an extravaganza called 'A Slap at the Gallant Tenths, or a Cut at the Sprigs of a No-a-Bility.' It has no obvious connection with the dramatic contents.

Scarecrows featured prominently in newspaper cartoons during the Second World War. Ronald Neibour ('NEB') often resorted to them in his witty pen and ink sketches. A portly farmer is taken aback when a voice from a spy concealed in a scarecrow with his arm pointing to the sky comments: "Nice little dog-fight up there guvnor" (*Daily Mail* 15 October 1940). A squire in a hacking jacket is caught off guard when a ragged scarecrow confronts him by asking: "I suppose this rationing business puts paid to that old suit you promised me" (*Daily Mail* 4 June 1941). Two crows perched on the arm of another scarecrow remark: "They're crying out for sparetime harvest labour – and all he does is stand around and flap" (*Daily Mail* 4 June 1942). One hilarious cartoon by Joseph Lee depicts two countrymen leaning over a fence watching women pull a team of shire horses or drive a tractor over a bumpy field: "Aye! There be queer changes on the farm since they Land Girls came." Central is a prancing female scarecrow (*Evening News* 18 September 1942).

Politicians in modern times have been pilloried in the press as scarecrows. Perhaps the most famous example was Michael Foot, former Leader of the Labour Party, who appeared wearing a donkey jacket at the Cenotaph on Remembrance Sunday. Apparently, this strange attire was in reality a high-quality Jaeger coat admired on that occasion by the Queen Mother. "A most sensible coat to wear in this rather inclement weather," Her Majesty was overheard to remark. But such royal approval did not save this luckless politician from being lampooned mercilessly by the media. Mr Foot's eccentric personality and shambling gait were further ammunition for satirists and cartoonists.

Private Eye launched an appeal: 'Save Britain's Scarecrows.' "Poor old Worzel," they scoffed. "Abandoned by society, he has now nowhere to go. Mr. Gummidge is only 68 – yet already people have written him off as a has-been. Even his friends admit that he is over the hill. When Worzel turned up

PRIVATE EYE

No.521
Friday
4 Dec. '81

40p.

CHRISTMAS ISSUE

Private Eye, 4 December 1981

opposite: Tony Blair at the Kettlewell Festival

recently for a Remembrance Day parade, he couldn't even afford the price of a decent donkey jacket. If you feel like sniggering, just remember that Worzel may soon be out of a job, with only a huge Government pension to help him in the eventide of his life. Worzel has served his country faithfully. Now it's your turn to show you care. Send old clothes, blankets, valuable antiquarian books to Jimmy Saville, Business Ladies House, Milton Keynes, Glos."

Wickedly, Richard Ingrams, editor, commissioned the television puppeteers, Peter Fluck and Roger Law from 'Spitting Images', to create a latex model of Michael 'Worzel' Foot. He appeared, wearing holly sprigs and brushed with snow, on the front cover of the Christmas Edition of *Private Eye* (4 December 1981). Prime Minister, Margaret Thatcher, who had recently ousted his party at the General Election, was modelled as a crow triumphantly perched on his bent shoulders. What happened to the overcoat? It was donated to the Museum of Labour History in Manchester.

Prime Ministers from Harold Wilson to Tony Blair have all been depicted in newspapers as literal 'stuffed shirts' while politicians from Enoch Powell to Anthony Wedgewood Benn have been portrayed as parasitical crows. Ted Heath is shown as a gardener planting seeds in three phases while crow 'miners' peck at scarecrow 'inflation' during the devisive miners' strike (*Daily Telegraph* 26 March 1973). Tony Blair is presented as a grinning scarecrow sporting a placard, 'New Labour Ban Fox Hunting. . . if there's time', beside a pair of panting foxes who despair, 'I don't think his heart his in it' (*Glasgow Herald* 5 November 1997). Two crows start at the sight of a genetically modified scarecrow transformed into Frankenstein (*Daily Express* 15 February 1999) while Bill Clinton as the Cowardly Lion hesitantly leads Tony Blair as the Tin Man and Robin Cook as the Scarecrow along the Yellow Brick Road to Kosovo (*Daily Telegraph* 8 April 1999). Giant scarecrows atop Dover's White Cliffs were New Labour's answer to combatting bird flu according to Paul Thomas, Political Cartoonist of the Year (*Daily Express* 21 February 2006).

DESIGNER SCARECROWS

Battalions of scarecrows were erected by farmers – often half a dozen to a field – in the immediate postwar period to combat the flocks of ravenous pigeons then flying into this country from the frozen mainland of Europe. Richard Mabey, author and broadcaster, in his *Nature Journal* (1991) notes their migration at that time. Revealingly, he propounds that scarecrows are the natural progression of rustic humour which found former expression in "irreverent misericords and rude topiary which now adds extra flourishes to corn circles."

Mabey recently toured the length and breadth of Britain searching for prime examples of scarecrows which, he insists, are no longer of the common or garden variety. Those he observed on his extensive travels were "done up in denim jackets and M&S shirts, topped off with chicly-tied scarves. They wore fashionable pastel shades and were arranged with the casual elegance of menswear window dummies. Some even sported sunglasses." And he concludes: "The age of the designer scarecrow has arrived."

In modern times the scarecrow has become so respectable an image that it has lent its name to a wide variety of products and organisations. Most successfully, a Scandinavian rock band performs as 'The Scarecrows.' The five musicians, who hail from Trondheim, Norway, demonstrate a truly dynamic attack on stage. Their style prowls between hard rock 'n' roll and classical country rock. . . and their logo is a jigging scarecrow.

A top American Junior Ice Hockey team is called 'The ScareCrows.' Formed in 1997, the players are based at Topeka, Kansas, and they practise at the ExpoCentre, Kansas City. The 'Crows' are an amateur group that compete in the American Central Hockey League. Their triangular logo features a ferocious scarecrow sporting a scarlet jerkin with a grey floppy hat and wielding a hockey stick. His head is a sack scored with a grim, determined expression. Inspiration for the name came from a legend about scarecrows that play hockey in the dead of winter on the frozen ponds of Kansas Plains. Best player is Haywire. He gives his name to the team's lucky mascot who poses for press photographs swiping the puck before faceoff.

First edition of the American 'Oz' series of alternative "dark side" graphic novels published in 1995 featured a violent cloaked scarecrow wielding a stave. The artist deliberately presented this pumpkin-head figure as a stark contrast to the lovable character from the film, *The Wizard of Oz*. Its rival magazine, *Mad*, has also repeatedly lampooned author, Frank Baum's wonderland. Earlier, a vicious scarecrow snatching a startled crow in his gloved hand had appeared on the grim cover of yet another American adult comic, *Fear* (May 1960).

The Topeka Scarecrows Ice Hockey logo, Kansas City, USA

'The Scarecrow' joined with The Joker, Two Face, The Riddler, Catwoman, Poison Ivy and The Penguin, as an arch villain to thwart the efforts of Batman to keep the peace in Gotham City. Batman was created by Bob Kane but The Scarecrow was the later invention of writer, Doug Moench, and illustrators Bret Blevins and Mike Manley. He first appeared in *World's Finest Comics* in 1940 but was later featured on the cover of several other comics. "I was always lanky and gangly, even as a youth, with a herky-jerky gait which never failed to draw derision and scorn," laments the Scarecrow who is the alter ego of bullied loner, Jonathan 'Ichabod' Crane. One gripping tale featuring this "bizarre tatterdemalion of fear" was included in 'Detective Comics' Annual 1995.' Batman is called to investigate the mysterious death by simultaneous cardiac arrest of five university professors where the only clue is a single dropped straw. The dramatic cover featured a torn and tattered Batman staked to a pole imitating a scarecrow lit by a full moon one Fall.

Another right-is-might superhero, 'The Scarecrow', featured in a brief series of Marvel Comics throughout the 1970s. Billed as 'The Most Mysterious Superhero of All', The Scarecrow had an unenviable upbringing since he had been born "in the darkest pits of Hell." He appeared by stepping out of the canvas of an oil painting in a Soho attic to right wrongs with the aid of journalist, Harmony, wrought across America by the evil god, Kalumai. These fairly incomprehensible stories recruited an army of fans from all walks of life across America.

Scarecrows have been used to promote a huge variety of products ranging from beer to cigarettes in Britain. Wychwood Brewery in Witney, Oxfordshire, whose logo is a witch flying on her broomstick, features a scarecrow on its label of 'Circle Master' organic ale. This genial scarecrow wearing a black coat, pink scarf and top hat rises majestically above a bine of ripe hops. A tawny owl perches on his shoulder watched, too close for comfort, by a stray fox. The bottled beer, which has a honey tincture with a hoppy aroma, is brewed by a company which has won awards from the 'Campaign for Real Ale.' A photograph of a model scarecrow dressed as an archer superimposed on a stylised painting of a bare field was selected to appear in advertisements inside colour supplements for Gallagher's low tar cigarettes, Silk Cut. This deliberately bold image was created by a team of designers from M and C Saatchi to be retained in the mind of readers at a time when restrictions on advertising tobacco were first introduced by the government.

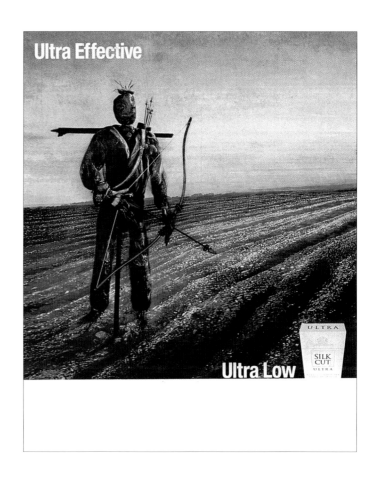

Silk Cut advertisement

House of Fraser advertisement

Rowntree's used the scarecrow image most successfully in their humorous 'Take a break, take a KitKat' series of television advertisements. A one minute colour film entitled *Scared Crows* (1984) featured comedian, Neil Innes, disguised as a scarecrow with a pure white face, black wig and carrot nose. He was dressed in a black coat, grey waistcoat, top hat and gloves. His scarecrow is glimpsed in the early morning standing in stark silhouette against a backdrop of bare trees in an isolated meadow. The bells of the village church peel mournfully. He stretches, yawns and decides to "take a break" from leaning against his perch by sitting on a grassy bank to eat a four-piece chocolate bar. Three or four crows join him for his picnic and one perches cheekily on his shoulder. He takes out his pocket watch and realises it is time to resume his duty, scaring crows in the open countryside.

One handsome scarecrow drew attention to Volkswagen's 'Passat' in both poster advertise-ments and colour supplements. This plush family saloon is parked on the gravel drive outside a suburban detached house. A scarecrow dressed in a trilby and trench coat stands incongruously on the front lawn strewn with autumn leaves. The juxtaposition of these two images is puzzling. Presumably, the artist's idea was that the scarecrow would keep the birds away from the gleaming bonnet.

A studious scarecrow wearing ill-fitting glasses appeared in advertisements for Boots the

Opticians in national newspaper and magazines. His rather unattractive appearance aimed to encourage short-sighted readers to attend Boot's Laser Eye Clinic in Central London and thus dispense with their unsightly spectacles.

A saucy scarecrow was employed by House of Fraser to introduce their range of casual female clothing, 'Therapy.' In their racy advertisements a scantily-clad girl, modelling a selection of the summer clothes, bends over a roadmap, having lost her way in the countryside. Her "edgy" attire has aroused a youthful scarecrow who stands nearby with a sly grin and a most obvious erection. Rooks, who seem also to have come under her spell, roost on this improvised perch. Above, appears the legend: "We aim to tease." Scarecrows, it would appear, have come full circle in the twenty-first century with this unintentional homage to the Greek God, Priapus.

A modern fable about a scarecrow who has lost his scare is related by Sir Ian Holme (Bilbo in 'Lord of the Rings') in a television advertisement for Weetabix. A kindly farmer feeds the banished scarecrow regular bowls of this 'nourishing breakfast cereal' so that not only is his confidence restored but he merrily cartwheels through the fields to the consternation of the crows. All the actors and a collie dog were recruited in Prague where the wheat field was specially created in a studio by art students.

Wychwood Brewery's 'Circle Master' organic ale

2. STONE THE CROWS

FARMERS realise that rooks and crows which have traditionally been thought of as enemies to crops may also be their friends in keeping down the numbers of insects which are harmful to young shoots. After experimenting for decades with a variety of ways of controlling the considerable damage caused by wild birds, farmers have conceded that the most humane method is also the most successful. Scarecrows are both cheap and effective while they preserve the balance of nature and their presence enhances rather than detracts from the natural beauty of the countryside.

FACTS AND FOIBLES

'Scarecrow' may, in fact, be a misnomer. 'Scarerooks' might be far more accurate. Crows are rarely seen in more than twos or threes, maybe fours, in the mating season. Often they fly solitary over a field and so are not exactly a threat to crops. They are scavengers and eat mainly carrion although they devour other eggs and young and therefore must be regarded as pests by gamekeepers wishing to protect laying pheasants and partridges. They build large, raggedy nests of sticks and bark high in tall trees and they collect shiny or bright trinkets found on the ground for furnishing their nests. From their treetop perches, crafty crows watch neighbouring birds building their nests, remember where they are, then rob them of eggs and even chicks while their parents are absent hunting for food.

Rooks, by contrast, are colonists. These birds swarm over fields in vast numbers and have generally been seen as a threat by farmers. They look eccentric with the ragged appearance of their plumage compared to the "svelte and glossy" crows. They are sociable in temperament, feed in groups and return at dusk to a communal roost. Before they settle for the night they sweep together through the evening skies in an aggressive, noisy display. Country parson, the Rev Gilbert White (1720–1793) remarked in his nature notes: "Rooks are continually fighting and pulling each other's nests to pieces: these proceedings are inconsistent with living in close community. And yet if a pair offers to build on a single tree, the nest is plundered and demolished at once". (*Journal* 10 March 1775)

There are two distinct types of crows, Carrion crows inhabit England, Wales and parts of Scotland.

opposite: Scarecrow in the snow, Kent.

'The Rook' by Thomas Bewick

They are the most visible crop-eating bird and they will eat mature corn and pull up young seedlings in search of kernels. Their most unpleasant trait is that, in addition to insects and vegetation, they are drawn to corpses although they will also devour small frogs and toads. Despite this, they are most impressive creatures. Carrion crows are jet black all over including the beak and they share with the raven a dark, brooding presence. "Typically a crow sits still, slightly hump-backed in a tree, closely observant of everything that happens around it," reveals ornithologist, Francesca Greenoak.

The Hooded crow inhabits Ireland (where it is called the 'Scald Crow') and north west Scotland (where it is known as 'Hoodie', 'Hoddie' or 'Corbie') The Hooded crow is distinguished by its grey mantle and underparts. They are far more sociable than the solitary Carrion Crows. Their diet and breeding habits are similar although the voice of the Hooded crow is not as distinct as its relative. The Hoodie is known in England and the more southerly parts of Scotland as a winter visitor which is why it has been referred to in the past as the 'Winter Crow.' An alternative appellation is 'Royston Crow.'

A gory picture of a Hooded crow preying on lesser birds is painted by Henry Williamson in his *The Story of a Norfolk Farm* (1941). Natives of Norfolk refer to the Hoodie as the 'Denchman' which is possibly a corruption of 'Danishman' since these birds cross the North Sea after migrating from Denmark and Norway. "The cunning old hoodie crow, the Denchman, sits on the sheep-bridge rails of the marshes and looks around him for food. He eats anything. Through glasses I saw one flapping after a small bird in the withered sea-lavender bushes growing above the mud flats. Perhaps it was a migrant robin or siskin, or one of the lesser wading birds which had been wounded by shot from some fowling-piece. I saw flapping dark wings and beak hammering down: then the Denchman was standing on its prey, pulling away beakfulls and swallowing."

Countrymen believe that nuisance birds such as rooks and crows have the altruistic ability to post sentries on guard looking for danger. Also they are thought to form rescue squads to retrieve wounded or distressed companions. Whether these beliefs are fact or fantasy, farmers are in full agreement that neither crows nor rooks are easily scared.

There are countless superstitions about both rooks and crows. For example, they are believed to forecast the weather. Rooks foretell rain and the signs are: a tumbling flight, roosting at midday, flying to the hills and standing on dead branches of trees. Here is one rhyme about what country folk commonly call "raincrows":

> Crow on the fence,
> Rain will go hence.
> Crow on the ground,
> Rain will come down.

'The Crow' by Thomas Bewick

Rural communities have great respect for these birds and know for sure that if a single crow caws near a house it announces a calamity. Fortunately, there is a counter charm. It is wise to raise your hat, or bow if bare headed, to forestall the danger that the crow signifies. If you see a crow fly through the air in an open field it means you will take a journey; if it flies to the right, be on your guard, but if it flies to the left you will definitely receive bad news. If the crow flies high, make a wish and if it does not flap its wings before it is out of sight your wish is certain to come true.

According to folklore, crows symbolise cunning, thievery, tale-bearing and foreknowledge. Crows, in fact and fiction, live their lives by their wit maintained by the labours of others. They are messengers of death and symbols of fertility and they are consulted by diviners. Yet they are capricious with their powers since they may also bring good luck. In Wales, for instance, it is thought that to see a pair of crows brings good fortune. And in heraldry, a crow signifies a quiet life and settled habitation.

Romans regarded the crow as a harbinger of the future because it cries "Cras, cras" ("tomorrow, tomorrow") Indeed, even the appearance of facial lines, "crows' feet", is an indication of the advent of old age and eventual death. The bird's cry jars on the ear and its proud, mocking tone gives the phrase, "something to crow about." Supposedly, crows can count up to seven (this assertion is based upon the number of caws used to identify themselves to their companions) and they employ almost two dozen different calls to communicate with one another. Certainly, the crow's raucous cawing renders it one of the most readily identifiable bird sounds. Crows also appear to be ventriloquists since they have the ability to make their voices sound as though they are coming from the opposite direction to which they are cawing. When tamed, wild crows may be taught to repeat certain words or phrases and when raised as fledglings they can easily be domesticated.

Both birds provide several phrases that colour the English language. The crow's skill in prising open food sources with its powerful beak gives us "crowbar" just as a beaked piece of iron hinged to the masts of ships used as a grappling hook was called by the Romans a "corvus". "Crow's nest" is another nautical term referring to a barrel fixed to the masthead of a sailing ship as a shelter for the look-out. "Crow's quill" is a calligraphy term for a steel pen for fine writing while "rook" (which derives from the Persian "rukh" meaning a chariot) is an alternative name for the castle in chess. The slang verb, "to rook" means to cheat someone at cards or dice while a "rookie" is a raw army recruit. The *Oxford English Dictionary* defines "rookeries" as a crowded cluster of tenements and offers an obsolete phrase, "a rook of prostitutes." Oddly, it is rooks with their steady, undeviating flight that provides the saying, "as the crow flies". (Crows never take the shortest route between two points except when migrating.)

There are two further curiosities. "Corvus" ("Crow") is a small, faint, ancient constellation in the southern sky, between Virgo and Hydra, best seen in the early evening in May. The Black tern, which was once a common bird in Britain breeding regularly in the south and southeast England, is colloquially called 'Scarecrow'. (The *Oxford English Dictionary* asserts this is also an alternative name for the Hooded Crow.)

LEGENDS AND SUPERSTITIONS

The crow shares with its cousin, the raven, a reputation for being a bird of ill omen and is associated with dark legends.

A Greek myth concerns Apollo, god of prophecy, and a crow which was his inseparable companion. At that time the crow was pure white. When Apollo fell in love with a nymph, Coronis, his pet crow informed him of her unfaithfulness. In a rage Apollo slew the nymph and turned the crow black. Despite its downfall, the crow could still talk and it also retained its gift of prophecy. Hence, the crow has, down the centuries, become famed as a prophet of ill tidings. Even today if a crow is seen before or after a wedding ceremony, superstitious guests believe that the marriage is destined to end in divorce.

Celtic mythology connects crows with several gods and goddesses. The Celts venerated Hooded Crows since they were seen either as the embodiment, or the emissaries of, the goddess of battle, Badbh. This sorceress was also known under a variety of names – 'Nemhain', 'Macha' or 'Madb' – but her influence was most potent as 'Morrigan, the Phantom Queen.' Described in Celtic literature as the "Battle Crow" or "Battle Raven" (she could assume either form) Morrigan combined the fundamental

opposite: Lady in red on an allotment, Exmoor, Devon.

elements of warfare and sexual conquest which were inexorably linked in Celtic culture. Bran, a rival warrior god, lived on after the advent of Christianity in the winged guise of 'Crawan' (or 'Crow') He was thought to have returned under the raven banner of the Norseman to scourge our land and return us to our pagan origins.

Scots of the Western Isles regarded this same crow as a symbol of evil. Their strong belief combined the notion that crows indicated the presence of one of the Celtic gods or goddesses of death with the evidence of horrific slaughter wreaked by marauding Vikings. Certainly, the Hooded Crow was greatly feared and distrusted throughout the Far Isles and the Western Highlands as a bird closely connected with the forces of Celtic darkness.

Traditions around the coast and on these islands concerned hoodies drinking human blood which may have derived from the fact that crows were often seen with bloodied beaks on the battlefield. It was also widely believed in such remote places as Orkney and Shetland that they could take on human form after dark while in the Inner and Outer Hebrides they were known to scour the countryside for victims to drink their blood. Thomas Pennant in *British Zoology* (1776) first records the name 'Hooded Crow' and mentions a ceremony whereby Scottish herdsmen made offerings to induce these birds to spare their flocks.

Crows were inextricably bound in primitive minds with death and destruction. They were regarded by warriors both as a sign of imminent victory or of impending doom. Their presence was deemed an ill omen by soldiers if they witnessed them flocking as they rode to battle yet, conversely, their image on a standard could rally an army to glorious valour. After a battle, crows were seen as ghouls picking indiscriminately at the decaying bodies of the slain. "European Battlefields were often black with feasting crows, filling the blood soaked air with their horrid squalling as they fought over succulent pieces of human flesh," grimly comments Bob Curran, an expert on Celtic folklore.

An Oxford scarecrow.

According to Dr Curran in 'Creatures of Celtic Myth' (2001) the medieval church combined all these superstitions and transformed them into one which closely associated the crow with the Devil. The Devil once scalded the crow's throat which left it with its harsh, rasping "caw"; the blackness of its plumage represented the scaly hide of its dark master while its alert, intelligent eyes were ever watchful to snatch lost souls. Only a holy man such as Saint Patrick of Ireland possessed the power necessary to withstand the harmful influence of these birds and there is one story how he frightened away threatening crows with a great bell.

It is a relief to find that there are a few legends concerning these birds which strike a happier note. Crows join with rooks to make an appearance in the Christian tradition and supposedly perch reverently in trees on Ascension Day. When Saint Cuthbert was forced to live alone in the Farne Islands off Northumberland, crows were among his welcome companions. King Arthur was said to have been turned into a "Crow by Inchantment" and would one day resume his former shape and recover his kingdom. For these reasons alone it was thought by some superstitious countrymen undesirable to kill a crow in former times.

Black and menacing, the crow retains its aura of menace even to the present day. Its strong and powerful beak is adequate defence against most predators. Indeed, two crows are more than a match for a hawk or a fox. Man is the bird's only serious enemy. "The creature's great cunning and sagacious character has earned man's hatred," affirms naturalist, Philip Clucas, in *Country Seasons* (1978) "Farmers dislike crows for stealing grain and seed, whilst gamekeepers persecute the birds in an effort to protect game-chicks. They are often confused with rooks, but the traditional rule of thumb, that solitary birds are crows, and those in flocks are rooks, generally runs true."

Trends are encountered even in bird life. Ornithologists now report that crows do tend to mass after breeding in mixed flocks of crows, rooks and jackdaws. This tends to take place in winter particularly around landfill sites on the coast which provide ample opportunites for scavenging. This reversal of fortune for farmers in recent times has given a new lease of life for scarecrows which are now employed almost exclusively for scaring flocks of ravenous winter crows.

CHARACTERISTICS OF CROWS

Ornithologists, past and present, have sometimes championed rooks and crows and have even dared to suggest that they may be more sinned against than sinning.

Thomas Bewick (1753–1828) in his monumental *History of British Land Birds* (1797) gave detailed descriptions of the appearance and habits of the family of corvidea whose members number jay, magpie, chough, jackdaw, raven, rook, carrion and hooded crow:

"Birds of this kind are found in every part of the known world, from Greenland to the Cape of Good Hope; and though their principal food is earth worms, they may be said to be of great benefit to mankind, not only be devouring putrid flesh, but by destroying great numbers of noxious insects, and reptiles. In general they are restless and noisy, easily tamed, and capable of being taught to articulate words, and to obey the voice of their master. They are sagacious, active and thievish: they are monogamous, and their mutual attachment is very strong and constant. They build mostly in trees, and form a kind of society, in which there appears something like a regular government: a sentinel watches for the general safety and on the approach of an enemy, or of a stranger, they act in concert, and drive him away with repeated attacks."

English farmers remained surprisingly acommodating over the years and even conceded that these birds could do some good by destroying harmful insects. *A Society of Gentlemen* (1786) claims that, although they do considerable damage to sprouting corn, "they never moleft the wheat which is fown about Michaelmas; because fo much grain of the late harvest then lies scattered about fields, that they find it much easier to pick up that, than to fearch for corn under ground in new-fown lands."

William Marshall, asserts in his *Rural Economy of Norfolk* (1787) that rooks are rarely shot as the notion prevails among farmers that they are more beneficial then harmful in picking up worms and grubs, "especially the grub of the cockchaffer."

More recently, Robin Page, in his *Journal of a Country Parish* (1980) presents an almost lyrical description of these birds:

"Rooks can damage crops, but they can also do much good, as they eat many wireworms and leatherjackets. Indeed as they fly on their ragged edged wings and then walk slowly about or hop from furrow to furrow, they look pompous and superior. With their thick thigh feathers they have the appearance of country gentlemen wearing fashionably cut plus-fours. Often, in wind, they seem to fly for the sheer enjoyment of tossing and tumbling in moving air, and it is possible to make weather predictions from their behaviour. They also seem to have a well developed communal life and social order, and because of the way in which they sit around in rookeries, there are stories of meetings, parliaments, rook courts and even evictions."

Despite such reassurances to the contrary, modern farmers insist that the damage caused by these birds to their crops is stupendous. It has been estimated that rooks alone devour fifty thousand tons of corn annually in Britain. And a single flock of wood pigeons can easily do a thousand pounds of crop

opposite: British Rail scarecrow, Dover.

damage in less than one hour. An enormous amount of time and research is therefore spent by agricultural scientists in dealing with the problem of wild birds and resultant crop damage.

A national survey of rooks was undertaken by the British Trust for Ornithology at the commencement of the Second world War. This important research was requested by the Ministry of Agriculture and Fisheries who were mindful of possible food shortages during hostilities with Germany. The survey was undertaken by volunteer observers who specifically enquired if the rook population was increasing and whether there was a change of habit in their feeding. Their findings demonstrated that corn featured more prominently in their diet and this was attributed to the large increase of cereal grown at home in the war years.

Also the adult rook population was shown to be just under three million birds which was an increase of about twenty per cent since the previous survey in the 1930's. It was tacitly assumed at that time that rooks were indeed harmful to agriculture.

Wild birds were once a source of free winter food for poor country folk. Indeed, in some rural areas rook pie is still considered a delicacy. Apparently, it is best made only from the breasts which are first simmered gently with onions until tender. Their dark, pungent meat is then placed in a pie dish lined with short crust pastry. Any discarded liquid can then be thickened with a tablespoon of flour with seasoning and poured over the meat before adding the top crust. It should then be cooked in a hot oven and served with root vegetables. Rook pie is said to be nourishing, wholesome and preferable even to grouse. Further, it is guaranteed to prevent hair from falling out or turning grey.

INTELLIGENCE OF CROWS

Naturalists rate the crow family (corvidae) as the most superior among birds. Crows are omnivrous and they will devour animal, fish and vegetables indiscriminately although they are particularly partial to fresh green shoots. Notorious for their craftiness, they will employ immense cunning to secure a hearty meal. Indeed, their intelligence has recently been the subject of research by Alex Kacelnik, Professor of Behavioural Ecology in the Department of Zoology at the University of Oxford. Surprisingly, it has been proved beyond doubt that it exceeds all wild birds and possibly even primates.

Caledonian crows (corvus moneduloides) from the Pacific Islands of New Caledonia between Fiji and the Solomon Islands are known to make tools from twigs in order to obtain large grubs or beetle larvae from trees. Adults teach this skill to their young. Two Caledonian crows ('Betty' and 'Abel') were bred in captivity to test their intelligence at Oxford University. They resemble jackdaws in appearance although their coats are blacker and more iridescent. The pair were repeatedly set a task in which they were required to manufacture a hook from a short length of wire. Then they had to dip the hook with their beaks into a narrow vertical glass tube to retrieve a miniature bucket containing meat or birdseed. Nine times out of ten the female crow managed this complicated task without coaching.

Professor Kacelnik commented: "Chimps and birds sometimes use tools but this is the first report of an animal systematically fashioning a tool for a new task out of unnatural materials without being taught. Experiments with primates, which are much closer relatives to humans than birds, have failed to show any deliberate, specific toolmaking and humanlike understanding of the basic physical laws. Toolmaking and tool use has always been considered one of the diagnostics of a superior intelligence. Now a bird is shown to have greater sophistication than many closer relatives to us humans." University scientists are now devising new experiments and logic tests to assess the extent of the intelligence of the British Carrion crow. (corvus corone)

High intelligence of these birds makes it all the more difficult for farmers to employ effective methods of scaring them away from their crops. "Birds will often avoid a new object or sound at first but unless their fear is reinforced by some unpleasant experience they quickly get used to the new situation, just as they do to traffic noise, aircraft engines and other everyday experiences which have no serious consequences," affirms R.K. Murton in his study, *Man and Birds* (1971) "Thus bangers and other noise machines and strange looking objects may initially cause a bird to prefer a field without such an object, but in the absence of choice hunger quickly overcomes any fear and it will ignore the device." Murton insists that the important lessons to be learned are the need to make model predators as lifelike as possible, to reinforce them with noxious stimulii and to alter their mode and frequency of presentation as much as possible. Needless to say, Murton is disdainful of farmers who do not regularly move their scarecrow but simply leave them to fall down.

Warning of response to a new stimulus was appreciated as far back as 1716 when a horticulturist named Worlidge penned *A Complete System of Husbandry and Gardening, or the Gentleman's Companion, in the Business and Pleasures of a Country Life*. He recommended a laborious task for farmers to scare rooks from their corn. This involved digging holes about two feet deep and four feet in diameter then placing long crow feathers round the circumference and in the bottom of these shallow pits. "I prefume the Reafon is, becaufe whilft they are feeding on the ground, the terrifying object is out of their fight; which is not ufual in other Scare-Crows, wherewith in a little time they grow familiar, by being always in view."

Scarecrow among the sunflowers
at Groombridge, Kent.

Gruesome devices which were formerly employed to frighten away pestilent birds included limbs of rooks scattered about the ground; their feathers stuck up on lines; dead crows swinging on sticks and a boy constantly tossing a dead bird into the air. Nuisance birds were scared off certain plots by the sight of strewn feathers and hung corpses of their own kind. Birds are territorial creatures and are thought to be daunted by the sight of another bird's feathers twirling in the wind whereas a dead bird nailed to a barn door or a tree stump is supposed to warn them of their impending fate. (These devices are all preferable to the rural custom of tethering live cats to a stake to ward off wild birds from fruit trees.)

Gardeners today often revert to that timeless trick of criss crossing strings of black thread or elastic twine on wooden pegs a few inches above a seed bed. The thread hums as it vibrates in the wind so that the birds sense a trap and fly away. Strips of newspaper, tin foil or even feathers tied to the string at short intervals is a further refinement. This is both a time honoured and time consuming method which does appear to be effective but it is only practical in modest plots such as allotments, gardens or small holding. A grisly alternative is for farmers to shoot several crows or rooks and suspend them from posts in fields as a warning to other birds. A row of shot birds displayed hanging from a barbed wire boundary fence is referred to by country folk as a 'Gamekeeper's larder.' More humane farmers shape small bundles of straw or hay with a few feathers stuck into it to hang on their fake gibbets.

Fear of predators is, of course, the basis of the scarecrow which models mankind. But cultivators realise that scarecrows must move otherwise birds will become accustomed to them. Amusing letters to contemporary gardening magazines highlight this problem. A lady complained that the birds had become so attached to her scarecrow they regarded it as a friend while another declared they were about as scared of it as her garden fork. One despondent farmer who had put up an effigy of a sportsman in a top hat and frock coat found that wild birds had actually built a nest in it! Farmers realise that they must ring the changes by altering the position of their creations. This keeps the birds guessing and in a constant state of alarm at the unfamiliar sight.

MECHANICAL SCARECROWS

Agricultural scientists have proved that there are four definite methods of deterring avian marauders: scarers producing noise; scarers producing movement; those that imitate natural enemies of the birds and devices which suggest a trap to any birds coming in contact with it.

Twentieth century inventors have experimented with a combination of all these principles to produce cheap, practical, efficient alternatives to traditional scarecrows. Their absurd devices have been generally a catalogue of valient failures fit to rank with the doomed efforts of the intrepid birdmen of past centuries. In 1966, the 'Merrydown Bird Scarer' made its inaugural – and valedictory – flight. This was a piece of plastic festooned with turkey feathers suspended thirty feet below a balloon tethered two hundred feet in the air above East Sussex. It was supposed to resemble a sparrowhawk but one pedantic ornithologist pointed out that it did not, not least because it lacked a head. A crosswind was blowing at the time which buffeted the balloon and caused the novel bird scarer to fly in vertical circles on its tail. The designer magnanimously agreed a passing blackbird would be struck more by curiosity than fear, but added lamely, "It behaves more convincingly high up."

In 1976, the 'Shoobird' made its brief appearance. This looked like a windmill and its manufacture trumpeted, "It can be assembled by a child in two minutes." (A doubtful virtue, one would have thought, for anything meant to be robust.) The following year a Leicester firm launched the 'Flyaway Peter.' This was a complicated structure consisting of three vanes, each of which presented a silhouette of a bird in different stages of flight. It was spectacularly ineffective. General Manager, Jim Lentell, admitted, with rare candour, "No bird scarer is perfect." Unabashed, Jim bounced back in 1980 with his 'Gentleman Jim' scarecrow which at least had a lifelike head. This was his breakthrough, he reckoned, since he now acknowledged that birds can tell the difference between a rotting turnip and a human skull. Jim's invention did a stint in Trafalgar Square where he was challenged to drive the pigeons away. They didn't budge. "Urban birds are accustomed to strange sights," was his disgruntled comment.

Michael Williams, a rival manufacturer from Essex, produced a real corker which was said to look like "an invading Martian." Standing eight feet high, it had four legs, a cylindrical head and long arms. And it wailed like banshee, emitting blinding flashes of light which were clearly visible for miles. "It is the nearest equivalent to a man running across the field waving his arms and shrieking at the top of his voice," pronounced Mr. Williams, optimistically. The birds, disdainfully, begged to differ. His sci-fi scarecrow was quickly lost in space.

An automated scarecrow was invented by Roy Rothery of Walcot which he unveiled at the Lincolnshire County Show in 1961. Farmer Rothery's hovercraft scarecrow was tethered to a post enabling it to circle freely above a field. An assortment of three dimensional shapes could be attached to his unique 'Scarecraft' including a terrier and a hawk. The revolutionary model was offered for one hundred pounds and his hope was that it would be used on airfields. Sadly, his idea did not take off but it beat a rival firm who marketed a mobile scarecrow powered by a humble lawnmower which travelled all day long in one continuous circuit.

A rare successful technological development combining several of these ideas is 'Scarey Man', which is readily available on the market. Powered by a battery operated fan, this is a bright red effigy made of flexible plastic which suddenly inflates to a commanding height of over five feet. In the process it flips several times, thrashes wildly and emits a loud wail. A timer permits this to occur at regular intervals from one to thirty minutes and between each bout 'Scarey Man' sinks back down to the ground. At night he blows up and glows red. Naturalist, Richard Mabey, comments that the bloated figure looks like "a large, inflatable doll whose face has an unnerving resemblance to an Identikit villain in a stocking mask." There is also a luminous model and a garden version, 'Scarey Boy.'

Clarratts, the manufacturers, make the bold claim that their 'Scarey Man' offers "day or night protection against most predators." It would seem that this is no idle boast for it successfully deters a multitude of destructive birds and animals including crows, pigeons, starlings, blackbirds, magpies, herons, rabbits and deer. This unique electronic scarecrow has been exported worldwide from the factory at 'Hollow Farm', Huntingdon, Cambridgeshire. The version used by Robert Royal of Mississippi has, apparently, changed the pattern of cormorant flocks which were devastating local fish farms. More dramatically, another model has been positioned on a farm in Kenya to scare away lions.

Fruit growers in America suspend large, orange hydrogen or helium filled balloons, painted with gigantic eyes, from poles by nylon lines attached to tall masts. These float over trees in the orchards and, because they are unfamiliar, tend to keep most birds at bay. Inflateable "Bug-eyed balloons", shaped like Chinese lanterns, have proved to be both both cheap and effective. A similar trick favoured by farmers in Britain is to fly kites shaped like eagles or hawks, which smaller birds fear, over young crops or fruit trees.

Experiments are currently taking place to prefect a 'Chemical Scarecrow.' Described as "an olfactory or gustatory repellent substance", it is aimed at preventing birds from feasting once it has been applied to a crop. The assumption is that wildfowl will be deterred by any noxious odour but so far all evidence indicates that most birds have a poorly developed sense of smell which, in any case, is of very little consequence in their lives.

Further, birds have few taste buds which means that they will remain oblivious to eating foul, yet harmless, substances. Such observations make it unreasonable for scientists to expect that any crude smell would provide meaningful scaring mechanisms, however repulsive they are to humans. Obviously, these trial chemical substances must not contaminate the crop they are intended to protect.

Farmers in recent times tend to favour automatic gas guns with time fuses that make loud bangs when placed in the centre of their fields. Alternatively, there are slow burning carbide bangers or squibs, rather like fireworks, which, when lit, make an occasional bang just when the birds are least expecting it.

These devices are most effective if the reports explode at irregular intervals. Generations of artful birds, however, have learned to eat their fill between explosions so that the noise is more likely to startle humans who are quick to complain. Frustrated residents of the Blackdown Hills of Devon recently called in local health officials after they had endured one farmer's repeated broadcast to the birds of a psychotic mix of rioting and trumpeting elephants.

LAW AND ORDER

Constant pounding by bottled gas guns and electronic warblers inevitably disturbs the tranquility of the countryside. This can cause acute distress to residents of remote villages and hamlets.

Suzy Gale, wife of the M.P. for Thanet North, found life became intolerable for her family after they were woken up at five o'clock every morning one summer while staying at their country retreat at Preston, near Canterbury. "There were so many salvoes it was like living through the Battle of the Somme," she wailed. "We found it quieter in London."

When Suzy aired her grievances in the national press she was surprised by the overwhelming response from the general public. Her mutinous mood had clearly caught the imagination of the shires and she began to lobby Parliament. She adduced in her support a report by the Apple and Pear Committee of the National Farmers' Union in which a certain Dr. Flegg of East Malling Research Station – hailed as the leading authority on bird damage – advised that "no sound device is of any real value for longer than two days." Furthermore, the Ministry of Agriculture Science Laboratories declared that the only period in which bangers are any use whatsover in the protection of oil-seed rape is between the approximate dates of 23 January and 7 March each year. "Even then they should be used sparingly for more extensive use results in the birds ignoring them."

Suzy Gale was triumphant. In 1987, she formed the Birdscarers Anti Nuisance Group (B.A.N.G.) to campaign for a restriction on audible birdscarers. She won approval from the Noise Abatement Society which opined that "acceptable, viable and silent" alternatives to the problem could readily be found. Her husband, Roger, had already succeeded in his efforts to bring straw and stubble burning under control thus preventing further scarring of the countryside in autumn.

Derek Pritchard, an award-winning wine grower, on the other hand, won approval when he appeared before the magistrates at Minehead accused of shattering the peace of his village with his high-tech birdscarers. He protested that only sensitive newcomers to the community had complained about his innovative machine which sounded, on average, twelve times per hour and boasted a range of two hundred noises including road drills, car horns, a ray gun, bird distress calls, dogs barking and human voices.

After investing £100,000 on his fertile vineyards at Wootton Courtenay, Somerset, Derek was determined to find a more humane alternative to the "barbaric" solution of shooting wild birds. Lamentably, his endeavours landed him in court when he was charged with failing to comply with a council noise abatement order.

The prosecution claimed that, after complaints were received from angry neighbours, an environmental health officer found the bird scarers produced fifteen decibels above the acceptable level of countryside noise. Mr. Pritchard argued that when he turned down the volume on his six acre estate he had lost half his remaining harvest to a flock of starlings. The magistrates listened to his side of the story sympathetically and dismissed the case.

Finally, a Staffordshire farmer was forced to resort to more traditional methods after his high-tech bird scarer caught fire! Firefighters were called to a field off Gorsty Lane, Little Wyrely, after a device similar to a cannon malfunctioned and it was set alight!

CAUTIONARY TALE

Bird scaring can be carried to extremes. Mao Tse-tung (1893–1976) was elected the first Chairman of the People's Republic which has governed China from 1948. The Communist dictator was the son of a farmer who pioneered disastrous reforms in industry and agriculture as part of his 'Great Leap Forward.'

One of the more ridiculous notions of his rural revolution was to declare flies, mosquitoes, rats and especially sparrows, that plagued rice fields, as 'pests.' Imperiously, Mao ordered their mass destruction. Peasants were encouraged to bang pots and pans ceaselessly to keep the sparrows awake until they died of exhaustion. True, these birds no longer ate the crops... but the insects that flourished without their existence caused havoc to the countryside. Harvests failed resulting in widespread famine and fluctuation of the economy. Ultimately, such foolish directives led to Mao's spectacular downfall.

Bird scarer rattle

3. SCARECROWS IN LITERATURE

STORIES FOR YOUNG CHILDREN often feature scarecrows although there are myriad references to them in adult poems, plays and novels. They appear in classics as diverse as 'Don Quixote' (1605) 'Rob Roy' (1817) and 'Adam Bede' (1859) and they are encountered by a host of characters from Sherlock Holmes to William Brown.

POETRY, PLAYS AND PROSE

The Bible contains what must surely be the earliest literary reference to a scarecrow. It appears in the Old Testament 'Book of Jeremiah.' Jeremiah was a reluctant prophet who lived in the second half of the seventh century B.C. He began his inspired career in the reign of King Josiah of Judah at a time when the state was corrupt and religion decadent. Jeremiah expressed his dismay that the Israelites had turned to idolatory and worshipped graven images no better than scarecrows made by men's hands and put together with hammer and nails. Such travesties of deities, he claims, cannot compare to the supremacy of the one, true, God of Israel. His poetic simile, however, is absent in the Authorised Version of King James (1611) and the more accurate Revised Version (1884) where the reference is to a palm tree carved into fantastic shapes, similar to a totem pole.

Mention of a scarecrow appears in all the later translations such as the Revised Standard Version and the New English Bible. (The New International Bible places the scarecrow in a melon patch)

Their idols are like scarecrows
in a cucumber field,
and they cannot speak;
they have to be carried,
for they cannot walk.
Be not afraid of them,

opposite: Max the Miller at Sarre Windmill, Kent.

for they cannot do evil,

neither is it in them to do good.

(Jer. 10 v 5)

Earliest reference to scarecrows in fiction appears in the epic poem, *The Faerie Queene*, by Edmund Spencer (1552–1599) This courtly romance was a thinly disguised eulogy extolling the virtues of Elizabeth I. The epic work transcends its immediate subject matter to become an enduring love poem and a haunting exploration of the mythology of Britain. Spenser was born in London, educated at Cambridge but eventually moved to Ireland when he was created Secretary to the new Lord Deputy. He took up permanent residence in Kilcolman Castle, near Cork, although he never forgot his devotion to Good Queen Bess in whose honour he composed his narrative verse. He was pursuaded by his neighbour, Sir Walter Raleigh, to travel to England to present the manuscript in person to the Virgin Queen. Her Majesty was duly flattered by the poetry and so she awarded Spencer a handsome pension.

In the poem (published 1590) valiant Sir Guyon, seeking to avenge his parents' murder, stumbles upon a ragged figure "sitting ydle on a sunny banck." He draws his sword and threatens him although the "scarecrow" proves harmless and agrees to become the nobleman's servant:

Thereat the Scarecrow wexed wondrous prowd,
Through fortune of his first adventure fayre,
And with big thundring voice revyld him lowd:
"Vile Caytive, vassall of dread and despayre,
Unworthie of the commune breathed ayre,
Why livest thou, dead dog, a lenger day,
And doest not unto death thyselfe prepayre?
Dy, or thyselfe my captive yield for ay.
Great favour I thee graunt for aunswere thus to stay."

(Book II, Canto III, Verse 7)

That "upstart crow", William Shakespeare (1564–1616) mentions scarecrows several times in his plays. An early reference appears in *Henry VI, Part One* (1591) where Lord Talbot, recently released from captivity, returns to London and describes his humiliation at the hands of the French:

In open market-place, produc'd they me,
To be a public spectacle to all:

Here, said they, is the terror of the French,

The scarecrow that affrights our children so.

   (Act I, Scene 3)

Falstaff privately admits in *Henry IV, Part One* (1597) that he has raised a ragged army of raw recruits for the King's service which he is far too ashamed to publicly present:

A mad fellow met me on the way, and told me I had unloaded all the gibbets and pressed the dead bodies. No eye hath seen such scarecrows. I'll not march through Coventry with them, that's flat.

   (Act IV, Scene 2)

Falstaff, himself, is fooled by the mischievous ladies in the comedy, *Merry Wives of Windsor* (1597) Mistress Page chides the rascal: "You little Jack-a-Lent, have you been true to us?" (Act III Scene III). At the close of the play he admits: "See now, how wit may be made a Jack-a-lent when 'tis upon ill employment!" (Act V Scene V). These are the first printed examples of the term for a scarecrow, 'Jack-a-Lent."

In the dark comedy, *Measure for Measure* (1603) the tyrannical Angelo, Deputy to Duke Vincentio, refuses to show mercy to Claudio, who is sentenced to be beheaded for his licentiousness. Instead he ferociously declares:

We must not make a scarecrow of the law,

Setting it up to fear the birds of prey,

And let it keep one shape, till custom make it

Their perch, and not their terror.

   (Act II, Scene 1)

Finally, in the tragedy, *King Lear* (1604/5) the mad king, in his ravings, hallucinates that he is addressing a vast army on the cliffs above Dover. "That fellow handles his bow like a crow-keeper," he yells into the salty air (Act IV Sc 6). The reference, here, is to the antiquated practice of shooting crows with bows and arrows.

Ben Jonson (1572–1637) – a friend of Shakespeare – makes several scattered references to scarecrows in his later plays. *The Staple of Newes* (first performed in 1625) is a satire that explores the idea of gathering, refining and promulgating information and parodies the absurdities among newsmongers of the time. Peni-Boy Senior, the Canter (or beggar) enters 'The Devil Tavern' wearing "a patched and ragged cloke" where he extolls the virtues of the soldier to impress his idle son. (Jonson had been a mercenery in his youth fighting in Flanders during the protracted wars of William the Silent against the Spanish):

> So, a true Souldier,
> He is his Countryes strength, his Soveraignes safety,
> And to secure his peace, he makes himself
> The heyre of danger, nay the subject of it,
> And runnes those vertuous hazards, that this Scarrecrow
> Cannot endure to heare of!
>
> (Act IV Scene 1)

In his more famous play, *A Tale of A Tub* (first performed in 1633 but probably a revision of an earlier comedy) there is a scene where Squire Tub and his governor, Hilts, accost Miles Metaphor, a young clerk, as he scampers across the countryside in the vicinity of Kentish Town. Hilts hurls insults at the dishevelled youth and compares him to a scarecrow set up at a country fair for folk to throw wooden balls at to win a prize:

> Thou cam'st but half a thing into the world,
> And wast made up of patches, parings, shreds:
> Thou, that when last thou wert put out of service,
> Travell'dst to Hampstead-heath on an Ash Wednesday,
> Where thou didst stand six weeks the Jack of Lent,
> For boys to hurl, three throws a penny, at thee,
> To make thee a purse.
>
> (Act IV Scene 3)

CLASSIC NOVELS

Daniel Defoe (1660–1731) sometimes regarded as the first English novelist, won worldwide acclaim for his fictional biography, *Robinson Crusoe* (1719). His exciting story of a shipwrecked mariner stranded on a desert island in the Caribbean Sea was based upon the factual experiences of a Scottish sailor, Alexander Selkirk, whose journal Defoe probably read. Crusoe's account of his survival and details of his self-sufficiency still make fascinating, if gruesome, reading. At one point he tells how he sowed corn rescued from his stricken ship but was dismayed to find that it was instantly devoured by the island's birds. After shooting three of these thieving natives, he notes,

> "... I took them up, and served them as we serve notorious thieves in England, viz, hanged them in chains for a terror to others. It is impossible to imagine almost, that this should have such an effect as it had; for the fowls wou'd not only come at the corn, but in short they forsook all that part of the island, and I could never see a bird near the place as long as my scare-crows hung there."

Defoe made another allusion to a scarecrow in his book, *The Political History of the Devil* (1726). The purpose of this book was to present an accurate portrait of Satan according to the scriptures which presented him in his fallen 'Angelic form.' Defoe dismissed the medieval trappings that painted him with "Bat's Wings, Horns, cloven Foot, long Tail, fork'd Tongue, and the like. . ." "Nor indeed should we have much Reason to be frighted at him, or at least none of those filly Things could be said of him which we now amuse ourselves about, and by which we set him up like a Scare-Crow to frighten children and old women, to fill up old Stories, make Songs and Ballads, and in a Word carry on the low priz'd Buffoonry of the Common People." (Part II Chapter III)

Henry Fielding (1707–1754) celebrated for his comic masterpiece, *Tom Jones*, created a more virtuous character, *Joseph Andrews* (1742) to be the hero of another farcical romp. Young Joey is introduced to the reader in a mock serious biographical chapter where he attempts to perform several menial tasks on Sir Thomas Booby's country estate with hilarious consequences:

> "At ten years old (by which time his education was advanced to writing and reading) he was bound an apprentice, according to the statute, to Sir Thomas Booby, an uncle of Mr. Booby's by the father's side. Sir Thomas having then an estate in his own hands, the young Andrews was at first employed in what in the country they call keeping birds. His office was to perform the part the antients assigned to the god Priapus, which deity the moderns call by the name Jack-o'-Lent: but his voice being so extremely musical, that it rather allured the birds than terrified them, he was soon transplanted from the fields into the dog-kennel, where he was placed under the huntsman, and made what sportsmen term a whipper-in."

(It is surely ironic that Joseph Andrews, paragon of chastity, was required to play the part of Priapus, god of promiscuity.)

Charles Dickens (1812–1870) made several literary allusions to scarecrows in his novels. The earliest occurs in *Nicholas Nickleby*, first printed serially in a periodical but published in book form in 1839. Nicholas naively travels to Yorkshire to be the new schoolmaster at 'Dotheboys Hall.' He reels in horror as the rascally headmaster, Wackford Squeers, triumphantly introduces him to his pathetic, starving charges: "Obedient to this summons there ranged themselves in front of the schoolmaster's desk, half-a-dozen scarecrows, out at knees and elbows, one of whom placed a torn and filthy book beneath his learned eye." (Chapter VIII).

A more dramatic mention of scarecrows occurs in *A Tale of Two Cities* (1859). This powerful drama concerns the ultimate sacrifice of the profligate, Sydney Carton, when he changes places with the handsome Charles Darney who is about to be guillotined during the French Revolution. Pampered aristocrats ignore signs that starving peasants are on the verge of revolt and their indifference to the inevitable tragedy is likened to exotic birds avoiding the threat of a scarecrow: "But, the time was not come yet; and every wind that blew over France shook the rags of the scarecrows in vain, for the birds, fine of song and feather, took no warning." (Chapter V).

Young Pip recalls working as a lad scaring birds from the marshland farms of North Kent in *Great Expectations* (1861). "I was not only odd-boy about the forge, but if any neighbour happened to want an extra boy to frighten birds, or pick up stones, or do any such job, I was favoured with the employment." (Chapter 7) Although this novel is supposedly set in the period of Dickens' boyhood it bears strong evidence of the mid Victorian period when it was actually published.

Thomas Hardy (1840–1928) makes an oblique reference to scarecrows in his romantic comedy, *The Distracted Preacher* contained in 'Wessex Tales' (1888). Mr. Stockdale, a young Methodist minister, arrives in the village of Nether-Moynton and promptly falls in love with the widowed Mrs Lizzy Newberry who just happens to be the leader of a smuggling fraternity. The itinerent preacher faces a dilemma between love and conscience which is rather too neatly resolved. A highpoint in the story is when one of the smugglers accidentally drops a tub of brandy and the Preventive Men follow the trail of the heady liquor. Their leader, Will Linton, instructs his officers to sniff any discarded soiled clothing which may lead them to their owner who will indisputably have had contact with the contraband. Among the objects he suggests they investigate for the smell of alcohol are scarecrows.

Hardy's final, bleak novel, *Jude The Obscure* (1896) opens with the orphaned youngster, Jude Fawley, earning sixpence a day scaring birds for the brutal Farmer Troutham. The scene is set in Marygreen, which corresponds with Fawley in Berkshire where Hardy's grandmother lived as a child. After his retiring schoolmaster charges him to be kind to animals and birds, Jude feels an empathy for the rooks, who, like him, have been displaced from their territory. He stands reluctantly early one morning in the newly ploughed fields of fictional Wessex:

> "The boy stood under the rick. . . and every few seconds used his clacker or rattle briskly. At each clack the rooks left off pecking, and rose and went away on their leisurely wings, burnished like tassels of mail, afterwards wheeling back and regarding him warily, and descending to feed at a more respectful distance.
>
> He sounded the clacker till his arm ached, and at length his heart grew sympathetic with the birds' thwarted desires. They seemed, like himself, to be living in a world which did not want them. Why should he frighten them away? They took upon them more and more the aspect of gentle friends and pensioners – the only friends he could claim as being in the least degree interested in him, for his aunt had often told him that she was not. He ceased his rattling and they alighted anew.
>
> 'Poor little dears!' said Jude, aloud. 'You shall have some dinner – you shall. There is enough for us all. Farmer Troutham can afford to let you have some. Eat then, my dear little birdies and make a good meal.'
>
> They stayed and ate, inky spots on the nut-brown soil, and Jude enjoyed their appetite. A magic thread of fellow-feeling united his own life with theirs. Puny and sorry as those lives were, they much resembled his own."

Young Jude is interrupted from his reveries by the irate farmer who appears suddenly out of the morning mist and "tickles his breeches" with the discarded clacker for idling his time.

Sir Arthur Conan Doyle (1859–1930) alludes to a scarecrow in *The Sign of Four* (1892) where the great detective, Sherlock Holmes, is visited at 221b Baker Street by his loyal band of street urchins who supply him with valuable information. "One of their number, taller and older than the others, stood forward with an air of superiority which was very funny in such a disreputable scarecrow." (Chapter 8)

NOVELS AND NOVELETTES

Hugh Walpole (1884–1941) wrote a whimsical novel, *The Golden Scarecrow* (1915). His slight tale centres upon the inhabitants of March Square in London who were helped through various crises in their infant lives by the presence of a fantasy "friend." A prologue relates how an impressionable boy, Hugh Seymour, befriends an elderly, eccentric, unsuccessful author, Mr Pigden, who is staying at a country vicarage one Christmas. The pair relate how they have both been encouraged during times of loneliness by the presence of a childhood "friend." As they tramp across the barren fields they notice on the horizon a scarecrow dramatically illuminated by the late winter sunshine. Momentarily, it seems, their mutual "friend" has manifested itself on the moor as a chivalrous knight:

> "The Scarecrow, perched on the high ridge, waved its tattered sleeves in the air. It was an old tin can that caught the light; the can hanging over the stake that supported it in drunken fashion seemed to wink at them. The shadows came streaming up from the sea and the dark woods below in the hollow drew closer to them.
>
> The Scarecrow seemed to lament the departure of the light. "Here, mind," he said to the two of them, "you saw me in my glory just now and don't you forget it. I may be a knight in shining armour after all. It only depends upon the point of view.
>
> The sun, at that instant, sank behind the hills and the world was grey."

Alfred Noyes (1880–1958) wrote a hilarious novel, *The Return of the Scarecrow* (1929). Noyes was a Staffordshire poet who composed the famous narrative verse, 'The Highwayman.' His farcical tale concerns the misadventures of a fastidious curate, Rev. Basil Strode, who returns to nature and is pursued by the eccentric inhabitants of the seaside village of Chalkdene, "a slumbering heap of gunpowder", on the coast of Sussex. This gentle satire explores the naked Anglican priest's transition from worship of the Christian to the Pagan Gods. When he returns to civilisation after countless mishaps, he has been turned into the semblance of a country scarecrow.

In the second chapter, Noyes describes the attempts by two villagers, Shepherd Thorn and Double Dick, a thieving tramp, to build a scarecrow on the rolling downs. Their original idea was to dress the scarecrow in castaway garments supplied by Thorn who opines that "worst clothes make best scarecrows." It turns out that the scarecrow's rags are superior to Dick's garments so he exchanges them for his own. The pair work indefatigably, knotting a beer-stained coat to the crosspiece and stuffing weathered trousers out with bracken. When completed the scarecrow is the spitting image of Double Dick.

> "Thorn went on with his task, glancing from time to time at Double Dick, as an artist glances at his model. He trimmed a big swede with his knife and fixed it securely on the central pole. He whitened the front half with chalk, leaving two dark circles for the eyes, a triangle for the nose, and a crescent for the mouth. Fronds of withered fern represented the hair, and were held in place by the hat. He turned up the coat collar to make the neck more realistic. He fastened to the back of the figure the windmill arrangement that gave a continuous clack and croak in a light breeze. And at last stood back a few yards to survey

the finished work. Double Dick sat up and also looked at it with interest.

There was a moment's silence, and then Double Dick said with simple conviction:

"Gord! It's me."

Ironically, when the naturist curate acquires clothes from a scarecrow to cover his embarrassment before he returns to conventional society, they are the very coat and trousers which Double Dick had swapped. It is with profound relief that he encounters that "rigid spectre, outstretched to bar his way... a wooden skeleton robed in rags and tatters." Unfortunately, hidden in the pockets are valuable pieces of stolen jewellery which adds to further complications when the curate is arrested for burglary. Eventually, the situations are resolved and the young curate's extraordinary exploits bring not only greater respect from his parishioners but the prospects of true romance.

Clemence Dane (1884–1960) wrote a compelling novel about a scarecrow, *The Arrogant History of White Ben* (1939) whose publication coincided with the commencement of hostilities with Germany. Her story is set in the near future after the cessation of a war which has ravaged England. The scarecrow – predictably, in novels – comes alive and dedicates his existence to annihilating crows from the face of the earth. A frenzy of "crow-fever" follows where the defenceless birds are either assassinated or incarcerated in concentration cages.

Clemence Dane (the pseudonym of Winifred Ashton) was not only an author and playwright but also an artist and sculptress. She was a great friend of the impressario, Val Gielgud, and her bust of Ivor Novello still stands prominently in the foyer of Drury Lane Theatre. Her most successful play was *Bill of Divorcement* although she won late recognition for *Eighty in the Shade* which she wrote for Sybil Thorndyke and Lewis Casson in their dotage. Celebrities were constantly welcomed at her untidy caravan packed with unfinished canvases in deepest Sussex.

The turnip-head scarecrow of her allegory stands in the "rook-haunted cornfields" of an imaginary village nestling below 'Campion's Hilltop.' He was made by an elderly gardener, George, assisted by a spoiled city child, Elly. George remembers a time when his brother fought in the previous war and became tangled in the barbed wires of 'No Man's Land.' When he was reached by rescuers, his decomposed body resembled a scarecrow dressed in a battle-scarred uniform. One day the gardener demands from his mistress a new outfit for his scarecrow which, he insists, must be pure white.

"There stood the scarecrow of the field, mounted on a hillock matted over by couch-grass

so coarse that its blades could draw blood. Through the loose root-stock white campions

rose up to flower about the scarecrow's wooden ankle, while sturdier briony writhed up him like a snake, hung from his black shoulders with a natural jewellery, and held firm his bowler hat. The rooks used him as a look-out, and beneath his arms the campion had grown the richer for their droppings.

The little girl admired the birds' daring; but it so infuriated the gardener that one hot day he marched down the cinder path to the back-door and demanded a new suit for the scarecrow.

"Have you anything white, missis? They're not afraid of black or colours."

Elly names her scarecrow, 'White Ben', because he stands in a field of white campion whose rural name is "white-ben." Unwisely, she places a magical mandrake root in his pocket which brings him to life. All the donated white garments assume a special significance the moment the scarecrow assumes human form. "He had been given flesh and bones. He had been garmented with religion, diplomacy, the art of war, the art of healing; for he wore a priest's vestment, a soldier's gauntlets, a civilian mackintosh, a gentleman's pleasure-hat, a surgeon's coat."

Culmination of White Ben's campaign is a rally in Trafalgar Square and the storming of Westminster Abbey by a hostile mob. Ironically, after ridding the world of crows, White Ben, drunk with power, returns to being a scarecrow once more but he is torn to pieces by pitiless children who invade his peaceful field. Clemence Dane's novel was intended as a parody of racial persecution under Hitler but modern critics have detected its universal significance in alerting readers to a cosmic malaise.

SHORT STORIES

An American short story featuring a scarecrow who comes to life appears in an anthology, *Mosses From An Old Manse* (1846) by Nathaniel Hawthorne (1804–1864). The author, whose great grandfather presided over the infamous witchcraft trials, drew on the customs concerning the occult of his rural hometown, Salem, Massachusetts. Mother Rigby constructs an aristocratic scarecrow to keep crows and blackbirds away from her patch of emerging Indian corn. She fashions his body from a broomstick, a flail, hoe handle, pudding spoon and broken rung of a chair. This wooden skeleton is then padded out with a mealbag stuffed with straw. She dresses him in a plum coloured, threadbare coat with embroidered cuffs, pockets and button holes, a velvet waistcoat, scarlet breeches and silk stockings. Final touch is to place her late husband's peruque on his pumpkin head and a tricorn hat decorated with the tail feather of a rooster. This inspires her to give the elegant scarecrow his name,

'Feathertop.' (It is also the name of a certain style of wig.)

Once complete, Mother Rigby, who just happens to be a witch, brings her creation to life by means of a charmed clay pipe. She charges Feathertop to pay a visit to her neighbour, Justice Gookin, who is also her arch enemy. She wishes to make a fool of him by allowing his daughter, Polly, to fall in love with such a stylish young gentleman without realising that he is, in reality, a scarecrow. The plot backfires when Polly glances in her mirror and sees that her suitor has no reflection. Feathertop returns home to Mother Rigby where he divests himself of his fine clothes and becomes a clutter of household utensils once more.

> "Snatching the pipe from his mouth, he flung it with all his might against the chimney, and at the same instant sank upon the floor, a medley of straw and tattered garments, with some sticks protruding from the heap and a shrivelled pumpkin in the midst. The eyeholes were now lustreless, but the rudely-carved gap that just before had been a mouth still seemed to twist itself into a despairing grin, and was so far human.
>
> "Poor fellow!" quoth Mother Rigby, with a rueful glance at the relics of her ill-fated contrivance. "My poor dear pretty Feathertop! There are thousands upon thousands of coxcombs and charlatans in the world made up of just such a jumble of worn-out, forgotten and good-for-nothing trash as he was, yet they live in fair repute, and never see themselves for what they are. And why should my poor puppet be the only one to know himself and perish for it?"

A theatrical version of 'Feathertop' was written by Percy MacKaye and presented in New York under the title, *The Scarecrow*, in 1910. There were minor alterations to Hawthorne's story. Goody Rickby, a vengeful witch, brings a scarecrow to life which she has fashioned in her forge. She names him 'Lord Ravensbane' and sends him to court the neice of Justice Merton, a devout Puritan, who had once spurned her. A jealous fiancé, Richard Talbot, exposes the dandy as a scarecrow but he chooses to discard his magic pipe and die an honest nobleman rather than seek revenge.

A television version of this play, starring zany actor, Gene Wilder (born 1934), who gave a strangely hypnotic performance as the scarecrow, was shown across America in 1971.

The success of the original play had also inspired a silent film, *Puritan Passions* (Film Guild/Hodkinson, 1923) This plot centred upon a cynical devil disguised as a scarecrow and the action took place during the notorious Salem witchhunts. An illegitimate child born to Gillead Wingate and Goody Rickby dies when the father refuses to seek medical aid for fear of scandal. Rickby swears revenge on Wingate whereupon a mysterious Dr. Nicholas ('Old Nick') arrives to offer his dubious services.

He breathes life into a scarecrow and turns him into a handsome suitor (Glenn Hunter) for Wingate's ward, Rachel (Mary Astor). The girl falls in love with him and their marriage is announced. Dr Nicholas intends to reveal the truth and expose both Wingate and Rachel for witchcraft. But the scarecrow foils Dr Nicholas' plan by laying down his life for the love of Rachel and thus he redeems his soul and dies a man.

"Deprived of sound and dialogue, director, Frank Tuttle, retained a good part of the play's poetic quality by making the picture strikingly visual and borrowing the barest of influence from German films," comments Carlos Clarens in his *Illustrated History of Horror and Science Fiction Films* (1997): "There were scenes of supernatural horror, as when the weird, misshapen creatures of the netherworld meet for the witches' Sabbath or the episode of the Mirror of Truth, borrowed from Goethe's *Faust*, where sinners see themselves as they really are . . ."

American anthologies of short stories frequently allude to scarecrows. One claustrophobic tale, *The Scarecrow*, appears in *The Scarecrow and Other Stories* (1918) by Gwendolyn Ranger Wormser. This inconsequential piece consists of little more than a dialogue between a widow and her wayward son who hates the farm on which he has been reared. The shivering figure of a scarecrow wearing his grandfather's military uniform beckons him from the cornfield one sultry, moonlit night, although there is no wind, and he makes his timely escape. Another succinct tale with a neat twist called *Scarecrow* by Paul Jones appears in *Famous Short Stories* (1966). This absorbing collection of "prize yarns by master entertainers" written in the twenties and thirties purports to present a dynamic picture of the United States just prior to World War II. Bank robber, Eddie Gann, holes up in a remote farm awaiting his share of the payout, kills the farmer and disguises his body as a scarecrow. He considers he is safe even when surrounded by state officials until the moment when a flock of buzzards swoop down into the cornfield and knock the scarecrow's hat off!

First British short story dedicated exclusively to a scarecrow was written by Kenneth Grahame (1859–1932) revered author of the children's classic, *Wind In The Willows*. Grahame was a Scotsman who acquired his great affinity with the English countryside when he was brought up by his grandmother at Cookham Dene, Berkshire, and when he attended school in Oxford. Even when he embarked on a banking career in the metropolis he would whisk off for long weekends with a friend on the Berkshire Downs.

Grahame's brief tale, *An Autumnal Encounter*, was first published in *National Observer* (25 March 1893) but reprinted in a collection, *Pagan Papers* (1898). It opens with a traveller crossing the Ridgeway when he encounters a scarecrow at dawn:

opposite: Witch at Sandwich, Kent.

"For yet another mile or two the hot dusty road runs through level fields, till it reaches yonder shoulder of the downs, already golden three-parts up with ripening corn. Thitherwards lies my inevitable way; and now that home is almost in sight it seems hard that the last part of the long day's sweltering and delightful tramp must needs be haunted by that hateful speck, black on the effulgence of the slope. Did I not know he was only a scarecrow, the thing might be in a way companionable: a pleasant suggestive surmise, piquing curiosity, gilding this last weary stage with some magic of expectancy. But I passed close by him on my way out. Early as I was, he was already up and doing, eager to introduce himself. He leered after me as I swung down the road, – mimicked my gait, as it seemed, in a most uncalled-for way: and when I looked back, he was blowing derisive kisses of farewell with his empty sleeve."

The anonymous traveller's mind casts back to the time when he was courting a young girl and they carved their initials on a wooden gate to mark their tryst eternally. When he returns at dusk, he is taunted by the scarecrow whose gyrating posture seems to express a variety of emotions – censorious, mocking and amorous – that conjure up painful thoughts of unrequited love. Close up, the traveller confronts the "heartless mummer" and surmises that his battered clothing was once worn by a similar male lover. "More than one supple waist has been circled by that tattered sleeve in days gone by; a throbbing heart once beat where sodden straw now fails to give a manly curve to the chest. Why should the coat survive, and not a particle of the passion that inspired it long ago?" Mundanely, the story ends with the traveller abandoning his fanciful thoughts and settling for a pint in the 'Dog and Duck.'

Baroness Orczy (1865–1947) Hungarian authoress, invented the fictitious hero, Sir Percy Blakeney, who, as the audacious 'Pimpernel', rescues innocent victims from the guillotine during the French Revolution. First performed as a stage play in 1905, *The Scarlet Pimpernel* fired the imagination of the British public and when it appeared in novel form that same year its publication marked the first of a string of international bestsellers. *The League of the Scarlet Pimpernel* (1920) includes a short story, *The Old Scarecrow*, which concerns the recovery of incriminating documents from the sinister citizen-deputy, Hériot. The devil-may-care perpetrator of this daring escapade is the elderly Public Letter-Writer whose shambling gait and squalid attire resemble a scarecrow. Avid readers of Orczy's novels will instantly recognise that this is merely another disguise of the courageous Pimpernel. "Demmed elusive."

Sir Pelham Grenville Wodehouse (1881–1975) lyricist, journalist and playwright, is celebrated as the author of over seventy sparkling novels and three hundred short stories. Inevitably, the creator of Jeeves and Wooster and Blandings Castle referred to scarecrows upon occasions as his memorable characters strayed into the English countryside. For instance, in *Summer Lightning* (1929) the waspish Lady Constance Keeble turns to her pig-rearing brother, Clarence, Lord Emsworth, and imperiously commands: "Dinner is at eight. And please see that your dress clothes are nicely pressed. Ring for Beach and tell him now. Last night you looked like a scarecrow."

And in another P.G. Wodehouse story, *Trouble Down at Tudesleigh*, a chapter within the title, *Men In Spats* (1936) Freddie Widgeon, a prominent member of the Drones Club, pursues his great love, April Carroway, with disastrous results. While courting this glamour puss Freddie finds himself trouserless in his rival's cottage. At the end of the convoluted tale he loses his girl but regains his modesty by stealing a pair of trousers from a scarecrow before driving back, forlornly, to London.

American humourist, James Thurber (1894–1961) compiled a collection of modern parables previously published in *The New Yorker* called *Further Fables of Our Time* (1956) One vignette, *The Crow and The Scarecrow*, concerns a farmer who disguises himself as a scarecrow in order to rid himself of "an armada of crows." His attempt has disastrous consequences when a kamikaze crow sets himself alight and aims straight for his trapped body. "The farmer was just about to blaze away at the squadron of crows with both barrels when the one that was on fire headed straight for him. The sight of the crow, dripping with what seemed to be blood, and flaring like a Halloween torch, gave the living scarecrow such a shock that he dropped dead in one beat less than the tick of a watch." The dubious moral Thurber draws for this particular fable is that: "All men kill the thing they hate unless, of course, it kills them first."

Perhaps the most stylish scarecrows mentioned in modern fiction are those by the journalist, J.B. Morton (1893–1979) who wrote a regular column, 'By The Way', for over fifty years in the *Daily Express* under the pseudonym, 'Beachcomber.' His reference to a distinctly upper crust scarecrow appeared in his wry essay, *A Foul Innuendo*, which even gains an entry in the *Penguin Dictionary of Modern Quotations*: "Not many of our old families can boast that a Savile Row tailor calls four times a year at their country estates to measure the scarecrows in the fields for new suits."

MURDER MYSTERIES

Margery Allingham (1904–1996) wrote a vastly entertaining novel which includes a pivotal scene involving a scarecrow. *The Case of the Late Pig* (1937) perfectly captures life in an English village 'between the wars.' Her stylish amateur sleuth, Albert Campion, attempts to unravel the mystery of the murder of his bullying school chum, 'Pig Peters', at a country house. The scheming uncle of the victim, Hayhoe, tries to extract money on the strength of incriminating knowledge he possesses but he soon mysteriously disappears. Campion borrows a telescope and surveys the scene from a hill where he notices a scarecrow in a distant cornfield. Far from frightening the rooks, it seems to be attracting them and upon investigation it proves to be the mutilated body of the missing blackmailer. BBC television (1988) presented a marvellous dramatisation of this tale starring Peter Davison as Campion and Michael Gough as the obnoxious Hayhoe.

Manxman, Nigel Kneale (born 1922) creator of the science fiction series, *Quatermass*, began his prolific career with a volume of short stories called *Tomato Cain and Other Stories* (1949). This atmospheric tale concerns a deranged person who steals a scarecrow from a windy ridge and becomes convinced it is telling him to murder the villagers one by one. The author demonstrates his masterly skill at building up tension in a few hundred words.

'Queen of Crime', Agatha Christie, (1890–1976) wrote a most satisfying short story in which a scarecrow presides over a scene where a murder is about to be committed. The creator of the two famous contrasting detectives, the retired Belgian, Monsieur Hercule Poirot, and the village spinster, Miss Jane Marple, invented another supernatural sleuth who she called Harley Quin. Whenever the elusive Mr. Quin makes an appearance his presence is heralded by some trick of the light which makes him seem to be dressed momentarily in the motley costume of Harlequin, the mischievous hero of the Italian Commedia dell'Arte, forerunner of British pantomime. When the illusion vanishes, Mr. Quin is revealed to be merely a tall, thin, dark, young man, conventionally attired. Mr. Quin, however, neither solves nor prevents crimes himself but operates through his human partner, Mr Satterthwaite, an elderly gentleman of substantial means but an onlooker whom life has passed by. . .

Mrs Christie enjoyed writing about this unlikely pair so much that she declined to contribute a series of stories to any one particular journal. She preferred rather to write about them at leisure over a period of time and therefore these stories were scattered about in magazines across Britain and America. Twelve of them were collected together and issued in one volume under the title, *The Mysterious Mr. Quin* (1930). Her archaeologist husband, Professor Max Mallowan, who called them "detection written in a fanciful vein, touching on the fairy story", casually mentioned in his memoirs that there was a fugitive tale, *The Harlequin Tea Set*, never published in Britain. It had appeared separately in two anthologies, *Winter's Crimes 3* (1971) and *Ellery Queen's Murdercade* (1975). *The Harlequin Tea Set*, the pendant to the series, is a murder story concerning colour. It is set in the olde-world village of Kingsbourne Ducis, which perhaps indicates the county of Devon. The intended victim is colour blind and therefore does not notice that his red teacup has been subsituted for a blue one, which contains poison, by a jealous mother who wishes her son to inherit the country estate, 'Doverton.' Mr. Satterwaite, who is taking tea at the same time in the garden with an old friend, swiftly acts to prevent this heinous crime. He is inspired by a scarecrow standing in a nearby field who is suddenly illuminated by the setting sun. Inexplicably, the scarecrow, which the family have named 'Harley Barley', later catches fire which event marks positively the last appearance of our mysterious, Harley Quin.

At one point in the story an obscure rhyme is sung in celebration by members of the garden party:

> Harley Barley, stands on guard,
> Harley Barley takes things hard.
> Guards the ricks and guards the hay,
> Keeps the trespassers away.

A superior detective story, *The Scarecrow Murders* (1939) by Frederick Arnold Kummer (1873–1943) was published in America. The opening chapter begins with the discovery of a mutilated body disguised as a scarecrow hidden in a field of squashes being pecked at by ravenous buzzards. A second body is discovered similarly disported and two lovers are wrongly accused before the final revelation of the maniacal murderer by an astute judge.

The discovery of the first murder is graphically described:

> "The original scarecrow had consisted of a ragged black coat, a pair of khaki trousers, stuffed with straw, and suspended by means of a crossbar to a stout hickory post set in the ground.
>
> The straw forming the scarecrow's body had been contained in an old potato sack, to keep it from being blown away by the wind.
>
> "Now coat, trousers and gunnysack all lay on the earth near the base of the post and in their place young Morrison's corpse hung limply from the crossbar, lashed to it with bits of rusty fence wire. Although of slight build his weight had been sufficient to tilt the post forward at an angle so that one of his arms, whether by accident or design, now pointed downward and directly at the house some five hundred or more yards away.
>
> "He wore a ducking outfit – boots, corduroy breeches, sweater and fleece-lined jacket of waterpoof canvas. The ancient derby hat which formed part of the original scarecrow had been jammed down over his head so that his eyes were just visible, peering out from beneath its tattered brim with an expression no longer human."

American suspense writer, Patricia Highsmith (1921–1995) wrote an intriguing murder story about a scarecrow, first published in *Ellery Queen's Mystery Magazine* (November 1976). Later, it was included in a book of short stories when it gave the title to the collection, *Slowly, Slowly In The Wind* (1979)

Edward 'Skip' Skipperton is insanely jealous of his neighbour, Peter Frosby, who he kills after a dispute over fishing rights of a stream which borders his farm. Artfully, he conceals the body inside a classic scarecrow which he has built to keep crows off his corn. His crime is eventually discovered by children intent on burning the scarecrow as a stunt for 'trick or treat' at Hallowe'en.

> "He had decided that broad daylight was the best time to carry out his idea, better than
> night when an oddly playing flashlight that he would have to use might have caught
> someone's eye. So Skip put one arm around Frosby's body and dragged him up the field
> towards his scarecrow. It was a haul of more than a mile. Skip had some rope and a knife
> in his back pockets. He cut down the old scarecrow, cut the strings that held the clothing
> to the cross, dressed Frosby in the old trousers and jacket, tied a burlap bag around his
> head and face, and jammed the hat on him. The hat wouldn't stay without being tied on,
> so Skip did this after punching holes in the brim of the hat with his knife point. Then Skip
> picked up his burlap bags and made his way back towards his house down the slope with
> many a backward look to admire his work, and many a smile. The scarecrow looked
> almost the same as before. He had solved a problem a lot of people thought difficult: what
> to do with the body. Furthermore, he could enjoy looking at it through his binoculars
> from his upstairs window."

American horror writer, Stephen King (born 1947) described gory human scarecrows in his short story, *Children of the Corn*, first published in *Penthouse* and later in his collection, *Night Shift* (1977). A quarrelsome husband and wife stop temporarily at a small town called Gatlin inhabited only by malevolent children. The husband is pursued by manic youngsters wielding axes and he hides among adjacent rows of corn which are miraculously free from weeds, blight and crows. He stumbles upon a clearing where he makes the horrific discovery of adults crucified in a circle to guarantee an abundant harvest. Among the victims is his wife:

> "She had been mounted on a crossbar like a hideous trophy, her arms held at the wrists
> and her legs at the ankles with twists of common barbed wire, seventy cents a yard at any
> hardware store in Nebraska. Her eyes had been ripped out. The sockets were filled with
> the moonflax of cornsilk. Her jaws were wrenched open in a silent scream, her mouth
> filled with cornhusks."

Children of the Corn was turned into a spine-chilling horror film by New World Pictures in 1984. The young couple, played by Peter Horton and Linda Hamilton, naively stray into the deserted town of Gatlin which lies in the centre of the drought-stricken prairie lands of Nebraska. Its only inhabitants are children who believe that human blood alone will restore life to the parched earth and revive the dying corn. The tension mounts as the sinister boy preacher, Isaac, and his teenage executioner, Malachi, relentlessly pursue their adult victims through the maze of cornfields, although the role of the living scarecrows is mercifully toned down. The supernatural element in the final reels is unconvincing and the special effects are outmoded. Nevertheless, *Children of the Corn* is a genuinely terrifying film which spawned a host of sequels that have achieved cult status among horror fanatics.

A woodcut by Colin Gibson for *Seeds in the wind: poems in Scots for children*, by William Soutar, 1948.

POETICAL SCARECROWS

George Mackay Brown (1921–1996) the sickly intellectual son of the tailor-cum-postman of Stromness, wrote a humorous ghost story that took place in Scotland's Orkney Islands. *Mister Scarecrow* featured in the *Fifth Ghost Book* (1969) edited by Rosemary Timperly. This regional writer, who won international acclaim through his novels, also wrote poetry anthologies. One early poem called 'The Scarecrow in the Schoolmaster's Oats' was included in *Fishermen with Ploughs* (1971):

> Hail, Mister Snowman. Farewell,
> Gray consumptive.
>
> Rain. A sleeve dripping.
> Broken mirrors all about me.
>
> A thrush laid eggs in my pocket.
> My April coat was one long rapture.
>
> I push back green spume, yellow breakers,
> King Canute.

One morning I handled infinite gold,
King Midas.
I did not trust Ikey the tinker.
He had a worse coat.

A Hogmanay sun the colour of whisky
Seeps through my rags.
I am – what you guess – King Barleycorn.

Two Scottish poets penned verses about "tattiebogles." William Soutar (1898–1943) a poet from Perth, included one humorous poem, 'Tattie Bogle', in an anthology in Scots for children, *Seeds in the Wind* (1932):

The tattie-bogle wags his airms:
Caw! Caw! Caw!
He hasna onie banes or thairms:
Caw! Caw! Caw!

We corbies wha hae taken tent,
And wamphl'd round, and glower'd asklent,
Noo gang hame lauchin owre the bent:
Caw! Caw! Caw!

'The Tattie Bogle' by W.D. Cocker was included in *Poems in Scots and English*, 1946 published by Brown, Son and Ferguson Ltd, Glasgow

Dramduff had a fine tattie-bogle,
Unmarrow'd on neebourin ferms,
A graip was his stumpie wee body,
The shank o' a besom his airms;
An' we buskit him braw for a bogle,
No' tatter'd, but tosh-like an' spruce;
Though his claes were a wee thing auld-farrant,
On his neep heid a lum hat was cockit,
An' he wore a wee sackie wi' frill.
He could fricht ony craw in the parish,
As he stood, a' his lane, mang the drills.

CHILDREN'S CLASSICS

English poet and novelist, Walter de la Mare (1873–1956) composed a considerable number of poems for children which were collected in an anthology, *Rhymes and Verse* (1944). "All his work is marked by exquisite craftsmanship," comments the compiler of the *Everyman Dictionary of Literary Biography*, "with a faerie atmosphere peculiarly his own." One poignant poem is 'The Scarecrow' which demonstrates de la Mare's characteristic charm and affection for the countryside:

> All winter through I bow my head
> Beneath the driving rain;
> The North Wind powders me with snow
> And blows me black again;
> At midnight 'neath a maze of stars
> I flame with glittering rime
> And stand, above the stubble, stiff
> As mail at morning prime.
> But when the child called Spring, and all
> His host of children, come,
> Scattering their buds and dew upon
> These acres of my home,
> Some rapture in my rags awakes;
> I lift void eyes and scan
> The skies for crows, those ravening foes
> Of my strange master, Man.
> I watch him striding lank behind
> His clashing team, and know
> Soon will the wheat swish body high
> Where once lay sterile snow;
> Soon shall I gaze across a sea
> Of sun-begotten grain
> Which my unflinching watch hath sealed
> For harvest once again.

Walter de la Mare also wrote a collection of tales for children, *The Scarecrow and Other Stories* (1945). The title story is an inconsequential piece that is little more than a dialogue between an elderly

gentleman and his neice. It concerns a scarecrow called Old Joe, "a mute lank ungainly figure", which Uncle Tim has improbably retained since childhood because it once sheltered a fairy. "He had been peacocked up in many a fine new suit of old clothes since then, and more hats than I could count on twice my fingers. But then he was in his hey-day, in the very bloom of his youth, the glass of fashion and the knave of trumps." Alas, Uncle Tim's experience of the supernatural was never repeated. Uncle Tim gives a vivid description of Old Joe when he was first made:

> "That morning, I remember, he was wearing a pair of slack black-and-white check trousers and a greenish black coat, very wide at the shoulders. Apart from the stick for his arm, another had been pushed into one of his coat-sleeves for a cudgel. Another with a lump at the top made his head and on that was a hat, a hard, battered, square black hat – like the hats farmers and churchwardens used to wear in those days. He was stooping forward a little, staring across at me as I crouched by the gate."

The lovely illustrations that accompanied the text were by Irene Hawkins.

One of the first books most children are given as a present is *The Tale of Peter Rabbit* written and illustrated by Beatrix Potter (1866–1943) It was conceived for the author's own amusement and published privately in 1901 but it proved to be such a huge success that it was professionally printed almost immediately afterwards by Frederick Warne. This first of her series of "little books" was immensely popular – it has been reprinted over one hundred times – and it was quickly followed by a further twenty-two titles. Much of the enduring charm of the classic series of children's tales is accounted for by the accurate representation of animals and birds in the charming watercolours that Miss Potter painted to accompany her lively text.

Beatrix Potter was born in a respectable Victorian terraced house in South Kensington where she spent a lonely childhood studying art and natural history in a bleak third-floor schoolroom. The original Peter Rabbit was a pet bought for the princely sum of 4s 6d from a London shop. Beatrix patiently taught her hungry rabbit a few tricks: "ringing a little bell and drumming on a tambourine" for titbits. She developed a great love of the countryside and its animal inhabitants during childhood holidays in Scotland. Later she became a respected farmer when she acquired 'Hill Top Farm' at Sawrey in Cumbria.

The delightful *Tale of Peter Rabbit* opens with a famous warning by Mrs Rabbit to her mischievous son: "You may go into the fields or down the lane, but don't go into Mr McGregor's garden . . ." Peter Rabbit ignores this stricture and strays into the cabbage patch where Mr McGregor is busy gardening. An exciting chase ensues whereby Peter loses first his new shoes and then his blue jacket held fast in a

opposite: White Rabbit, Wray Festival.
overleaf: Alice in Scarecrowland and the Mad Hatter, Wray Festival.

gooseberry net by its brass buttons. Peter returns home to be scolded by his mother – it was the second jacket he had lost in a fortnight! – and he is sent tearfully to bed with soothing camomile tea.

Meanwhile Mr McGregor had put Peter's discarded shoes and jacket to good use as an improvised scarecrow. Miss Potter's vignette to accompany this incident shows Peter's jacket draped over crossed sticks with his shoes gently swaying on strings below. Inquisitive blackbirds and a brave robin stare at the pathetic apparel while Mr McGregor resumes his work, hoeing onions.

Peter's lost clothes provided a sequel which Beatrix Potter dedicated to 'the children of Sawrey.' *The Tale of Benjamin Bunny* (1904) concerns Peter and Benjamin's attempt to reclaim them from the scarecrow while Mr and Mrs McGregor are away visiting relatives in their gig. The intrepid pair manage to retrieve the shrunken coat and soggy shoes before a mischievous cat traps them underneath a discarded straw hat. Old Mr. Bunny, wielding his cane and smoking his pipe, comes to their rescue. He whips both bunnies and cat indiscriminately in a surprisingly violent ending. He sends Peter home with a sore bottom and some onions wrapped up in a pocket-handkerchief to give to his widowed mother. Meanwhile, Mr McGregor, upon his return, is perplexed to find only his own tam-o-shanter is left atop crossed sticks in his vegetable patch. Perhaps Mrs Potter intended this tale to be a warning to the local children to keep their distance from her own private garden at 'Hill Top'?

Rupert Bear, who first appeared in the *Daily Express* on 8 November 1920, was the creation of Mary Tourtel née Caldwell (1874–1948) She was born in Canterbury where both her father and brother designed and restored stained glass for Christ Church Cathedral. Mary, herself, an intrepid traveller and pioneer aviator, trained as an artist at The Sidney Cooper Gallery of Art which became Canterbury Art College. Her art master was Britain's leading cattle painter, Thomas Sidney Cooper R.A., who taught Mary animal and landscape painting. When she married Herbert Tourtell, a night editor for the *Daily Express*, Mary was encouraged to create a cartoon character which would rival Teddy Tail in the *Daily Mail* and 'Pip, Squeak and Wilfred' in the *Daily*

'Mr. McGregor hung up the little jacket and the shoes for a scare-crow to frighten the blackbirds.' From *The Tale of Peter Rabbit* by Beatrix Potter. Copyright © Frederick Warne & Co,. 1902, 2002. Reproduced by kind permission of Frederick Warne & Co.

Mirror. She invented Rupert Bear. His adventures, told in single monochrome frames, appealed to children and adults alike and boosted the newspaper's circulation.

At first Rupert resembled a real bear and he wore a blue jersey with a grey scarf and trousers. His escapades catapulted him all over the world bravely fighting dragons, ogres, witches and wolves. His pals included Bill Badger, Edward Trunk, Algy Pug, Podgy Pig and the Wise Old Goat from Nutwood. They inhabited a timeless world where medieval fantasy juxtaposed with modern settings and animals interacted with humans. Even during the Second World War, when there was a severe shortage of paper, Rupert was retained to boost the national morale although there was a marked absence in the sketches of food rationing, black outs and army manoeuvres.

When Mary was forced to retire through failing eyesight her place was taken by the gifted Alfred Bestall who produced Rupert strips and annuals from 1936. Bestall, son of a Methodist missionary, had been born in Mandalay, Burma, but after a crippling accident he was brought to England where he studied at the Central School of Art in London. His contribution to the Rupert series was immense since he drew the characters with imagination and flair and elevated the stories and rhymes to a certain literary merit.

Gradually, Rupert Bear evolved into the character known and loved today wearing a bright red jumper and yellow-checkered scarf and trousers. Although he officially retired in 1965, Bestall was still contributing to the annuals in 1982 at the age of ninety after which the character was handed over to a team of talented writers and illustrators.

Rupert finds employment as a scarecrow.
Couresy of Express Newspapers

Alfred Bestall first drew an animated scarecrow named 'Odmedod' during 1940 in a Rupert adventure for the newspaper which was subsequently repeated in the *Rupert Annual* for 1942. His episodic wartime tale is fervently patriotic with Rupert helping to thwart a pair of spies hiding in a cave. Odmedod masquerades as a ghost and terrifies the men who escape from their lair and retreat across the English Channel. There is an amusing moment where Rupert is forced by an irate farmer to pose as a scarecrow and he charges across the fields armed with flag and rattle.

Characteristically, the tale is told in both prose and rhyming couplet:

> As Rupert won't his friend betray,
> To learn his job he's led away.
> He's given, in the farmer's shed,
> A rattle, and a flag that's red.
> And though the rattle's noise is grim,
> 'Don't stop,' the farmer orders him.
> At first he finds the job great fun,
> But soon he wishes it was done.

The most popular boy in fiction is undoubtedly William Brown. This scruffy, exuberant, rumbustious middle-class boy was the creation of Richmal Crompton (1890–1969) a Lancashire schoolmistress who first recorded his hilarious escapades in *Just William* (1922). Curiously, the stories, which first appeared in serial form in women's magazines, were intended to amuse adults but the adventures of William and his Outlaws have been relished by children of all ages over six decades. A great deal of the saga's appeal lies in their timeless quality, the vivid encapsulation of boyhood and the period detail of life in an undisclosed English village 'between the wars.'

William, who constantly roams the countryside accompanied by his mongrel, Jumble, encounters numerous scarecrows on his travels. When William is escorted to Ireland to visit an elderly relative for the last time in *The Cure*, he puts a farmer's scarecrow in front of the fire so that his short-sighted aunt mistakes it for her husband and talks to it in the half gloom. And in *William and the Secret Society*, he pursuades his companions to take revenge by dressing up a scarecrow in the exact likeness of the squire who chased him out of his orchard (*William Again*, 1923). In *William and the Returned Traveller*, he assists his friend, the dishevelled artist, Archie, to evade a stalker by draping his distinctive grubby raincoat, in which a diamond ring has been secreted, over Farmer Jenk's scarecrow (*William and the Tramp*, 1922). William declares war on all scarecrows by shooting relentlessly at them with bows and arrows in *William and the Archers* (*William The Good*, 1928) while his Outlaws take possession of no less than five outsize jackets including one from a scarecrow in *The Brown Checked Sports Coat* (*William The Bold*, 1950).

One cracking good story is *William's Midsummer Eve* contained in *William Carries On* (1942). This story, set in the middle of the war, is packed with period detail. William and his Outlaws try to outwit their arch rival, the odious and obese Hubert Lane, who has acquired the best shrapnel collection in the district. Out of spite, Hubert has stolen a garden fork from a land girl working on Farmer Jenk's farm. A further complication is that Farmer Jenks has confiscated William's prize trophy, a defused German bomb stick. William, playing on Midsummer superstitions, tricks Hubert Lane into returning the fork by dressing up as the scarecrow from Six Acre Meadow which has come to haunt the thief. His scarecrow wore a battered old slouch hat and a capelike ulster which had once been worn by the irritable farmer. By chance, William also discovers the hiding place of the bomb stick. Farmer Jenks has used it for the upright to hold the scarecrow's head! A real bonus is that the story contains an illustration of William disguised as the scarecrow by Thomas Henry, a commercial artist who was also responsible for the sailor trademark on Player's Navy Cut cigarette packets.

WORZEL GUMMIDGE

Worzel Gummidge, indisputably, the most famous literary scarecrow of all time, was the creation of Barbara Euphan Todd (1897–1976) who was born in the Vicarage at Arksey, a small farming village in South Yorkshire. Her father, the Rev. Thomas Todd, was the Vicar of All Saints', a handsome twelfth-century church which stands just a stone's throw away from the Victorian Vicarage. (Parish records charmingly show that Barbara was baptised on St. Valentine's Day). The Vicar fostered his daughter's creative talents and encouraged her to write stories while she was quite young. One early composition was about a scarecrow that stood in a smallholding opposite and which could be viewed through the high gothic windows of the Vicarage. Perhaps this anonymous scarecrow also served as the model for the rascally Worzel.

William Brown as a scarecrow. From *William carries on* by Richmal Crompton with illustrations by Thomas Henry Fisher. Reproduced by kind permission of PFD on behalf of the Thomas Henry Fisher Estate.

During the Great War, Barbara enrolled in the Voluntary Aid Detachment where she met and married Commander John Graham Bower who also wrote adventure stories, often set in a submarine, under the pseudonym, 'Klaxon.' Shortly afterwards, Barbara was widowed but she became absorbed in her writing and was a prolific author of books and plays. She wrote over thirty magical novels for children and was a regular contributor of witty verses to *Punch*. Sadly, Barbara Euphan Todd died a matter of months before Worzel shuffled to worldwide fame on television.

Worzel Gummidge was originally created for radio and only later appeared in print. Barbara was the first to admit that her manuscript might never have been published. "Worzel kept coming back to me like a homing pigeon," she revealed. "He then sulked in a Hampshire drawer until I unpacked him in

Berkshire and sent him to the BBC." He made his debut in 1935 on 'Children's Hour' where his character was brought to life by a succession of actors – Hugh E. Wright, Philip Wade and the ubiquitous, Norman Shelley. Narration was by the celebrated raconteur, David Kossoff. The "cross, moody scarecrow with a heart of gold" soon caught the imagination of millions of listeners who willingly joined in singing his ridiculous songs. Barbara's first book, *Worzel Gummidge*, was published by public demand the following year with illustrations by Elizabeth Alldridge.

Worzel Gummidge has the distinction of being the first title to appear under the banner of 'Puffin.' It was published during wartime alongside four other titles which were considered to represent "the best of new work then being done for children." Sir Allen Lane, publisher of the phenomenally successful Penguin paperbacks, pursuaded his friend, Eleanor Graham, to edit a revolutionary series of quality, portable books aimed at capturing the imagination of children. Despite the deprivations of war – paper rationing was rigorously enforced – she successfully marketed affordable paperbacks which proved ideal to accompany children being evacuated to the countryside. The paperback version of *Worzel Gummidge, The Scarecrow of Scatterbrook* (1941) priced sixpence, featured distinctive broad horizontal orange bands, a sketch of the irascible scarecrow nursing a stolen baby and the obligatory Puffin symbol. (An advert for durable children's shoes appeared on the back cover). Publication was cleverly timed for Christmas.

The first adventure starts when two children, John and Susan, are sent with their nurse to convalesce at Scatterbrook Farm. They notice a scarecrow in Ten Acre Field and borrow his umbrella when they are caught in a rainstorm. Pandemonium erupts when Worzel turns up at the farmhouse to collect his possession which the children have failed to return. He introduces himself as Worzel Gummidge, an ugly name he invented that very morning to suit his rude appearance, and he describes himself as a "betwixt and between" person, neither a child nor a man, who can come to life at will. Also, he refers to himself as a "stand still" since that is what he is required to do all day long while scaring rooks. Best of all, he possesses magical powers because he also happens to be a wizard!

The first time John and Susan encounter the irrepressible scarecrow they are intrigued by his strange appearance:

"The children stood quite still, and stared at the figure in the middle of the field. It was a good long way off from them, but they could see that the scarecrow was dressed in an old black coat and long trousers, and that its hat was tilted on the back of its head. Its arms were stuck straight out from its shoulders. Susan saw that the scarecrow had a most friendly and pleasant face. It was cut out of a turnip, and one or two green leaves stuck out from under his black bowler hat. She looked more closely, and saw that the scarecrow hadn't got a hand. The round, polished end of a broom-handle showed beyond his ragged cuff."

Worzel acquires an extensive wardrobe by pinching clothes from washing lines so that he can parade in a variety of accesories and is constantly able to cut a dash. His working clothes consist of "a shirt and a weskit and a pair of string braces, and a hat and a pair o' bottle boots." He smokes a pipe and keeps a nest of robins inside his top pocket which is handy because he can use their wings as a feathery "handkychiff." He is proud of the fact that he was "made backwards" by being created specially to fit the available secondhand clothing. Worzel is bemused by the fact that he can celebrate numerous birthdays because parts of his body were made at different times. "My face is one age, and my feet are another, and my arms are the oldest of all. 'Tis usual with scarerows. I get a lot of birthdays, one for my face and another for my middle and another for my hands."

Barbara Euphan Todd introduced a host of character scarecrows in the series of eight books about Worzel Gummidge. These include Mildew Turmut, Scairey Gummidge, Soggy Bogart and Granfer Bogle. Earthy Mangold is his coy fiancée who, although professionally inept, "allus tries to be comforting." Typical of her goodness is her attempt to shoo away the hens so that sparrows may eat the grain. Further, she cannot think of her hedgerow origins without longing to shelter small birds and feel their wings flutter among her boughs. Little Upsidaisy, carved from a milking stool, is simple but cheerful while hypochondriacal Hannah Harrow suffers from a variety of alarming complaints ranging from "damping off" to "the mice" – for which her chums recommend swallowing a mousetrap! A favourite character is undoubtedly the spiteful Aunt Sally who has escaped from a sideshow in a travelling fair. She is pert, petite and precocious – Worzel is terrified of her – and her selfish exploits provide an abundance of hilarity. Credible tension is provided by John and Susan's constant attempts to protect Worzel and his companions from discovery by the adults, particularly the patronising, Mrs. Bloomsbury-Barton.

Worzel made his transformation to black and white television in 1953. He appeared on 'Children's Television' in an adaptation by Joy Harrington (assisted by her friend Barbara Euphan Todd) who also produced the series. Earthy Mangold was played by Mabel Constanduros, who had previously played the part in radio versions, but Frank Atkinson was elevated from the minor character of Farmer Braithwaite to Worzel, himself. He wore a greatcoat with a battered bowler and his face peeped through a balaclava representing sacking covering his head. The series, which went out live, was broadcast from Lime Grove Studios and, consequently, there was a decided "stagey" feel to the production.

A more enduring version of the stories was made by Southern Television when colour programmes were still a novelty. This time Worzel was played by the talented Jon Pertwee (1919–1996) known to millions as the star of radio's *The Navy Lark* and television's *Doctor Who*. (Originally, the idea was to make a film but this was cancelled owing to lack of financial backing.) Pertwee was the ideal choice of actor since he mastered all the nuances of Todd's zany character which ensured the series worked on several levels and appealed to audiences of both children and adults. Unpredicatable, devious, exasperating, childish, prone to sulks yet full of professional pride. . . Worzel manages to extricate himself from all his outrageous escapades and his perverse reckoning invariably proves irritatingly right. Only rarely does he admit defeat and confess to being "bumswizzled."

Scripts were provided by the talented partnership of Keith Waterhouse and Willis Hall who had created the phenomenally successful fantasy character, *Billy Liar*, which they presented as a book, play and film. They made subtle changes to Todd's vast literary cast of characters, most notably by replacing the children's nanny by their ineffectual father (Mike Berry) and making Aunt Sally (Una Stubbs) his girlfriend despite her haughty, pretentious nature. Worzel and all the other scarecrows are made by the sinister Crowman (Geoffrey Bayldon) who appears in a worn dark suit and a topper bedecked with crow feathers. And there is a cameo perfomance by the outrageous Joan Sims as Mrs Bloomsbury-Barton. The children (Charlotte Coleman and Jeremy Austin) manage to hold their own amongst such a cast of seasoned character actors.

The scriptwriters, recognising that a great deal of fun is provided by Worzel's irrefutable logic from quaint premises, presented an abundance of his wise saws. "Furniture don't mind the rain," he opines after stealing half the village's furnishings

Jon Pertwee as Worzel Gummidge.

and plonking them in the middle of a field to create his own home. "Except beds. Yes, beds have feelings 'cos they're made of straw, same as scarecrows. Stands to reason." Perhaps, today, though, his exploitation of wildlife – robin handkerchief and hedgehog hairbrush – might be banned by campaigners for Animal Rights. Inevitably, there would also be the removal of mildly sexist and racist quips.

A key attraction of the television series was the location sequences filmed around the scattered village of Braishfield, four miles north of Romsey in Hampshire. Pucknall Farm provided the setting for the children's holiday residence although the field where Worzel stood was a little further away on Bailey's Down. Certainly, the rural atmosphere and seasonal landscapes add an air of authenticity to these vintage programmes. There is also a hint of period charm although the series was only shot towards the end of the 1970s. Morris Minors, bobbies on bicycles, rag and bone men and travelling fairgrounds were even at that time familiar components of the British countryside.

Pertwee's countenance was remarkable. The actor was ingeniously transformed into a humanised scarecrow by a skilful make-up artist. A carrot was shaped to extend his nose; carrot tops were applied to make a scraggy beard; sugar puffs were glued on to represent warts and raffia was twisted into his own hair for a scruffy wig. Plaited corn formed the scarecrow's eyebrows; his teeth were painted with black enamel and his face was liberally splattered with mud. Lastly, an orange complexion gave the illusion of a turnip head.

Jon Pertwee had devoured the books as a boy and expressed complete empathy with the character. He recognised aspects of Worzel's character which compared to his own and secretly admired him for being "sullen, touching, vulgar, rude, smelly, with not one redeeming feature" although, like all great comedy actors, he could not resist bringing a sense of pathos to the role. His unique contribution was the invention of a complicated language spoken only by scarecrows and this was perfectly matched by his talent for dialect acquired during his childhood in Devonshire. In addition the scriptwriters introduced a variety of heads – "thinking", "learning", "riddle-me-ree" and a ludicrous "handsome" visage guaranteed to frighten rather than woo any suitor – which showed off the many facets of the scarecrow and they also composed a variety of songs with nonsensical words for Worzel to teach to the children.

The popularity of the television series prompted a host of merchandise including games, annuals and a long-playing record featuring Worzel's songs. A Christmas Special entitled, *A Cup o' Tea an' a Slice o' Cake*, was a musical romp with celebrity guests screened in December 1980. Barbara Windsor appeared as Saucy Nancy, a vivacious figurehead from a pantomime pirate ship, while Billy Connolly played a belligerent Scottish scarecrow, Bogle McNeep, who despises Christmas in favour of Hogmanay. Wily Worzel's antics with Aunt Sally in the snowbound countryside end with a sentimental pronouncement from the Crowman and a joyous scarecrow ball. A further three collections of stories, adapted from their television scripts, were penned by Waterhouse – Hall for Puffin Books.

4. SCARECROWS ON STAGE, FILM AND TELEVISION

SCARECROWS both comical and scary have made their mark on the silver screen and have become familiar to cinema audiences in both Britain and America. A few have made the transference to British television where they have appeared in programmes as diverse as Bob the Builder to Midsommer Murders, from Eastenders to The Big Read. Even the radio programme, The Archers, reflected the current trend for scarecrow festivals when residents organised a competition for making lookalike characters one summer in the fictitious village of Ambridge.

SILENT FILMS

In the early years of cinematography there was a succession of silent black and white films featuring scarecrows worldwide. Plots and storylines were often similar since there was an absence of copyright laws to prohibit such blatant borrowing. When these early 'shorts' were released in cinemas across Britain they were listed in a London weekly trade newspaper, *The Bioscope*, which is now often the only clue to their content.

First known moving picture to bear the title, *The Scarecrow*, was produced by a Frenchman, Charles Pathé (1863–1957) This pioneer film maker founded the film company, 'Pathé Fréres', whose logo was a crowing cockerel surmounting the globe. Pathé is credited with developing a primitive colour process but he is better remembered for producing the weekly newsreel, Pathé News. He also made the first 'long' film consisting of four reels, *Les Misérables*, in 1909.

Earlier that same year Pathé's *The Scarecrow* had been released. Unfortunately, no copies of his 610 feet long monochrome film, which was shot entirely upon location in the French countryside, have survived. The scenario of this simple, romantic comedy was rehearsed in *The Bioscope*:

Opposite: Pirate Johnny Depp, Wray Festival.

"Herein we watch the ravages made by thieves and schoolchildren upon a farmer's orchard. The latter, realising that his scarecrow of rag and stick is no good, himself takes its place and awaits events. The marauders, heedless of what they think to be still a lump of wood, are about to despoil the trees when the farmer makes known his presence and gives a lusty drubbing to those he can capture. Resuming his pose, he is surprised to see his daughter holding amorous converse with a sportsman who has been staying at the farm and who has captured the girl's affections by soft speeches and fair looks. The farmer, furiously angry, captures the pair, asking the man whether he intends to take his child as his wife. The other laughingly scorns the idea, and the old man is about to rush upon him with a gun when a farm hand, who has long been enamoured by the girl, runs up, stays the farmer's hand and offers himself as a bridegroom. Although she has rejected him before, the daughter now accepts his proposals, and the picture ends with a scene depicting general satisfaction"

(21 October 1909).

The following year the Danish film company, 'Nordisk', produced a slightly longer film, *The Scarecrow* (715 feet) alas, also lost. A brief storyline appeared in *The Bioscope*: "The film relates the story of a thief's ruse and his capture by a smart detective" (29 October 1910).

The first British film called *The Scarecrow* was made in 1911 by Cecil Hepworth (1874–1953). This financially successful film producer who specialised in sentimental and historical stories wrote the first book on cinema, *Animated Photography* (1897) His autobiography, *Came The Dawn*, (1951) mentions that his proudest moment was when King Edward VII halted the funeral procession of Queen Victoria so that he could record it for posterity. By contrast, *The Scarecrow* was a light, short film (350 feet) released through his own company, 'Hepwix', based at Walton-on-Thames. According to *The Bisoscope* this third, lost, silent film was "a comedy describing the adventures of a gentleman who is unfortunately forced to represent a scarecrow" (14 September 1911).

An Italian film, *The Scarecrow*, was made by the 'Cines' company in 1912. It was a much longer film (980 feet) with a far more complicted storyline which was detailed in *The Bioscope* (1 August 1912). A farmer is ambushed by two ruffians who steal his money and cast him into a river. They hide their false beards and booty in the pocket of a scarecrow so that the police are unable to arrest them. Later, a kindly neighbour lends the unfortunate victim the coat from the very same scarecrow to protect him from the cold. When he puts his hands in its pockets he discovers both the beards and his money. The police lay a trap for the criminals when they return to the scene of the crime. As they approach the scarecrow it suddenly throws its arms tightly around one of them. A police sergeant has been substituted for the effigy! This lively foreign film was successfully distributed in cinemas throughout Britain since, obviously, there were no language barriers with silent films.

A fifth film, *The Scarecrow*, was produced by a modest French studio, 'Nizza', in 1913, and released through its rival company, 'Pathé.' It is a shame that this film (455 feet) is lost, too, because *The Bioscope* gives a tantalising synopsis: "A scarecrow meets with many surprising adventures, and is responsible for some very comical situations" (10 April 1913).

One of America's great silent clowns, Buster Keaton (1895–1966) wrote, directed and starred in a two-reeler film, *The Scarecrow*, in 1920. Keaton, who had trained in vaudeville with his family act, turned to movies when he teamed up with a rotund partner, Fatty Arbuckle. Later, he began to devise his own material after he had formed his own company, 'The Keaton Studio'. Invariably, the comic featured as the unsmiling hero who manages to overcome insurmountable problems. He brought stillness to the screen in the way that Hancock later brought silence to the radio. Keaton did not easily convert to talkies although he was planning a comeback at the time of his death.

Keaton's *The Scarecrow*, which took around six weeks to film, is regarded as a classic of the silent screen. Keaton was a perfectionist who mapped out the improvised storyline in fine detail before he would allow the cameras to start rolling. His ingenious plot – a fantasy highlighting man's struggle with machinery – shows his talents to perfection. Our hero lives like a hermit in a shack packed with hilarious homemade devices. Every appliance doubles up: the gramophone converts into a gas stove, the bath becomes a sofa and the bed becomes an organ. There is even a toy train running round the breakfast table supplying rolls and butter. At one point Keaton is chased by a mad dog and falls into a harvest machine which shreds all his clothes. Through necessity, he steals an outfit from a scarecrow but is then forced by the farmer to take its place. There is a joyous ending when Buster kneels to tie up his shoelace and the girl he has been pursuing (Sybil Sealey) mistakes this action as a proposal and agrees to marry him. "It is an unearthly little comedy," claims Keaton's biographer, Rudi Blesh. "In it is the poetry of memory."

THE WIZARD OF OZ

The world's most famous and best loved scarecrow appears in an American fairy tale, *The Wizard of Oz*, invented by a humble story teller, Frank Baum. His enchanting fantasy, told on the spur of the moment to entertain his own children, has brought pleasure to millions as it has been translated from the page onto stage and screen.

L. Frank Baum (1856–1919) the self-appointed 'Royal Historian of Oz', had a rollercoaster life. (He declined to use his first name, 'Lyman', which he intensely disliked.) His father was a dairy farmer cum oil baron who brought up his family in Chittenango, New York. Baum inherited a string of theatres from his millionaire father but lost all of them through his own improvidence. He attempted a dozen careers ranging from chicken farmer to crockery salesman. He married Maud Gage, a suffragette and spiritualist, who bore him four sons. A high point in Baum's life was when he was appointed editor of a trade magazine devoted to shop window displays published in Chicago. This gave him temporary financial stability with time to write "wonder tales" for children.

Baum was a natural story teller possessed with wit, charm and intelligence. He held his own children in raptures when he devised extempore fairy tales to amuse them and their friends. His classic tale, 'The Wonderful Wizard of Oz', which brought him sudden and enduring fame, evolved from one such bedtime story. At first, he struggled to find a title but his grandson, Robert, later revealed the strange place from which he drew inspiration. "One day he was sitting at his desk and looking at his filing cabinet. The first drawer was A–N and the second O–Z. That made 'OZ', which he thought would be an excellent title for an imaginary land."

The Wonderful Wizard of Oz was written in laborious longhand and delivered to an unenthusiastic publisher who insisted Baum invest his own money to fund the illustrations. When it was belatedly published in 1900 the book was an instant success and the public clamoured for more. It was recognised as an original fairy story and hailed as a native American folk tale. 'The Wizard of Oz' ('Wonderful' was soon dropped from its title) was followed by a further forty volumes – Baum wrote the first fourteen and a succession of authors penned the rest which were of diminishing quality. The original character drawings were by William Wallace Denslow (1856–1915) but when the pair fell out over royalties for a stage play subsequent illustrations were undertaken by John R. Neill (1877–1943) an artist from Philadelphia. Denslow continued to write and illustrate children's books, some of which featured scarecrows.

The Wizard of Oz relates the adventures of Dorothy, an orphan who lives on a farm in Kansas. A prairie cyclone transports her house to the land of Oz where she is proclaimed a heroine by the Munchkins after she accidentally kills the Wicked Witch of the East. Glinda, the kindly Witch of the North, tells Dorothy she must follow the Yellow Brick Road to the Emerald City where the Wizard of Oz will help her to return to her beloved home. Along the way she meets a Scarecrow who lacks a brain, a Tin Woodman who lacks a heart and a Cowardly Lion who lacks courage. All the time Dorothy is pursued by the Wicked Witch of the West who covets the magical slippers which belonged to her tyrannical sister. (Dorothy is prone to killing witches because she accidentally disposes of this one too!). It becomes evident that this is a story of self discovery for the four friends already possess the qualities they seek . . .

The plot unfolds at a rapid pace – it is surprisingly violent in places – and the story is full of incident and drama. Baum invents a host of original and imaginative characters of whom the most popular is the Scarecrow. There is only a cursory description of his appearance but his personality is revealed as gentle, humorous and resourceful. His daring exploits in the novel include taking a tumble from the ferocious Hammer-Heads; covering the friends with straw from his own body to protect them from a swarm of bees and twisting the necks of forty crows sent by the Witch to peck out the strangers' eyes. His only fear is of a lighted match. At the end of the story he is rewarded for his bravery by the Wizard who fashions him a brain from pins and needles mixed with bran and proclaims him King of Oz. Baum's childhood farm in upstate New York had been populated with scarecrows and one of his earliest scribblings was an acrostic poem, published in the *Rose Lawn Home Journal* that reveals the answer 'SCARECROW'.

After the spectacular reception of his book, Frank Baum, who had a marvellous instinct for theatre, was determined to turn *The Wizard of Oz* into a musical comedy. He wrote both the book and the lyrics but commissioned a talented young composer, Paul Tietjens, to provide the music. The producer was Fred Hamlin and the director was Julian Mitchell, who immediately recognised the possibility of a lavish musical extravaganza. Baum's comic opera was first produced at the Grand Opera House, Chicago, in 1902 and then transferred to the Majestic Theater, New York, the following year before touring America. His plot was drastically changed during its long run and eventually altered beyond recognition. Dorothy had become an amorous young woman, the Wizard was a wise cracking Irishman while even Toto had been replaced by a pet cow, Imogene. There were breathtaking transformation scenes – The Kansas Cornfield, the Wizard's Palace and a beautiful Deadly Poppy Field – the scenery presented "a flare of colour." Despite mixed reviews the show, which was aimed mainly at adults, was a surefire winner.

Undoubtedly, the success of the show which toured for eight years rested primarily on the comic partnership of Fred Stone as the Scarecrow and David Montgomery as the Tin Woodman. Fred Stone (1873–1959) had been a circus performer, acrobat, dancer and minstrel performer. He first teamed up with fellow minstrel, Montgomery, in 1894 and the inventive pair were soon lauded as star vaudeville entertainers. Critics raved over their uproarous antics in *The Wizard of Oz* which ran for over 1400 performances and turned them into national celebrities.

The *Chicago Tribune* trumpeted: "Montgomery and Stone are pioneers in absolutely original comedy." Stone was constantly singled out for his impersonation of the brainless Scarecrow because his

FRED R. HAMLINS MUSICAL EXTRAVAGANZA

THE WIZARD OF OZ

FRED A. STONE

Otto Sarony Co.

1177 BROADWAY N.Y.

Fred Stone as the inimitable
Scarecrow on stage.

fluid movements and rubbery legs enabled him to flop around the stage seemingly without joints. One contemporary critic, Amy Leslie, reported: "His makeup, his wonderful command of every expression, every muscle, every queer tone and a perfect fusilade of brand-new steps, acrobatic tumbles and his famous repartee quick as a flash, were revelations," and she declared that Stone was simply "the greatest burlesque comedian of his generation." (*Chicago Daily News*)

Fred Stone's makeup for the Scarecrow consisted of a tight chamois leather skull cap which he painted with rough stitches and then varnished. Nightly, he daubed his face with thick layers of pink greasepaint, obliterating all traces of his own eyebrows, and then criss-crossed his face with black greasepaint markings to simulate sewn material. Final touches were to draw one eyebrow higher than the other, paint a black triangle on his nose and blacken his mouth so that it appeared to be a frayed slit in the cloth. When his makeup was complete it was identical to the familiar illustrations by Denslow.

The Scarecrow's working costume was also inspired by Denslow. He wore blue shirt and trousers stuffed with real straw which protruded from parts of his body. A large, floppy hat, oversize white gloves and rope tied around his waist, wrists and ankles completed this outfit. The actor took immense pride in his appearance on stage and worked hard to authenticate parts of his bizarre wardrobe by the addition of tears, patches and repairs. "I tore and wore and smeared and mended till they began to show up right," he boasted.

Speciality songs were a feature of the stage show and these were performed by the principals wearing outrageous costumes. The Scarecrow made a spectacular appearance as an Indian Chief to perform a number, 'Sitting Bull', but then incongruously pinned playing cards to his costume to deliver a nonsense ditty, 'The Lobster.' When partnered by Montgomery his costumes were even more outlandish. Stone wore a sailor's suit for a rousing chorus, 'Hurrah For Baffin's Bay', which involved the agile duo sailing across the stage in a tiny sailboat, and full sporting gear for a satirical song, 'Football', where the routine involved such energetic stunts that a doctor was kept on hand in the wings in case of accidents. Undoubtedly, their comic duets were among the most popular numbers in the musical and the flexibility of the production allowed for numerous encores.

Comic business became so highly developed that it resembled pure pantomime. A golfer misdirected a ball in an opening scene which Dorothy later retrieved from the Scarecrow's ear while Imogene nibbled on the straw which she had tugged from inside his costume. Stone's first appearance drew a huge response from the audience. He stood perfectly still as the Scarecrow stage centre throughout Dorothy's song and when the rag dummy came to life it caused gasps of astonishment that resounded round the auditorium. A far more spectacular special effect was when the Scarecrow was dismembered to escape from prison and then reassembled in a sentry box positioned in another part of the stage, which feat was invariably greeted with thunderous applause.

Baum's stage version of *The Wizard of Oz* was a wild, gorgeously mounted fantasy brimming with unrelated songs and speciality acts. It took America by storm. Oddly, the show bore only a peripheral relationship to the 1900 fairy tale and most of the themes including friendship, self-discovery and longing for home were eliminated from the stage adaptation. Yet its strong comic plot and well-defined characters were embraced by an adoring public while the spectacular stage effects – cyclones and snowstorms – ensured box office takings.

Encouraged by the success of the musical, Baum devised a further entertainment based on his stories which he called *Fairylogue and Radio Play* in 1908. This multi-media show – a travelogue through fairyland – combined fantastic stories with trick effects and extolled the marvels of the Land of Oz. It combined early silent motion pictures, hand coloured lantern slides, live narration and an orchestral accompaniment. All the figures were first presented in black and white but then they burst into colour as they stepped off the pages. Snippets of film were shot in Chicago by Selig Polyscope Company and one of the studio's stock players, Frank Burns, posed for the Scarecrow. The show won instant acclaim from an admiring public but in the realistic world of finance it proved a cumbersome show to tour and high production costs led, inevitably, to Baum's insolvency.

Two years later, William Selig produced a one-reeler silent film, *The Wizard of Oz* (1,000 feet). A rare copy of this vintage movie, described as "an excellent film, well acted and clearly photographed," has been preserved by the George Eastman House International Museum of Photography and Film, New York. Dorothy was played by a juvenile performer, Bebe Daniels (1901–1971) who later became a leading lady of the silent screen. Born Phyllis Daniels, Bebe married Ben Lyon and the couple moved to Britain with their family to appear in comedy programmes on radio and television, *Life with the Lyons*. The studio's major character actor, Hobart Bosworth (1867–1943) played the Scarecrow.

Selig telescoped Baum's tale and added scenes which do not appear in the novel. The title, for instance, *Meet the Wonderful Scarecrow*, heralds a scene where Dorothy releases the Scarecrow from his pole in a Kansas cornfield. His ungainly antics scare a mule, a cow and the cairn terrier, Toto, who were all recruited from the studio's menageree. A cyclone approaches and the two friends plus the farm animals seek refuge in a haystack. This is whisked away to the Land of Oz where Dorothy and the Scarecrow experience further adventures. Evidentally, the producers regarded the Scarecrow, who is far from bungling, as a key character and therefore introduced him early on in the film. This is an odd change in Baum's narrative since it invests Kansas with a magical quality and detracts from the wonder of Oz while the distinction between the two places becomes blurred. Selig made two sequels – *The Land of Oz* and *Dorothy and the Scarecrow in Oz*, in which the Wizard finally bestows brains upon the intrepid Scarecrow. The first film was released as a family entertainment for Easter and there is thought to have been a superior tinted version which appeared later.

Frank Baum devised further musicals, *The Woggle-Bug*, based on *The Marvellous Land of Oz* (1904) which had been dedicated to Stone and Montgomery, and *The Tik Tok Man of Oz*, derived from *Ozma of Oz* (1907) which were both moderately successful. Unwisely, he was compelled to invest his earnings in building his own grand studios, 'The Oz Manufacturing Company', in 1914. He produced a trio of short silent films based on his fantasies. The first was *The Patchwork Girl of Oz*, a romantic comedy featuring the Scarecrow played by Herbert Glennon (1895–1967). Its sequel was *The Magic Cloak of Oz*, taken from *Queen Zixi of Ix*. The third was a longer five reel feature, *His Majesty the Scarecrow of Oz*, which proved to be both ambitious and costly.

Highlight of this third film was the scene when Dorothy, the Tin Woodman and the Scarecrow, this time played by Frank Moore (1888–1960) are pursued by the witch, Mombi, as they escape on a raft. The Scarecrow steers the raft but his pole becomes stuck in the river bed. He clings to the pole and becomes stranded in deep water as the raft continues gayly on without him. Eventually, he is rescued by a huge crow which snatches him to safety. This scene is recounted in the original book where the Scarecrow laments the irony of his situation which has left him in a worse state than when Dorothy found him stuck to a pole in a cornfield! Despite a series of similar misfortunes the Scarecrow is proclaimed king at the end of the film. Prints of all three films miraculously survive. Predictably, the success of the film venture was short lived and Baum was declared bankrupt.

Frank Baum, who had been the prolific author of fairy tales, teenage books, adult novels, short stories, stage plays and film scripts, retired with his wife to what was then a quiet suburb of Los Angeles called Hollywood. They lived in a modest villa, 'Ozcot', where Frank contentedly raised chickens, practised archery, played golf and pottered in the garden. After two bedridden years he died, aged sixty-two, having achieved his greatest ambition which was to write stories that would simply "please a child." Upon his demise, the mantle of 'Chronicler of Oz' was assumed by a talented young author, Ruth Plumly Thomson (1891–1976) who kept up the tradition of writing a new Oz book each year until 1940. Afterwards, the series continued more feebly in less capable hands – illustrator, John Neill, produced three lavish volumes – until they were finally abandoned in 1986.

A seven reel silent version of *The Wizard of Oz* (6,300 feet) was produced by the modest 'Chadwick Film Company' in 1925. It was written, produced and directed by Larry Semon (1889–1928). Semon also starred as the Scarecrow while his wife, Dorothy Dwan, played a winsome Dorothy. The film strayed far from the spirit and content of the original story without repeating its magic formula for success. Its revised plot, which opens with an aged toymaker reading the book to his granddaughter, centres upon court intrigue and romance. Dorothy, abandoned as a baby on the doorstep of a Kansas farm, discovers on her sixteenth birthday that she is the true Queen of Oz. Three hired hands assist her to regain her throne, which has been usurped by Prime Minister Kruel, aided by Ambassador Wikked and Countess Vishuss. There is a fleeting appearance by an unconvincing Wizard who readily admits he is a fake.

Dorothy and her companions are reluctantly transported to Oz when the barn they are sheltering in is blown away by a cyclone. It is only when they arrive there that the friends assume various disguises – a Lion, a Tin Woodman and a Scarecrow. The Scarecrow is involved in several amusing chase sequences including being trapped inside a lions' den. After deposing the dictator with the help of a reformed Wizard, Queen Dorothy predictably lives "happily ever after."

Emphasis of this film is firmly on slapstick which is delivered with such a heavy hand that it is difficult now to believe that its star once rivalled Chaplin, Lloyd and Keaton. Semon's Scarecrow imitated Stone's costume and makeup but his own spirited performance was calculated to appeal to the Jazz Age. Alas, Larry Semon, who had been born into a showbusiness family from Mississippi, came to a sad end only three years after making this artificial comedy which was only his second feature film. In the course of a single year he was declared bankrupt, suffered a nervous breakdown and died from pneumonia. Chief interest in the film now lies in the brief appearance of a young Oliver Hardy as the Tin Woodman.

There were further adaptations of the timeless classic. The Meglin Kiddies, a children's performing troup from California, appeared in a short film, *Scarecrow of Oz* in 1931. Two years later a cartoon version of *The Wizard of Oz* was produced by Ted Eshbaugh, a Canadian animator, which began in monochrome then burst into colour when Dorothy arrived in Oz, but this was never released. More faithful to Baum's stories were the series of fifteen minute radio shows broadcast throughout the early 1930s by NBC Radio. They starred Nancy Keel as Dorothy supported by Bill Adams as the Scarecrow. These programmes were sponsored by 'Jell-O.'

Landmark version of *The Wizard of Oz* was produced by 'Metro-Goldwyn-Mayer' that same decade. It featured Ray Bolger (1904–1987) in the singing-dancing role of the rubber-legged Scarecrow who wanted little more than a brain to while away the hours. The role, which won him great acclaim from the contemporary press, dominated the actor's career for the rest of his life. *Variety* instantly summed up the enduring quality of his performance and the appeal of the film when it announced: "There's an audience for it wherever there's a projector and a screen."

'Metro-Goldwyn-Mayer' had started looking for a fantasy film to rival the phenomenally successful pioneering 'Walt Disney' feature cartoon, *Snow White and the Seven Dwarfs* (1937). This prestigious company was willing to invest around three million dollars in producing an opulant version of *The Wizard of Oz* in 1939. It was the studio's most expensive production to date but the risk was worth taking since it assembled a dream cast headed by newcomer, Judy Garland, as Dorothy, which ensured the film broke several records: It has had the longest continuous exposure of any feature film, it has never been off release since it opened and it has been piling up revenue non stop for MGM.

This was a magic year for cinema. Among the enduring classics to appear were *Stagecoach*, *Beau Geste*, *Wuthering Heights* and *Gone With The Wind*, which set box office records for decades. The premier of MGM's *The Wizard of Oz*, which took place at Grauman's Chinese Theater in Hollywood, was an occasion for celebration. The cinema's forecourt was transformed into a Kansas cornfield complete with cellophane cornstalks and a stuffed scarecrow while a Yellow Brick Road extended to the foyer. Guest of honour was the original Scarecrow from the stage show, Fred Stone.

Ironically, it was only when it was shown on television that the film became popular with mass audiences across America. First televised screening took place in November 1956 when the film held over forty-five million viewers spellbound. It was screened on British television for Christmas Day 1975 and drew an audience of twenty million. When it became evident that the film was a surefire hit, an unbroken tradition was set up of it being shown as an annual festive treat on both sides of the Atlantic. Evidentally, the film still worked its magic despite the fact that, initially, it could only be broadcast in black and white. Millions more fell under its spell when it was translated into foreign languages and shown in cinemas and on television around the world. By 1970, it had been estimated that more people had seen 'Oz' than any other entertainment in history. In 1989, The Library of Congress and National Film Registry announced that it was one of twenty-five motion pictures designated a 'National Treasure.' Today, it is estimated that MGM's *The Wizard of Oz* has been seen by over one billion people worldwide.

This is remarkable since at the time of its release critics were divided over its merit. Their descriptions of the film varied from "a movie milestone" (*Los Angeles Times*) to "it's a stinkeroo" (*The New Yorker*). Generally, it was hailed as a triumph. Typical was the notice in the *Chicago Daily Tribune*: "It is gorgeous, fantastic, radiant with Technicolor. It teams with midgets, it is alive with trick photography and is jeweled with hummable tunes." *Time* had only one reservation: "When it descends to earth, it collapses like a scarecrow in a cloudburst." More succinctly, *The New York Mirror* commanded imperiously: "Borrow a child and see it."

The Wizard of Oz was filmed in an expensive light-intensive process known as 'Technicolor.' Cinema audiences, however, had to wait for the breathtaking moment when colour floods the screen. It is not until Dorothy's house lands and she emerges into Munchkinland with Toto in her arms that the joyous moment is reached. (This effective device had been borrowed both from the *Fairylogue* and the earlier animated cartoon.) Afterwards, the storybook colour is presented in profusion – yellow for the Yellow Brick Road, red for the potent Poppy Field and green for the Emerald City. Even the silver shoes of the original book were changed to ruby slippers because the producer thought they would look brighter in Technicolor.

Garland's biographer, Christopher Finch, explains: "specifically this is the sensuality of the late thirties tri-pack Technicolor with its distinctive blush, its noonday warmth, its faint deepening of the spectrum." The Art Deco sets and the saccharine backdrops heighten the film's artifice and render this a classic of colour photography. "You stood with awe when you saw the sets and the costumes," sighed Bolger years later as he remembered being daily filled with "wonderment."

The making of the film, which had been shot entirely upon MGM's sound stages, was fraught with difficulties. A succession of fourteen screenwriters attempted to adapt Baum's story for the screen although the final version by Noel Langley was easily the most imaginative. There were no less than five directors with an ambitious young producer, Mervyn LeRoy, assuming overall responsibility for the project. Principal director was Victor Fleming but even he left before completion of the film to make the

Ray Bolger as Baum's Scarecrow.
© 1939 by Loew's Incorporated

epic, *Gone With The Wind*. Fleming did not shy from making tough decisions and he boldy scrapped all footage shot by previous directors and insisted on shooting the film from the beginning. The first scene he directed was the meeting between Dorothy and the Scarecrow (in fresh makeup). Incidentally, this sequence required the services of Jim, billed as "the world's only trained raven", who unprofessionally made a hasty exit to the studio rafters immediately the cameras rolled for the first time.

Music for the film was a collaboration of two young men from Broadway – E.Y. 'Yip' Harburg, who wrote the lyrics, and Harold Arlen, who composed the melodies. Their marching song, 'We're Off To See The Wizard, the Wonderful Wizard of Oz' was guaranteed to set audiences swaying as their screen counterparts danced – with a hoppity skip and a skippity hop – along the Yellow Brick Road. (British cinemas now present a 'Sing-a-long-a-Oz' where audiences are encouraged to dress up as characters from the film and sing the words of the song flashed up on the screen in a mass karaoke).

A few songs were jettisoned during post-production editing including a rousing chorus when the companions are being pursued by flying insects known as 'Jitter Bugs' on their way to the witch's castle and almost all of 'Lions and Tigers and Bears' which survives only as a chant as they travel through the haunted forest. Even Judy Garland's soulful rendition of 'Somewhere Over the Rainbow', which catapulted her into an international superstar, was scheduled for the cutting room floor because the producers considered the film was overlong. Ironically, it was this poignant number which has become identified with Baum's fairytale although nowhere in any of his books is there a reference to a rainbow. One true casualty was a knockabout routine performed by the Scarecrow when he first meets Dorothy to accompany his song, 'If I Only Had A Brain.' A dramatic stunt involved Bolger being suspended on wires to appear as if he had been scooped up into the air by the wind. Discovered in MGM's vaults this inventive sequence choreographed by Busby Berkeley was eventually included in the compilation, *That's Dancing* (1985).

Undeniably, the whole enterprise depended upon the talents of the little girl who wandered through this "wonderment". A host of child stars were considered for the part of Dorothy Gale (her surname, a pun on the cataclysmic cyclone, was added for the purpose of the film) including Shirley Temple, Helen Hayes, Deanna Durban and Mary Pickford. MGM soon settled on a rising young film actor cum jazz singer, Judy Garland (1922–1969) whose awkward grace and plump figure were considered ideal for the role of the sunny, brave and resourceful heroine. There was strong support from such stalwart actors as Billie Burke (1885–1970) as Glinda, the Good Witch of the South; Margaret Hamilton (1902–1985) as the Wicked Witch of the West and Frank Morgan (1890–1949) as the Wizard of Oz. Toto was played by a female cairn terrier who was already a veteran of the silver screen.

Perfectly cast were the rude mechanicals. They consisted of a trio of vaudevillian performers: Ray Bolger as the Scarecrow, Jack Haley (1899–1979) as the Tin Woodman and Bert Lahr (1895–1967) as the Cowardly Lion who stole practically all the notices with his inspired clowning. Langley's script acknowledges the principals' broad style of delivery:

> SCARECROW:
> They took my legs off and they threw them over there.
> Then they took my chest out and they threw it over there.
>
> TIN MAN:
> Well, that's you all over.

Ray Bolger had a variety of jobs – a bank clerk, a vacuum cleaner salesman and an accoutant – before he made a success in theatre.

After a spell in vaudeville, he shot to fame as a pliable tap dancer in the film, *The Great Ziegfeld* (1936). Halliwell describes him as "A rubber-legged American eccentric dancer, a stage star who made far too few films." Original choice for the part of the Scarecrow was Buddy Ebsen who late became famous as the patriach of television's 'Beverly Hillibillies.' His role was switched with Ray Bolger who didn't want to play the Tin Woodman. Bad luck plagued Ebsen because he became desperately ill after inhaling the pure aluminium spray that was applied to his skin for his character makeup. While he was recovering in hospital MGM callously replaced him with Jack Haley whose face was dusted with a gentler form of silver powder.

Bolger based his performance on his idol, Fred Stone, who until that time had been the definitive Scarecrow. He recalled watching him as a child in a play, *Jack-O-Lantern*, in Boston. "All I remember now is that I saw this man save a girl from a fate worse than death," he recounted. "He bounded on a trampoline out of the haystack looking just like a scarecrow, put his hand on his head and said, 'Just in time!' I've never forgotten it. That moment opened up a whole new world for me."

Studio artist, Jack Dawn, had the challenging task of humanising all the characters for the film. He endeavoured to reproduce almost exactly the original drawings by Denslow. Dawn devised an elaborate character makeup for Ray Bolger. This consisted mainly of a rubber mask wrinkled to simulate burlap. The actor took delight in telling fans: "The only unfortunate thing was that it closed up all the pores in my face and when the lights got really hot it ate up all the oxygen and I couldn't breathe."

Each morning it took an hour to glue the mask to Bolger's head and another hour to blend the face paint to match it exactly. Then character lines were added to resemble a realistic scarecrow and lastly straw was placed precisely about his body to match the last shot filmed. All of the principal actors dreaded the daily application of their makeup for which they had to report to the studio at 4.30 a.m. six days a week. And to top it all MGM bossses considered their makeup looked so alarming they were banned from eating publicly in the canteen.

Despite such trials and torments the principal cast enjoyed lasting fame for their performances. They were constantly in demand for film, stage and, later, television roles. In 1948, Ray Bolger scored a smash hit on Broadway with *Where's Charley?*, a musical version of the farce, *Charley's Aunt*. He made several more minor films and was a welcome guest artist on numerous television programmes before he finally retired to his villa in Beverley Hills.

Editorial cartoons in American newspapers underscored public sympathy for the passing of each actor and indicated the deep affection held for all the fictional characters from Oz. Caricatures of the Scarecrow featured prominently as the press noted the successive deaths of Bert Lahr (1967) Judy Garland (1969) Jack Haley (1979) and Margaret Hamilton (1985). Finally, Ray Bolger, himself, was gathered up "somewhere over the rainbow" on 15 January 1987. He had always delighted in his own conviction that his performance as the Scarecrow would lend him immortality.

Bolger bequeathed one of his raggedy costumes (there were triplicates of every major costume for the film) designed by Gilbert Adrian, to the National Museum of American Film History at the Smithsonian Institution in Washington. It consists of a dozen items including a black felt hat, green woollen pants, green flannel jacket, ecru work gloves, suede boots, twine belt, straw wig and even a bag of straw for stuffing. Apparently, this costume is displayed sparingly because of its fragility. Recently, it formed part of the touring exhibition, 'Red, Hot and Blue – A Salute to the American Musical.'

Souvenirs of the MGM film were cheaply made and of inferior quality yet paradoxically these are much sought after by collectors for their rarity. Oz memorabilia include character dolls, novelty soaps, beach towels, jewellery caskets, nursery wallpaper, children's stationery, baby carriages and carpet sweepers. Among treasured ephemera are Valentine cards featuring the Scarecrow with the dubious legend, "I wish I had a brain so I could think of you."

More imaginative products were marketed on each special anniversary of the film or television revival. The Knowles China Company produced a limited edition collection of eight plates – the first to feature characters from a film – one of which depicts the Scarecrow singing and dancing at the crossroads. Elton John produced a yellow vinyl tribute album, 'Goodbye Yellow Brick Road' whose cover presented the flamboyant artist stepping out in stack heels and flared trousers along the eternal highway while recently Monopoly brought out a limited edition 'Wizard of Oz' board game.

Baum's stories and characters figured prominently in a variety of presentations in both Britain and America. Situations from the books have been parodied in comics, magazines and computer games and themes have inspired everything from evangelical sermons to AIDS awareness campaigns. The simple plots have formed the basis of radio plays, puppet shows, ice dances, circus acts and even a ballet. Impresario, Tom Arnold, chose 'The Wizard of Oz' as the topic of his annual 'Holiday On Ice' at the Empire Pool at London's Wembley Stadium in 1962.

The Royal Shakespeare Company staged a spectacular musical of *The Wizard of Oz* at London's Barbican Theatre in 1987. The script by John Kane Fox was the first theatrical adaptation to incorporate most of the film's dialogue plus original songs from Harburg and Arlen. This show was directed by Ian Judge, the sets were designed by Mark Thompson and the choreography was by Sheila Falconer. A cast of seasoned actors was headed by Imelda Staunton as Dorothy. There was a full orchestra and all the film's songs and dances were restored including "If I Only Had A Brain" and "The Jitterbug." (The Jitterbug was a colourful mosquito whose bite gave one the jitters causing a wild dance.) A versatile young actor, Paul Greenwood, played the Scarecrow dressed in a dapper costume of straw and stripes in the style of a faded English gentleman.

There was an inspired all black film version of Baum's tale called, *The Wiz* ('Universal', 1978) It was based on a glossy musical that had been a hit on Broadway. The film script was written by Joel Schumacher, the songs were composed by Charlie Smalls and the film was directed by Sidney Lumet. It starred Diana Ross as Dorothy, a shy Harlem kindergarten teacher who is whisked away during a blizzard while searching for her stray dog, Toto, to a futuristic land of Oz. Modern settings provided a touch of realism to this extravaganza based in New York – a subway station, an abandoned amusement

Paul Greenwood as the Scarecrow in the RSC's 'Wizard of Oz', Barbican 1988
Photograph: Reg Wilson
© Royal Shakespeare Company

park, a motel, the rooftop of a perfume factory, an underground car park and a sweatshop presided over by the wicked Evelinna. Lena Horne appeared as Glinda the Good and Richard Pryor played The Wiz.

The great surprise in this lavish Motown production was a young Michael Jackson as the Scarecrow. Dorothy encounters him suspended from a television aerial on a building site where he is being taunted by a quartet of crows. His opening number accompanied by their extraordinary gyrations is a highpoint of the film. Dorothy recognises that this Scarecrow is a true philosopher who just lacks confidence. "Just a product of some negative thinking," she announces. She accepts him as a worthy companion on her journey along the Yellow Brick Road which at one point crosses Brooklyn Bridge. The star-studded picture, which had cost a phenomenal twenty-four million dollars to make, was an immediate box office hit. Mark Ewan Swartz, author of *Oz Before The Rainbow*, considered the producers had masterfully transformed Baum's classic into an "urban fairy tale based on black vernacular culture."

An animated film, *Journey Back To Oz*, was produced by 'Filmation' in association with 'Warner Brothers' in 1971. An absorbing plot concentrates on Dorothy's battles to thwart the evil witch, Mombi, from her attempts to dethrone the Scarecrow, now King of Oz. There are several new characters including a mischievous talking signpost, a rocking horse and Jack-o'-Lantern. Voices are provided by Judy Garland's daughter, Liza Minnelli, as Dorothy, Margaret Hamilton as Aunt Em, Ethel Merman as Mombi and Mickey Rooney as the Scarecrow King.

'Walt Disney', which had acquired the rights to a dozen Oz titles, produced a long-heralded sequel, *Return to Oz*, in 1985. This was a twenty-seven million dollars live action film incorporating electronic puppets but there was an inexplicable absence of songs. A stellar cast includes Jean Marsh, Nicol Williamson, Piper Laurie and newcomer, Fairuza Balk, as a sincere Dorothy. The hybrid plot, based on two Baum fables, *Land of Oz* and *Ozma of Oz*, is most strange. Dorothy suffers traumas because of her previous experiences in Oz and relives further nightmares under shock treatment. The film introduces intriguing new characters such as Jack Pumpkinhead, the Nome King and the Tik Tok Man, but Toto is inexplicably replaced by a talking chicken. His Majesty the Scarecrow of Oz made a late appearance wearing a colourful costume consisting of a checkered jacket and trousers with a lopsided silver crown designed by Michael Floog. Alas, even his amusing antics failed to enliven this lacklustre film. "A weird way to treat a children's classic," opined Halliwell. "Disney should have known better."

The Muppets caused mayhem with Baum's timeless tale when Disney's version of *The Muppets' Wizard of Oz* was released in 2005. It starred Miss Piggy as the Witch and Kermit the frog as the Scarecrow. The musical, *Wicked*, which tells the tale of all four witches, flew in from Broadway to London in 2006. Inevitably, the Scarecrow makes his appearance in the final scenes.

DR SYN ALIAS 'THE SCARECROW'

A trio of exciting films featured Dr Christopher Syn, the saintly parson of Dymchurch in Kent who turns into the spectral figure of 'The Scarecrow' at night to lead his gang of smugglers across Romney Marsh. Dr Syn was the creation of Russell Thorndike (1885–1972) an eccentric actor with a rich sense of the macabre. He and his celebrated sister, Sybil, were the children of a Canon of Rochester Cathedral. Russell was educated at St. George's School, Windsor, where he trained as a boy soloist and performed before Queen Victoria. As an adult, he became a talented actor and played such diverse roles as the first English Peer Gynt and Smee, the comical pirate in J.M. Barry's *Peter Pan*. Russell frequently stayed in a coastguard cottage (since demolished) in Marine Terrace, Dymchurch, where Sybil and her husband, Lewis Casson, joined him for invigorating seaside holidays.

It was while touring America during the First World War that Russell conceived the character of Dr. Syn. Apparently, Russell and his sister shared the same room in a hotel during a trip to Spartanburg, South Carolina. One night there was a murder immediately outside their window, Sybil recalled, and the pair were "too frightened to go to bed." Russell invented the macabre tale of the eigthteenth-century smuggler to entertain his sister and while away the long hours.

According to the story, Christopher Syn was born in 1729, the son of a Kentish solicitor who studied at Oxford. He was introduced to Imogene, the daughter of a Spanish lady, and won her hand in a duel with a bullying landowner who had attempted to kidnap her and her mother. After a hasty marriage to Syn, Imogene was seduced and eloped with the landowner's son, Nicholas Tappitt. Syn vowed revenge and pursued the couple across the high seas where he assumed the identity of the pirate, Captain Clegg.

After repeated attempts to intercept the lovers, Christopher Syn admitted defeat and resumed residence in Dymchurch where he began a belated career in the priesthood. The anonymity he desired was soon compromised by the arrival of his wily first mate, Didymus Mipps, with whom he had shared countless bloodthirsty adventures. The pair teamed up as parson and sexton by day but they became leaders of a smuggling fraternity at night. Dr Syn adopted the role of 'The Scarecrow' and rode a pure black stallion, 'Gehenna', while leading his gang, known as 'The Nightriders', across Romney Marsh. They wore face masks and ragged clothing and daubed their horses with luminous paint so that they appeared as spectres to terrify gullible marshfolk. Dr Syn was ably assisted by Lieutenants Hellspite (Mr Mipps, the sexton) and Beelzebub (Jimmie Bone, the highwayman)

Christopher Syn was indeed a complex character. A learned cleric and revered author, he travels the desolate marsh to comfort the sick and dying, and yet as 'The Scarecrow' he will hang a man for treachery or order the murder of a zealous Revenue Officer without remorse.

When Thorndike returned from America, he turned his tale into a novel and added such colourful characters as Jerry Jerk, the schoolboy who dreams of becoming a hangman; Dr Sennacherib Pepper (a name borrowed from a local tombstone); the blustery squire, Anthony Cobtree; Cornet Blackenbury, who wishes to marry Kate, daughter of Sir Henry Pembury, Lord of Lympne Castle and General Troubridge, Commander of Dragoons at Dover Castle, sworn adversary of 'The Scarecrow.' *Dr Syn – A Tale of Romney Marsh* was an instant hit with the public upon its publication in 1915. Six more ingenious volumes followed to complete the saga although they appeared as a retrospective sequel since Thorndike had unwisely killed off his hero in the first novel. The first book was turned into a successful stage play in 1926 with Thorndike, himself, playing the title role.

Thorndike's stories were obvious material for adventure films and there have been three different versions. The first, *Dr Syn* (British Gaumont 1937) starred George Arliss (1868–1946) as a rather elderly parson who is also the leader of the smuggling cartel on Romney Marsh. A young Margaret Lockwood took a minor role as his secret daughter while matinée idol, John Loder, played her admirer, the Squire's son, Denis. Another youthful actor, Graham Moffatt, who would have been instantly recognised by cinema audiences as Will Hay's stooge, appeared as the chubby potboy, Jerry Jerk. The film was shot almost entirely upon location so that marsh characters and local landmarks have been preserved for posterity. Although the acting style now appears distinctly "stagey", the film remains an exciting romp with a dramatic denoument. During a tense courtroom scene Dr Syn's true identity is revealed by the tenacious Captain Collyer, leader of the Revenue Men. The village mob rises to defend their benevolent parson who escapes by ship to resume his lucrative career as the pirate, Captain Clegg. The scarecrow element is underplayed but there is a mildly comic scene when the hero and villain dine off the same pigeon pie. A sequel was planned but Arliss retired from acting for personal reasons almost as soon as the film was completed.

Hammer Horror Films produced a far more robust colour version of Thorndike's tale in 1962. There was a dispute over copyright since Walt Disney announced that his studios were also preparing an identical film and had not only bought the rights to all of the books but had even copyrighted the name, 'Dr Syn.' Unabashed, Hammer simply changed the title of their film to *Captain Clegg* and the name of the hero from Syn to 'Blyn.' (The film was released in America as *Night Creatures'*.)

Peter Cushing fitted the role of the parson-cum-pirate like a smuggled glove. An excellent supporting cast included Patrick Allen as Captain Collier, Michael Ripper as Sexton Mipps and a young Oliver Reed

Terry Hyson as the ferocious 'Scarecrow' of Romney Marsh and Rev. Roger Ellis as Dymchurch's saintly Dr. Syn at Dymchurch's 'Day of Syn'.

as the Squire's son, Harry, who marries Clegg's clandestine daughter, Imogene. The film was shot mainly on location in Buckinghamshire. Denham served for Dymchurch and Copstone Mill on Thurville Heath provided the smugglers' hideaway. The parish church, village square and tropical island were all conveniently located in the vicinity of Bray Studios.

Captain Clegg concentrated far more on the theme of smuggling and the parson's cunning disguise as 'The Scarecrow.' The opening sequence where an informer is pursued across the fog-enshrouded marshes by fluorescent skeletons riding spectral horses is truly terrifying. The name of the nocturnal fraternity was changed to 'Marsh Phantoms' because it sounded spookier! The film included several scenes of smugglers disguised as scarecrows to act as look-outs (one was named 'Worzel') and these provided lighter moments. Otherwise, the film was hammered by the critics for its inclusion of sickening "blood and gore" for which Hammer, after all, has become synonymous.

A third title, *Dr Syn, Alias the Scarecrow*, was made simultaneously by 'Walt Disney.' It starred American actor, Patrick McGoohan (born 1928) who was famous for his British television appearances in two long-running series, *Danger Man* and *The Prisoner*. A cast of stalwart British character actors included Michael Hordern, Patrick Wymark and Alan Dobie. The script was based on the last book in the series, *Christopher Syn*, completed by William Buchanan after Thorndike's death. Their intricate plot involved the attempts by the tyrannical General Pugh (Geoffrey Keen) to root out the smugglers along the Kent and Sussex coast during the reign of George III. Highlights of the film are a court case with a surprising twist after the verdict and a daring rescue of prisoners from Dover Castle.

Patrick McGoohan as Dr. Syn alias
'The Scarecrow'.
© Walt Disney Productions

Disney's film was a rip-roaring adventure which had a true period flavour and an authentic local setting around Romney Marsh. 'The Scarecrow' was a striking figure with a luminous mask and a cruel laugh which set terror into the heart of his victims. His Robin Hood lifestyle – robbing the rich to pay the poor – was echoed in the catchy theme tune, 'The Scarecrow's Song', composed by Terry Gilkyson. Here 'The Scarecrow' not only managed to evade justice but maintained his secret identity thus allowing for the possibility of a further film. At one time the film was adapted in three parts for screening on American television as *The Scarecrow of Romney Marsh* but Disney did not consider the ratings were sufficiently high to warrant a sequel.

All the Dr Syn titles have long been out of print although they are revered by Marsh folk who biennially bring the characters to life in a pageant ambiguously named, 'Day of Syn'. (The first event involving the whole village of Dymchurch took place on August Bank Holiday, 1963.) The fun begins on the previous Sunday afternoon with costumed militia and townsfolk attending the parish church of SS. Peter and Paul for Evensong. The service is sometimes accompanied by a violin and clarinet. On the Monday various scenes from the Syn novels are reenacted at points around the village including that of a smuggler escaping from a gaol, a duel and a beach landing resisted by the Revenue Men. There are also mummers' plays at the three pubs: The Ship Hotel, The Ocean and The City of London. A procession to the recreation ground takes place during the afternoon with the threat of a skirmish between smugglers and dragoons. Traditionally, the character of the benign parson, Dr Syn, is taken by the Vicar of Dymchurch (currently Rev. Roger Ellis) while his alter ego, 'The Scarecrow' is portrayed by a younger man (Terry Hyson).

THE TALKIES

Scarecrows have made their mark on several classic talking films. Brilliant special effects contributed towards the success of the screen adaptation of H.G. Wells' *The Invisible Man* ('Universal', 1933). The film made a star of the suave British actor, Claude Rains (1889–1967) who is glimpsed only momentarily in his screen debut. (Horror veteran, Boris Karloff, turned the role down for this very reason) Rains played a scientist who discovers a drug which renders him invisible but the side effects turn him into a megalomaniac. A sequel was inevitable. Vincent Price took over the role in *The Invisible Man Returns* ('Universal', 1940). He plays a man who is wrongly imprisoned for the murder of his brother but then uses his invisibility to track down the real culprit. This time the plot is tortuous and the special effects are repetitive. There is one marvellous sequence, undeniably, towards the end of the film where the hero is being pursued by the police across the lonely moors in the bitter cold. To keep himself warm he steals a suit from a scarecrow. "Mind if I borrow your clothes? I'm cold and a bit shaky." It is regarded as one of the great moments in screen history.

Leslie Howard (1890–1943) produced, directed and starred in *Pimpernel Smith* (British National 1941) an update of the classic story, *The Scarlet Pimpernel*, by Baroness Orzy. Howard plays an absent-minded professor of archaeology in charge of a party of Cambridge undergraduates researching in Berlin. When the Second World War begins he gallantly goes undercover to rescue refugees in war-torn Europe. After helping a scientist flee the Nazis, the professor escorts his students onto a train with the intention of joining them further along the line after first rescuing a world famous pianist from a German labour camp. A soldier notices a scarecrow in an adjacent field and idly shoots at it. Blood is seen dripping from its wrist. . . The scarecrow is, as might be guessed, Pimpernel Smith in one of his inpenetrable disguises. (How the professor managed to get back onto the train remains a mystery.)

The eighth James Bond adventure, *Live and Let Die*, ('United Artists', 1973) marked the debut of Roger Moore as 007. Bond is sent to San Monique in Jamaica to track down the evil Dr Kanaga (Yaphet Kotto) who plans to flood the market with free heroin and thus create millions more drug addicts. The beautiful psychic, Solitaire, (Jane Seymour) guides Bond across Kanaga's private island to trace his poppy fields guarded by voodoo scarecrows. Their revolving heads are equipped with cameras concealed in their eyes and guns in their mouths. After a pursuit by helicopter through the jungle, the pair make their escape aboard a double decker bus which careers headlong towards a low bridge. . .

The most frightening movie of all time is generally agreed to be *The Wicker Man* (British Lion 1973) The story concerns a pious policeman, Sergeant Howie, played by Edward Woodward, who is sent to a remote island in West Scotland to investigate the supposed disappearance of a young girl. He is drawn into an erotic world of pagan rituals, superstition and sacrifice which appears normal routine to the islanders. Culmination of events is when the omnipotent Lord Summerisle, played with relish by Christopher Lee, shepherds Howie to the brow of a commanding hill where the community plan to burn him alive in a giant, faceless, wicker effigy.

Director, Robin Hardy, described *The Wicker Man* as a "film fantastic." It opens in a most sophisticated manner by thanking the fictional Lord Summerisle for his cooperation in making the film which adds to the air of realism in this makebelieve island. But this devastating film soon starts to awaken a kind of tribal memory in the viewer who willingly accepts the ambient lifestyle of the islanders which involves naked women jumping over bonfires, yokels wearing animal masks and the ultimate sacrifice of a human being to ensure their island's fertility.

"We wanted to get to the old religion, the pagan underground behind the black magic, pentagrams and garlic that you were used to seeing in Hammer movies," explained Hardy. It harks back to the ancient custom of sacrificing victims before straw men were substituted in the fields although for cinematic effect the burning wicker effigy appears gigantic. The impact of the film was described by Tom Cox in an article for *The Sunday Times* 'Culture' magazine: "The wooden head topples, the sun goes down and life is a little more vivid – and terrifying – forever." (14 April 2002).

Magazine cover of 'The Wicker Man'.

The Wicker Man was written by Anthony Shaffer who loosely based it upon David Pinner's novel, *Ritual*, and folklore customs detailed in Sir James George Frazer's *The Golden Bough*. The film, which has achieved cult status, was shot at twenty-five locations in South West Scotland. Now there are regular 'Wicker Man' festivals held at various places associated with the film and the highlight is the burning of a replica giant figure. *The Wicker Man* was refilmed starring Nicholas Cage and released by Warner in 2006.

Absolution is a strangely discomforting melodrama also scripted by Anthony Schaffer ('Bulldog Films', 1978). Richard Burton plays a tormented priest, Father Goddard, working as a tutor in a Roman Catholic Boys' School. His sanity is challenged by a manipulative pupil (Dominic Guard) who confesses to the murder of a traveller (Billy Connolly). When the priest digs up the body in a nearby wood he finds that it is merely a scarecrow. The pupil admits that his confession was a prank but when the real body is discovered, Father Goddard, bound by the confidentiality of the confessional, is trapped into committing murder. The complicated plot is weakened by the final revelation that the school contains not one but two psychopaths among its pupils.

Another disturbing film made for television, *Dark Night of The Scarecrow* ('Wizan', 1981) has gained cult status in the U.S.A. Possibly, this is because its director, Frank De Felitta, went on to make such horror masterpieces as *Hallowe'en* and *Friday the 13th*. A suspenseful plot focuses on the relationship of a young girl with a mentally retarded man called Bubba which is frowned on by the inhabitants of a small farming town in Mid-West America. When the girl is mauled by a savage dog the townsfolk assume that Bubba has molested her and they track him down. He hides inside a scarecrow but he is soon found and shot dead by the vigilantes, leader of whom is a murderous mailman played by burly film actor, Charles Durling. Bubba's malevolent spirit seeks revenge on each of his executioners with bizarre consequences. The most haunting scene is the sight of Bubba's eyes staring through the scarecrow's hood when he is surrounded by his tormentors.

A tense drama, *The Scarecrow* ('Oasis Films', 1982) directed by Sam Pillsbury was made in New Zealand. It concerns a confused adolescent, Ned, growing up in an idyllic town with his older sister, Pru, and their oppressive farming family. Ned's chickens are stolen from the coop on the day a young girl is raped and murdered. Shortly afterwards, a mysterious stranger appears who mesmerises the townsfolk with his displays of conjuring. He is first glimpsed one dark winter's night shrouded in steam from a railway train on the secluded platform. Ned slowly realises the connection between young girls disappearing and the arrival of the stranger and he begins to suspect that Pru is his next victim. Horror veteran, John Carradine, gives a chilling performance as the hypnotic stranger known as 'The Scarecrow.'

An American television programme screened throughout the 1980s was *Scarecrow and Mrs. King*. This stylish comedy adventure series starred Kate Jackson ('Charlie's Angels') as the brave, resourceful housewife, Amanda King, and Bruce Boxleiter as Lee, a handsome, dapper intelligence operative who works for a top secret United States Government Agency. There were oblique references to *The Wizard of Oz*. In the episode, 'We're Off To See The Wizard', Amanda helps to solve a case by studying Baum's book and she also learns how Lee earned his perplexing codename, 'Scarecrow.' In another episode,

'The First Time', she discovers a notepad fixed to her fridge door that reads, "Toto, I have a feeling we're not in Kansas anymore." And propped up against the refrigerator is a scarecrow. . .

Alfred Hitchcock personally introduced a series of television programmes hailed as classic tales of terror on ITV between 1957 and 1966. They were revived briefly throughout the 1980s after the death of the portly Master. 'Alfred Hitchcock Presents' is still shown on television around the world and certain fans regard the series of absorbing tales as even better than his feature films. Three hundred episodes were produced involving top directors, top stars and top writers including Roald Dahl, Eric Ambler, Ed McBain and Ellery Queen. Their tales with a twist were full of irony since villainy went unpunished and virtue went unrewarded. Hitchcock, himself, was fascinated by the weird and wonderful. He habitually employed his dry wit by presenting the epilogue in a bizarre setting – ensconced in an electric chair or impaled as a scarecrow. Once he aptly demonstrated his flair for self promotion by posing as a human scarecrow with three large crows perched on his outstretched arms for *Life Magazine* (1 February 1963) to publicise his film adaptation of Daphne du Maurier's short story, *The Birds* ('Universal', 1963).

A vindictive scarecrow made a fleeting appearance in the controversial BBC television serial, *The Singing Detective* by the experimental dramatist, Dennis Potter (1935–1994) in 1986. This multi-layered mystery starred Michael Gambon as a writer of detective novels suffering from a painful skin disease who literally makes "a song and dance" of his pitiful condition. He hallucinates while in hospital and fantasises that he is the hero of one of his own pulp thrillers as a crooning 1940s detective enmeshed in a baffling murder case. When he consults a psychotherapist he reverts to his guilt-ridden wartime childhood. He travels with his mother by steam train to visit relatives in Wales and through the steamy carriage windows he sees a scarecrow who patriotically salutes him. Puzzlingly, the train seems to be going round in circles for at one point the scarecrow turns into Adolf Hitler and a troop of British soldiers use it for target practice. Eventually, the scarecrow becomes his venomous schoolmistress (Janet Henfrey) who pursues him relentlessly with her blanched face around the hospital ward in the final episode.

A bizarre horror movie, *Scarecrows* was produced by the aptly named, 'Effigy Films', in 1988. "When it comes to terror," pronounced the producers, emphatically, "their (sic) in a field of their own." The opening sequence is highly dramatic. Five commandos turned robbers hijack an aircraft and escape with three million dollars in stolen banknotes. Greed soon materialises which drives one of their company to hurl the loot from the plane and parachute after it while his enraged accomplices follow in hot pursuit. He lands in a cornfield populated by a ragged circle of hideous scarecrows who possess supernatural powers. All this thrilling action takes place before the opening titles have rolled. . .

opposite: Marilyn Monroe wearing her famous windy dress and '007 Licensed to kill weeds', Faversham Festival;

Phantom of the Opera, Kettlewell Festival.

The film is truly scary. One by one the villains are murdered by the scarecrows whose moulded faces are swathed in hessian. The bodies of their victims are stuffed with straw before being brought to life and made to turn against their comrades. They have now become indestructible and impervious to gunfire. There are some moments of real humour both planned and unintentional. The villains take refuge in a dilapidated farmhouse stuffed with dead crows owned by a Mr Fowler; a telephone call is made by a dismembered straw head in a fridge and the heroine screams in terror when threatened by a manic scarecrow stowaway while she coolly manages to fly an aeroplane, singlehandedly. . .

Scarecrows pop up imtermittently in Tim Burton's supernatural chiller, *Sleepy Hollow* (Mandalay Pictures 1999). This cult fantasy drama is loosely based upon a 19th century gothic tale by Washington Irving, *The Legend of Sleepy Hollow*. Constable Ichabod Crane (Johnny Depp) is sent to investigate a series of murders by decapitation in an isolated community on the outskirts of New York in 1799. Critics agree that although *Sleepy Hollow* lacks the imaginative weirdness of Burton's earlier films (*Batman* and *Edward Scissorhands*) its style, elegance and black humour raise it far above the level of a pedestrian slasher movie.

In the exciting pre-credit sequence a Dutch aristocrat rides in his carriage through the evening mist across remote farmland when his coachman is beheaded by a headless horseman. He flees in terror through fields of maize where he is confronted by a scarecrow with raised arms, tattered drapes and a pumpkin head. The scarecrow manages to keep his head while the aristocrat's own is severed. A second scarecrow swivelling in the wind surrounded by

Opposite: Glinda, Good Witch of the North, Wray Festival.
Above: Frankenstein, Kettlewell Festival.
Left: Inspector Clouseau and the Pink Panther, Wray Festival.

cornstooks is interpreted as an ill omen by a magistrate seeking to escape from the claustrophobic community. He, too, falls victim to the headless horseman. Later, Constable Crane is startled when the scarecrow's flaming head is hurled at him as he gallops through dense woodland. He deduces that the supernatural creature is being summoned up by a sorceress who plans to inherit a fortune.

Tim Burton also wrote a dark, eccentric, narrative poem and drew sketches of the main characters which were turned into a feature length stop-motion animated film, *Nightmare Before Christmas* (Disney 1993). In the elaborate opening sequence the scarecrow, Pumpkin King of Hallowe'en, is pulled through the streets astride a straw horse before he sets himself on fire and leaps into a fountain to rematerialise as the spindly Jack Skellington. One day, by chance, Jack discovers Christmas and the plot concerns his misguided attempts to bring all the excitement of that season to his own ghoulish town, 'Halloweenland.' This triggers an hilarious sequence of events. The complex and ambitious musical fantasy film was directed by Henry Selick, the screenplay was by Caroline Thompson and both music and lyrics were by Danny Elfman who also provided Jack's haunting singing voice. This was a brave departure for the Disney studios where Tim Burton was once one of the animators of cuter two-dimensional cartoon characters. "The setting may be odd and a little unsettling," admitted Tim Burton, "but it's a celebration of my two favourite holidays – Christmas and Hallowe'en."

Accolades have been bestowed upon Peter Jackson's epic production of Tolkein's trilogy, *The Lord of the Rings*. In the first episode, *The Fellowship of the Ring* ('New Line'/'Wingnut' 2001) two hobbit friends, Frodo Baggins (Elijah Wood) and Sam (Sean Astin) attempt to smuggle the powerful, magical ring out of the Shire. A scarecrow with three crows perched on its shoulders stands in the lush fields against a mountain backdrop as they steal through the countryside. New Zealand provided the spectacular scenery for Tolkein's Middle Earth.

Francis Ford Coppola's *Jeepers Creepers* ('Myriad'/'United Artists', 2002) was promoted as 'The Best U.S. horror movie of the last ten years' upon its release. The incomprehensible story concerns two college teenagers, Trish (Gina Philips) and Darry (Justin Long) driving home along a deserted highway when they watch a mysterious stranger disposing of bodies down a chute. They investigate and discover numerous decomposing bodies in the crypt of a ramshackle church. The killer gives chase. They should have taken warning from the mocking crows in the belfry. For it turns out that their pursuer is a rapacious demon who devours parts of the human anatomy to survive. The petrified pair seek shelter in a wayside bungalow inhabited by a strange lady who runs a cat sanctuary. Lurking behind the scarecrow in her overgrown garden is the Creeper (Jonathan Breck) wielding a battleaxe.

The sequel, *Jeepers Creepers II* (2003) despite inconsistencies, far surpasses the original film for thrills

opposite: Rocky the Rooster, Wray Festival.

and excitement. A tense opening sequence involves a young boy staking out scarecrows in a field of maize. He notices one of them has grown claws and he runs away. The scarecrow leaps high into the air, pounces on the terrified boy and carries him off to his lair. The Creeper has metamorphosed into a flesh eating crow! The real fun starts when the monster picks off members of a basketball team trapped inside a bus that breaks down on a deserted highway. This is definitely the most frightening film to date to feature a scarecrow and not one to watch late at night or alone.

MUSICAL SCARECROWS

'The Scarecrow' is the title of a song written by the acclaimed husband and wife team, Mike and (the late) Lal Waterson. Although it is a modern composition, 'The Watersons' were steeped in the evolution of folk music and naturally incorporated traditional imagery in this haunting song. Their own recording of 'The Scarecrow', which appears on 'Bright Phoebus', is most elusive but a cover version by June Tabor is included in her album, 'Abyssinians' (1989) obtainable from Topic Records.

June Tabor's rendering is wistful and melodious whereas the lyrics would appear to be cruel and taunting. They express a woman's despair at her husband's impotence through old age. Her agony is compounded by the sight of a ragged scarecrow in a field who has lost his power to frighten the crows. The forlorn figure seems to express the lifecycle of mankind through the imagery of a scarecrow inevitably replaced by a younger version once its impact has been lost:

> As I walked out one summer's morn,
> I saw a scarecrow tied to a pole in a field of corn.
> His coat was black, his head was bare,
> And as the wind shook him, the crows took into the air.
>
> Ah, but you'd lay me down and love me,
> Ah, but you'd lay me down and love me, if you could.
> But you're only a bag of bones in an overall
> That the wind sways so the crows fly away
> And the corn can grow tall. . .

'A Field of Scarecrows' (Carnyx) is a bizarre piece of modern classical mood music, combining lyrical delicacy with disembodied eeriness, composed by Paul Keenan (1956–2001) This contemporary composition combines alto and tenor trombone (John Kenney) and piano (George Nicholson) with fragments of spoken text – an Anglo Saxon poem, 'The Ruin.' The original idea came from a dream in which scarecrows were dancing in a summer field full of hay bales. Paul visualised a motorbike riding at speed along a leafy lane and captured the soundbites of the countryside, wind whipped at speed. "Imagine the ear as a camera snapping each fraction of present time as you travel," suggested Paul. "The field of the title is a harmonic field and the scarecrows are all in the mind's ear."

Is it a bird? Is it a plane? No, it's a scarecrow!
(Kettlewell Festival)

5. SCARECROWS IN ART

ARTISTS AND SCULPTORS have been inspired to depict scarecrows over the centuries. Their lure is threefold. The addition of a scarecrow adds colour and humour to an otherwise bleak landscape; their torn and tattered attire flapping in the breeze provides movement to a picture while just a few props arranged on crossed sticks instantly creates a character which many artists find irresistible.

MINIATURE MASTERPIECE

Earliest known representation of a scarecrow in the world of art is a miniature painting in a medieval manuscript: *Les Trés Riches Heures du duc de Berry*. Jean, duc de Berry (1340–1416) was born in the Château de Vincennes, the third son of Jean II, 'le Bon', King of France. The duc was an extravagant patron and plunderer of the arts who owned eighteen illuminated 'Books of Hours'. The most precious was the *Trés Riches Heures* which included a unique Zodiacal or Astrological Map that probably had medical significance. This masterpiece, whose purpose was to outline a daily regime of pious devotion, is known principally for its calendar which sets out in fine detail the agricultural year.

The month of October features tilling and sowing. A rider dressed in scarlet cracks a whip to steer a horse pulling a harrow across the field. This primitive instrument simply consists of a wooden grid weighed down with a boulder to make its pegs penetrate the soil more deeply. In the foreground a second peasant wearing a blue tunic broadcasts seeds from his bulky white apron or "sowing sheet." A seed bag and leather water bottle lie beside the hedgerow where a clutch of magpies and crows are pecking at the scattered corn.

The far field has been staked off after it has just been sown. Feathers are tied to strings which criss-cross the land to ward off thieving birds. In the centre stands the profile of a scarecrow equipped as an archer. He has a carved wooden face and wears a grey smock with a vibrant blue tabard and a pot helmet. He prepares to fire an arrow over his right shoulder from the taut string of his longbow. This unique

opposite: Lloyd le Blanc's bronze 'Scarecrow'.

October: sowing the winter grain from *Les Trés Riches Heures du duc de Berry*.
Victoria & Albert Museum, London/The Bridgeman Art Library

military scarecrow casts a short shadow on the soil from the soft noonday sun.

Courtiers stroll in the background beneath the ramparts of the magnificent Chateau of the Louvre built by the duc de Berry's eldest brother, King Charles V of France. A central tower, commonly called 'Le Tour de Louvre', serves not only as a dungeon but a store for the royal treasure. It is surrounded by myriad towers and turrets whose blue spires are surmounted with gilded weather vanes. Hidden from view is the north-west tower which contained Charles V's precious manuscripts that formed his famous library. A high curtain wall enlivened by parapets and balconies protects the château while a postern gives access to the quay. Figures are stepping into boats drawn up along the bank of the River Seine which serves as a moat. This scene of country life in the shadow of the royal residence presents a vivid image of the outskirts of Paris at the beginning of the fifteenth century.

Experts attribute the majority of the decoration of this most celebrated 'Book of Hours' to Pol de Limbourg (*c*.1385–1416) assisted by his two younger brothers, Herman and Jean, who were all born in Nimwegen, in the Duchy of Guelders, between the Meuse and the Rhine. Their exquisite handiwork was completed by their artistic successor, Jean Colombe (*c*1435–1493) and the estimated date of completion is the mid to late fifteenth century, long after the duc de Berry had died. The style of the Limbourg brothers is marked by its unprecedented attention to detail, its realistic representation of the countryside, its marvellous sense of narrative and its carnival of colour. Their work is often regarded as the first true landscape painting. The duc's 'Book of Hours' is now owned by the Musée Condé, Chantilly, France.

EUROPEAN ARTISTS

Avant-garde artists of the twentieth century were often inspired by scarecrows. Among the most revolutionary designs were the illustrations for a German children's story, *Die Scheuche* ('The Scarecrow') published by Kate Steinitz in 1925. This experimental book was a collaboration between the writer, Kurt Schwitters (1887–1948) and the designer, Theo van Doesburg (1883–1931). Schwitters had already made his mark with eccentric book covers incorporating typographical designs while Van Doesburg was the founder of the magazine, *De Stilj*. "I pasted words and sentences into poems in such a way as to produce a rhythmical design," he explained.

Apparently, the innovative style of this bizarre German fairytale was "conceptualised and visualised" on the spur of the moment. Miss Steinitz was present at a meeting between the author and the ilustrator, who were already close friends, where she watched as the style of the book unfolded. She recalled how Schwitters recited his story from memory and "while Kurt declaimed, Theo van Doesburg laid some matches on the tablecloth and arranged them in the shape of a scarecrow. Then he drew a terrifically naturalistic tailcoat and a very stylised one. Kurt took the big scissors and cut them out." Later, these sketches of a matchstick figure were translated into a Chaplinesque scarecrow on the page surrounded by unrelated typographical signs and symbols.

Schwitters' experimental plot concerns an old-fashioned scarecrow who sports a tuxedo, lace shawl and top hat. He also flourishes a walking stick, incessantly pecked at by a courageous rooster and chicks. The scarecrow experiences real terror when a bullying farmer threatens to kill him. At the end of the story ghosts of former owners come to retrieve all their accessories from the scarecrow for they are to be regarded as symbols of an outmoded civilised society. The tale is intended as a parable for young children who are encouraged to eliminate the past represented by the scarecrow – and embrace a Brave New World.

The prophetic book, which has now become a collectors' item, was printed in just two colours – red and blue – with sans serif text. Letterforms on every page become the characters acting out the story which echoes themes in the 'Book of Genesis.' Who, though, is the farmer that could strike fear into such an inoffensive scarecrow? At the time of its publication the book was hailed by art critics as an "explosion of interactive creative ability" although no one has recorded whether these radical illustrations were fully appreciated or even understood by impressionable child readers in pre-Nazi Germany.

Ivan Generalic (1914–1992) founder of Croatian Naive Art, produced a vibrant painting of a scarecrow on glass. He was the most productive of the 'peasant painters' from the 'School of Hlebine' in the Podravina region of Northern Croatia. Generalic completed over eight hundred naive paintings, many of which have been exhibited in galleries throughout the world. This cowherd turned painter hailed from the Hlebine, a village near the Hungarian border boasting little more than a row of stone cottages, an inn and a tiny church with an onion dome. Despite such an uninspiring background, he was able to derive inspiration from the surrounding countryside and his rural themes included vineyards, stables, markets, anglers, gypsies, weddings, funerals and festivals. Croatian Naive Art first gained recognition in the 1950s when it commanded high prices and Generalic's paintings, in particular, have continued to escalate in value.

Generalic's 'Scarecrow' (1964) is a dandified figure presented against fertile farmland beneath a threatening sky. It is tied to a treestump which stands in the centre of two banks of cornsheafs. His flowing garments consist of a burgundy jacket, lemon shirt, grey pants and a floppy hat bedecked with a trio of feathers. A dead crow hangs from his angular arm formed from a branch of a tree and he wears a pale, mournful expression. This painting perfectly demonstrates Generalic's "gift for colour and ability for developing significant form."

AMERICAN AND CANADIAN ARTISTS

William Sidney Mount (1807–1868) is celebrated as the first "absolutely American artist." He was born on Long Island, New York, and made a prosperous career from his representations of Yankee farmers. One of his most famous paintings is an engaging scene where a vagabond exchanges his battered chapeau for a superior Panama worn by a scarecrow propped up in a barrel. At first glance it might appear that this colourful oil painting, 'Fair Exchange No Robbery' (c.1865) is simply an amusing narrative picture. It might even be assumed that the humorous subject points to Mount's sunny disposition. But art historian, Elizabeth Johns, who has made a study of American genre painting, insists that this is actually an example of the artist's darker side. She has meticulously examined Mount's series of paintings on agricultural themes and has convincingly demonstrated how his seemingly innocuous topics often disguised devastating criticisms of unsavoury practices in rural America.

'Fair Exchange No Robbery' apparently focuses on the friction caused by the arrival of a party of anarchists on Long Island. Their eccentric behaviour was ridiculed by the wary inhabitants of the surrounding villages and the artist was enticed to take up his brush and palette to join his neighbours in the fun. Mount was a man of staunch political, social and religious views and this mild act was a demonstration of his orthodox pursuasions. He became a master at camouflaging his principles in deceptively innocent pictorial language.

Josiah Warren, a reformer whose Utopian theories earned him considerable notoriety, pledged himself to eradicating social injustice by attacking its roots – money. Currency made speculation possible and therefore permitted unscrupulous middlemen to manipulate prices on basic commodities. Warren further believed it encouraged the elite to live, parasitically, off the sweat and toil of the working classes and boldly claimed: "Money represents robbery." Spurning monetary transactions, Warren sought a fairer means of exchange.

Acting on his principles, Warren opened an Equity Store at Cincinnati in 1827. There, labour could simply be exchanged for labour. Promissory notes were issued instead of bank notes and these could be redeemed for either labour or corn. Every customer had the option of bartering his wares for those of others but most preferred labour notes with which the holder could require an agreed amount of work from the person who had affixed his name to the bill. This venture precluded the need for cash and prevented the middleman from profiting significantly from any exchange between producer and consumer.

Warren's store flourished although sceptics observed certain loopholes in his system. Most criticism related to

William Sidney Mount's
'Fair Exchange, No Robbery', 1865
oil on panel.
The Long Island Museum of American
Art, History and Carriages. Gift of
Mr and Mrs Ward Melville, 1958

time for time since it is obvious that not every person's labours are equal. Inherently, there is a marked imbalance in society; for instance, between skilled artisans and casual labourers whose exchange of work would render Warren's system totally unfair. Unabashed, Warren and his disciples gathered in the spring of 1851 to found their self-sufficient community in the pine tree hinterlands of Long Island. The village they founded was called 'Modern Times' but it changed its name to 'Brentwood' during the Civil War. Mount's home at 'Stony Brook' was just twelve miles from the community where he was able to observe Warren and his followers' peculiar lifestyle at firsthand.

The artist expressed his disdain for the Warrenites' homespun philosophy in his painting which he named after an adage current in the nineteenth century relating to equitable transactions: 'A fair exchange is not robbery.' The vagabond who stands with his hound beside a cornfield in the centre of the picture practises the type of barter common at the time store in operation at Modern Times. He simply exchanges one item for another. But, Mount asks, is it a fair exchange?

"Mount suggests that the vagabond's labours were worth no more than those of the scarecrow, or, since the exchange is decidedly unequal, even less," suggests art critic, Charles Colbert, in *American Art* (Summer/Fall 1994): "From this perspective, the artist expressed in paint precisely the same criticism levelled by the society's detractors: Warren's Utopian schemes provided no safeguard against those whose profligacy encouraged them to take advantage of the system"

Another critic, Donald Keyes, observed: "Mount's schemes are carefully controlled theaters in which the actors happily partake in the humorous anecdote while reinforcing the standards of popular morality." Presumably, the artist regaled his circle of friends with the precise circumstances which prompted this complicated painting but the work's provincialism and narrow frame of reference may explain why it was left abandoned in his studio after his untimely demise since no buyer was ever found during his lifetime.

James Wells Champney (1843–1903) produced a delightful oil painting of a scarecrow which can be admired purely for pleasure. Champney, born in Boston, Massachusetts, was apprenticed at the age of sixteen to a wood engraver. At the outbreak of the Civil War he enlisted with the 45th Massachusetts Regiment but after a few months contracted malaria. He was forced to return to his career of wood engraving but his eyes soon became weakened by the drawing and fine pencilling.

In 1866, he toured Europe where he first studied under Edouard Frére in Paris and then at the Academy in Antwerp before wintering in Rome. When he returned to America he opened his own studio in Boston and churned out genre paintings which he signed, 'Champ.' A feature of these paintings was the relationship between old and young people. This comes to the fore in his oil painting, 'Making The Scarecrow' (1880) which shows an elderly farmer putting the finishing touches to a scarecrow assisted by three youngsters on a smallholding in spring.

James Wells Champney's, 'Making the Scarecrow'.

Not long afterwards Champney began to experiment in pastels. He was attracted by the "ease, rapidity and certainty" of this medium and he was regarded as the foremost pastelist of his day. Portraits of high society and theatre personalities boosted his popularity and to sit for Champney was an affirmation of status. His self portrait reveals him as a dandy wearing a smart suit with a stetson and sporting a ginger beard and whiskers. His artistic skills were diverse and he was in great demand as a lecturer, illustrator, watercolourist and photographer. He died in a freak elevator accident while leaving the Camera Club in New York in 1903.

Daniel Fowler (1810–1894) was a Georgian English artist who became Canada's foremost Victorian watercolourist. Born in Kent, where he was a school friend of Benjamin Disraeli, he came from a wealthy middle class family. Determined to become a painter, he moved to London where part of his training was to tour the Continent to study European Masters. At one time he was appointed art master to an elderly daughter of George III, Princess Mary, Duchess of Gloucester. He exhibited at the Royal Academy in 1839 and was elected a member of the British Artists, 1836–1842.

In 1843, Fowler emigrated to Canada because of poor health and there he strove to become a successful farmer on Amherst Island. He did not paint again until after a return visit to England in 1857. He had become stimulated by the Pre-Raphaelite Movement because he shared their interest in poetry, simplicity and naturalism. For the rest of his life, Fowler painted in every moment spared from his family and farming commitments. Eventually, he earned the epithet, 'Canada's Pride.'

Farming, naturally, gave Fowler an unique insight into landscape painting. His depictions of wild flowers and dead game are expressed with accurate detail, vivid colouring and arresting realism. Invariably, he worked in the open air which enabled him to confront nature and almost all his still life paintings are set against a realistic background. While exploring the region where he farmed, he honed his artistic talent and mined the beauty surrounding the serene Bay of Quinte.

Fowler's watercolour, 'Scarecrow, Amherst Island' (c.1890) was executed towards the end of his life. The commanding figure wears a mask and stands, plump and distorted, against a ricketty wooden fence. "The scarecrow stands rooted in stabbing brushstrokes and a calligraphy of broken lines that create receding planes to a rail fence. This, then, articulates in the definition of space with the scarecrow's outstretched arms and the distant trees beyond the field," notes art critic, Dr. J. Alan Walters. "It is a North American scene by a North American farmer whose British eyes have been sharpened by forty-seven years in the atmosphere, geography and ecology of the South Eastern Ontario limestone plain."

Canadian painter-poet, Maxwell Bates (1921–1971) was born at Calgary, Alberta, surrounded by lumber mills, oil refineries, ranches and tanneries. He is, paradoxically, regarded as a European artist since he travelled across England before being taken P.O.W. in Germany and resettling in New York immediately after World War II. After a paralysing stroke, this bleak artist took a sombre view of existence and he was marked by the art world as a "perpetually blasted man." His paintings, like his poems, deal with tragic themes and reflect his personal irony, fantasy and fascination with people, most freely expressed in his disturbing portraits.

"Bates' main concern is the fate of man," propounds art critic, Joan Lowndes. "His most ambitious painting aims to create a metaphor for the human condition and his puppets, clowns, scarecrows and crucifixions are classic symbols." Further, he shows "a strong penchant for decoration," she declares, "and when the picture calls for it, a joy in handling sumptuous color."

This view is aptly demonstrated in Bates' abstract watercolour, 'Scarecrow' (1967) now in the collection of The Canada Council Art Bank. This is a striking, if puzzling, composition where three buxom beauties romp through a field, viewed in amazement by a white sheeted scarecrow. Ms. Lowndes observes: "A startled scarecrow watches, impotent while a rout of hoydens – smashed raspberry mouths, flushed scarlet flesh, skirts hoisted above their crotch – cavort about as though maddened with aphrodisiac."

America's favourite contemporary watercolourist, Andrew Wyeth (born 1917) finds inspiration for his exquisite landscapes in the immediate environment of Chadds Ford, Pennsylvania, and Cushing, Maine. He is clearly fascinated by crows and scarecrows and has made them both the subject of several of his paintings. 'Winter Field' (1942) presents a dead crow lying across the foreground with distant bare fields and isolated farm buildings against a cold, grey skyline. Wyeth is often dismissed by his critics for his narrative approach and commitment to realism but, given the radical low viewpoint and the fantastic scale of the crow, he has introduced here a magical sense of abstract beauty. Frequently, Wyeth invokes death which is evident in the sketch of a pair of dead crows, his study for 'Woodshed' (1944) and also a distant flock of crows, a study for 'Snow Flurries' (1953).

'The Scarecrow' (1947) features the startling image of a derelict scarecrow reduced by time to jagged sticks from which torn strips of material flutter in the breeze against a backdrop of burnt stubble and oppressive clouds. This stark image is truly menacing. His second scarecrow painting entitled, 'Gull Scarecrow' (1954) plays around with perspective making the image of a dead seagull staked to a pole the overpowering feature of a rugged landscape, with a farmhouse appearing tiny by comparison, in the far distance. Wyeth noticed the gruesome gibbet scarecrow guarding blueberry fields from the window of an upstairs studio where he was painting while staying with friends in their house overlooking the George River, New England. A third simple but effective painting is called 'Benny's Scarecrow' (1955).

This striking watercolour focuses on a coat blowing in a high wind draped over a stout stick in a sloping field. It is tantalisingly subtitled, 'Jim Loper's Coat.'

Wyeth's fourth watercolour to feature a scarecrow is 'Witch Country, Cushing' (1973) This time Wyeth chooses a distressed straw effigy which takes the form of a witch riding a broomstick. A strong anecdotal quality is expressed in this finely executed painting. A pedestal of pumpkins banked beneath the scarecrow and the sparse autumnal landscape remind the viewer of America's unique harvest traditions and Hallowe'en customs. Further, there is an obvious visual association between the black-robed scarecrow and rural witchcraft which is made explicit by the painting's ominous title. Art critics now concede "the artist possesses the ability to present the commonplace in a strange and mysterious manner" but the American public, who recognise him as the undisputed master of disturbing agrarian images, regard Wyeth as an icon.

Phil Berkman's mixed media sculpture, 'Thoreau's Scarecrows', was exhibited at the N.A.M.E. Gallery, Chicago, in 1981. Berkman is a low profile artist whose daytime job is chief of security at Chicago's Museum of Contemporary Art. He exhibits infrequently, enjoys "games of correspondence and contradiction" and endeavours to "make art out of life." His 'Thoreau's Scarecrows' is a complicated composition, difficult to interpret or understand. It is a plywood construction consisting of two intersecting walls, about seven feet tall, creating eight surfaces and four corners. The edges of these walls are exaggeratedly jagged and frayed suggesting pages ripped out of an upright book. Visitors are encouraged to walk into this 'cornerama', touch and examine the artefacts positioned on the stark white walls and so 'read' the puzzling pages.

The hotchpotch of objects displayed on these plain walls provide "a satirical slice of museum experience in a benign fabrication designed to mock security with its cartoon like profile," according to one critic, Judith Russi Kirshner. A variety of handles from brushes, buckets, knives, hammers and umbrellas are displayed on two adjacent walls. The functional part of these handles have been replaced by colour photographs of information plaques at a Braille Trail near Aspen, Colorado. A blind person will be able to "perceive" the complete picture by feeling the signs whose meaning is concealed from the ordinary sighted viewer who can only guess the mundane function of each incomplete object.

Mounted on the wall is a crossbow-pistol arrow. Its lethal tip has been replaced with an everyday key that fits the lock of the narrow door framed in the opposite wall. This door opens into the next corner and faces a red fire extinguisher installed like sculpture on a pedestal. Lastly, in the fourth corner, an artist's sketch of a black man (a stereotype "suspicious character") confronts the generalised yellow "smile" face of a kitchen clock, "another benign mask for the tyranny of the time." "Thoreau's

David Carlin's scarecrow netsuke.

Scarecrows", asserts Kirshner, "not only refers to the ordering of the museum experience but also to ideas of trust and security that order everyday experiences."

Californian artist, David Carlin (born 1944) specialises in carving miniatures in the style and function of the Japanese netsuke. Netsuke are ornamental buttons traditionally carved from ivory which has now become a prohibited material. Therefore David exclusively adopts non-endangered species of American hardwoods which he colours to achieve an individual character for each of his minute creations. David was inspired by his extensive journeys across Japan and he has created over six hundred miniature buttons since his return some thirty years ago. Subjects include frogs, snails, turtles, ladybirds, cowboys, footballers and lovers sailing in a walnut shell. He has carved several scarecrows including one from boxwood and coca bola (a Central American hardwood renowned for its colour range and poisonous qualities) wearing a straw hat and a buttoned shirt tied with rope around its waist (5.5 x 1.5. cms) An exhibition of David's work was presented at the Los Angeles County Museum of Art in the summer of 1994 entitled: 'Treasured Miniatures – Contemporary Netsuke.'

BRITISH ARTISTS

A well-known work of the Georgian watercolourist, John Sell Cotman (1782–1842) representing his early period is 'A Ploughed Field' (c.1808). As its title suggests, the subject of the watercolour is a sweeping view of a newly ploughed field in the vicinity of the artist's home in Norwich. Above is a lowering sky, in the centre are bright green meadows dotted with dark trees while in the lowest part of the picture is an expanse of ribbed fallow land. A self-satisfied farmer surveys this quiet landscape which is empty of scavengers on account of the row of dead crows hanging limply from a stick. His severe critic, Sydney Kitson, writing his only book, uncharacteristically proclaimed that this painting was "one of the loveliest glimpses of an imaginative landscape ever created by Cotman's mind and hand."

William Kiddier (1859–1934) was born in Loughborough but moved to Nottingham where he joined the family firm as a brushmaker. Luckily, this mundane career allowed him plenty of time to pursue his creative talents as an artist. Eventually, his paintings were exhibited at the Royal Academy and he produced a series of manuals on the subject of art. His work was held in high esteem although as a person he was known to be arrogant and haughty. Also, he had a strong self-destructive strain. After an unsuccessful exhibition of his paintings at the Fine Art Society's gallery in 1919, he burned all the unsold canvases in a fit of rage.

Consequently, early examples of Kiddier's work are rare but several late paintings are displayed at Nottingham Castle Museum. They include a vibrant oil painting of a scarecrow (*c*.1928) nailed to the crosstrees, his clothes flapping wildly and the figure bent double against the wind. The scarecrow has turned his back to the viewer which heightens the impact. The ground is barren, the landscape bare and one or two birds struggle to fly against the strong breeze. Kiddier was noted for his exaggerated colouring and the rich red soil and vibrant orange sunrise makes this a powerful painting.

Stanley Spencer (1891–1959) painted a dramatic representation of a scarecrow in 1934. This dark, disturbing oil painting which is privately owned, has been exhibited at the Stanley Spencer Gallery housed in a converted Methodist Chapel in Cookham near Maidenhead, Berkshire. Spencer's scarecrow, which occupies the entire frame of the canvas, consists of little more than a brown striped shirt on which is plonked a straw hat attached with string to a rusty pole rising from a bank of sweet peas. It stood in a plot of land next to 'Rowborough', a grand villa which still stands in Terry's Lane, where there is a sweeping view over the village towards the war memorial and straggling houses at the far end of the High Street which are all depicted in the painting. (The inclusion of the war memorial may be an oblique reference by Spencer to the sufferings of British soldiers during the Great War)

'The Scarecrow' was one of three paintings by Spencer which the Royal Academy displayed in their summer exhibition the following year. The artist was asked to

William Kiddier's 'Scarecrow'.
oil on canvas
Nottingham Castle Museum

Stanley Spencer's 'The Scarecrow, Cookham', 1934.

Stanley Spencer Gallery, Cookham. Private owner.

© Estate of Stanley Spencer/Dacs 2006

comment upon this unusual choice of topic: "Left and deserted as it was (the scarecrow) seemed daily to become more a part of its surroundings. It was like watching a person slowly changing into a part of nature. And I liked the feeling of it always being there . . . In the evening he faded into the gloaming like a Cheshire cat."

Whilst he was painting, it occurred to Spencer that there was a Christian implication in the subject. Later that same year he made this idea more explicit when he adapted his forlorn scarecrow into a depiction of Christ on the cross for a painting of 'The Crucifixion.' The abandoned plot of land which had become little more than a dump ideally served as a modern Golgotha. His new painting also featured a rear view of the subject although the artist added several local figures and the background was expanded to include Cookham Church and Cliveden Woods. Spencer's painting is extraordinary in that the grotesque posture of the crucified Christ perfectly mirrors the scarecrow.

A larger than life bronze sculpture, 'The Scarecrow', by Benno Schotz (1891–1984) was displayed at the 'Virtue and Vision' exhibition organised by the National Galleries of Scotland at the Royal Scottish Academy, Edinburgh, in 1991. Schotz was born in Estonia, moved to Germany but emigrated to Scotland to study engineering with his brother at Glasgow Technical College. He worked as a draughtsman for John Brown's Shipyard at Clydesdale where his knowledge of the Russian language proved invaluable to the company which was then engaged in building the Russian fleet. After visiting an exhibition at the Victoria and Albert Museum in London, Schotz decided to become a sculptor and he quickly gained a considerable reputation for being the leading modeller of portraits in Scotland.

Schotz wrote a spirited autobiography, *Bronze In My Blood* (1981) which details the sufferings of his relatives in the Holocaust. Despite these personal tragedies, he remained compassionate, vivacious, generous and hardworking. He developed a distinctive, romantic and expressive style of modelling busts which was greatly influenced by Rodin and Epstein. In 1938, he was appointed Head of the School of Sculpture for the Ceramics Department at Glasgow Art School and, in 1963, he was made Queen's Sculptor-in-Ordinary for Scotland. Schotz's 'Scarecrow' presents an elongated figure with outstretched arms dressed in a jacket with high collar, baggy trousers and a cap tilted over a blank face which echoes the abstract style typical of the 1960s. When the exhibition opened, the giant sculpture had just been recovered by the police after it had been stolen from the owner's garden.

WOOD ENGRAVERS

Thomas Bewick (1753–1828) penned fascinating descriptions of *British Land and Sea Birds* which he published in two volumes in 1797 and 1804, respectively. The lively text was accompanied by his exquisite wood engravings which illustrate north country life towards the end of the eighteenth century. Bewick, the son of a farmer and collier, was born at 'Cherryburn', a modest farm on the south bank of the River Tyne, twelve miles west of Newcastle. He became a self-taught artist who eventually set up his

'Scarecrow' by Thomas Bewick

own phenomenally successful wood-engraving business in the city. His celebrated "tail-pieces of gaity and humour", which were later published separately as *Vignettes* (1827) have sometimes a grisly tone such as children leapfrogging over tombstones, a horned devil preaching from a pulpit or a hanged man suspended over a stream. On a more cheerful note – once or twice – this miniaturist's includes illustrations of scarecrows.

One fine engraving in *Land Birds* features a totally ineffectual scarecrow that is being studied by a bemused crow while his companions feast on corn. It is dressed in a military coat and a tricorn hat. Most extraordinarily, the original owner of these cast-off clothes can still be identified. Bewick, in his *Memoir* (published posthumously in 1862) says they belonged to John Cowie, a tall, stout, elderly gentleman who inhabited the village of Ovington. He had served in the corps, 'Napier's

Grenadiers', and even in ripe old age displayed all the vigour of youth. "Cowie appeared occasionally in his old Military Coat & as long as he lived, & after he died this coat, which had been shot at both at Minden & else where, was, at last hung up – on a Stake on the corn Rigs as a scare Crow."

American artist, Gregory Lago (born 1949) "grew up in western New York and came of age along the Erie Canal." He insists he is proud of his Franco/American heritage since he claims his ancestors lived on the Canadian-American border in northern New York State from the time of the French and Indian Wars. Gregory, a former U.S. Army Sergeant who was awarded a bronze star for valour in the Vietnam War, describes himself variously as a cabdriver, carpenter, dishwasher, bouncer, quarryman, model, deckhand and drifter. He has now become internationally known as a wood engraver whose work has been included in exhibitions in Los Angeles, San Franscisco, Washington D.C. and New York City. In 1988, he established 'The Winged Bull Studio', a gallery with an emphasis on printmakers, in Clayton, New York. He promotes his own images as a haunting mixture of dark humour and illuminating truth. "Lago's work seems to speak of the desperation and insanity of a cruel existence, and of the struggle for calm," affirms critic, Simon Brett. "He has an eye for human frailties and nationalistic boastings."

Gregory Lago's 'Effigy'.

Gregory's first solo show, 'Just Prints', included one striking engraving, 'Effigy', which depicts a man struggling uphill on his hands and knees over the landscape and rivals other figures on distant hills beneath billowing clouds. Gregory explains the inspiration for this disturbing subject which clearly relates to ancient druid rites: "Shortly after Christmas, but before the full moon in January, I begin to pile old timber and hay into the shape of a twenty foot man. We rig the structure with bags of pitch and balsam, fireworks and sparklers. In St. Lawrence river valley, the first full moon of the year is called Wolf Moon because it is a time when large mammals mate. Frequently, it is twenty degrees below zero with three feet of snow on the flats, and crystal clear. After a fair amount of libation, in the dark and cold, the fire is set, and spreads rapidly skyward. Folks bring stuff to throw in the fire. I have seen restraining orders against rogue husbands, paid off mortgage papers and bank notes. One guy brought the old couch that his dog died on. Any bad karma or evil spirits one wishes to dismiss are added to the fire. The flames suck everything up, shooting a column of sparks high into the frigid and starry night sky. Everyone stands with their neck craned until the sparks and the stars become indistinguishable from each other. . . in some ways like good and bad luck."

British artist, Linda Holmes (born 1950) lives in Walpole, Halesworth, Suffolk, where she is surrounded by scarecrows. Linda was commissioned by Whittington Press to illustrate a passage written by a seventeenth-century Hungarian for their publication, *Matrix*, (No. 13, 1993) an annual review journal for printers and bibliophiles. The writer was Nicholas Kis of Totfalusi (1650–1702) a reformer who set out from his native Transylvania (then part of Hungary) to travel to Amsterdam where he taught himself printing with the aim of producing an accurate translation of *The Bible* into Hungarian. Today, Kis is celebrated in the world of books for having designed a typeface known as 'Ehrhardt' which has been described as "one of the greatest of source type designs."

When he returned to Hungary, Kis wrote his 'Monologue', which he called 'My Justification.' Basically, it was a tirade against the Reformed Church in his home town for treating him with contempt when he had been hailed as an innovator in Holland. His writing echoes Christ's bitter comment that a prophet lacks honour in his own country (Luke 4 v 24): "The esteem with which I was first regarded was lost bit by bit because of my slow start; they treated me like a scarecrow." Linda judged Kis' writing to be "fairly earthy" yet "full of passion and wit."

Linda was struck by Kis' analogy of the scarecrow to express how the clergy dismissed him. She also considered the passage was strongly visual and so chose to represent the Hungarian patriot as a crucified figure dressed in national costume for her own wood engraving. Kis holds a compositor's stick – used for setting type – in one hand and a spherical ink dabber in the other. Torn pages from his manuscripts lie scattered about the bare field bown by the wind. Crows circle the shingle spire of a distant church and represent the clergy of the Reformed Church who dress entirely in black. Linda asserts that her own interest is principally the human condition "whether comic or tragic or pleasantly humdrum."

A third member of 'The Society of Wood Engravers' who has produced an image of a scarecrow is Claire Dalby (born 1944). Claire was born at St. Andrew's, Fife, but she spent her childhood in Ealing when her parents moved to London. She studied at the City and Guilds of London Art School and now specialises in watercolour drawings and botanical illustrations for which she was presented with a Gold Medal by the Royal Horticultural Society. Recently, she was awarded a Shackleton Scholarship to draw and paint landscapes in the Falkland Islands. Claire came across her scarecrow closer to home since it had been made by one of the holders to amuse his grandchildren on an allotment in Camberley, Surrey. Her vibrant engraving shows a strident figure wearing a shirt, baggy trousers and Wellington boots with a floppy hat pulled over a faceless sack. In the background are allotment sheds and the inevitable compost heap. This particular engraving was displayed at the Royal Academy Summer Exhibition in 1997. Claire has since returned to Scotland where she hopes to find more scarecrows to pose for her. She admits that, apart from "a very sad, sagging and soggy looking specimen", so far, she has had little luck.

Miriam Macgregor (born 1935) who lives in Whittington Village near Cheltenham, Gloucestershire, worked for several years in the art department of Batsford publishers. In 1977, she joined the

Claire Dalby's 'Scarecrow.'

Whittington Press where she continues to work as a part time compositor and engraver. Miriam was commissioned by Whittington to illustrate a delightful sequence of books including one called simply, *Allotments* (1991) with text and poems by R.P. Lister. She depicted shabby sheds, compost heaps, wonky wheelbarrows, water butts, straggly bean poles, men digging and hoeing. . . A couple of her engravings feature scarecrows. One sorrowful character stands shivering beside a cold frame protecting lettuces. "I used to love that makeshift construction made from anything that came to hand," Miriam remembers. Another scarecrow mimics the stance of a sturdy young gardener resting against his bicycle loaded with vegetables. "No one taught me to engrave," she admits. "I practically learned it from one quick demonstration over the counter."

CONTEMPORARY ARTISTS

Peter Szumowski (born 1954) a commercial artist whose commissions have ranged from designing tea caddies to science fiction paperback covers, now runs his own design and print business. He produced two acrylic paintings featuring scarecrows towards the end of the 20th century. 'Out On The Edge' has a shepherdess with a sheep standing beside a field of ripe corn. She is facing a tall brick smock mill whose sails stand out against a summer sky. The second painting, 'Going Home' shows a lady with a parasol wandering down a leafy lane towards a distant village. A smock mill looms in this picture, too, but this time it is painted white and is lacking its sails. A scarecrow appears almost incidentally in both paintings. They are so perfectly placed, however, that they cannot fail to catch the eye.

Peter, who is of Polish descent, was brought up in Sheffield. His grandparents used to take him as a child for bus rides into the country for a treat and they often stopped off at a village called Anston. At one time a scarecrow caught his young eye and he insisted on walking out to the field where it stood. "I was drawn to that scarecrow which I found both fascinating and terrifying," Peter admits. "Even now I find them frivolous and repellent but I am compelled to include one in my idyllic landscapes as a kind of trademark."

Simon Palmer (born 1956) is a visionary artist who sometimes slips a scarecrow into his complicated landscapes. Currently, his studio is a garage next to his house in the hamlet of Ellingstring, near the prosperous market town of Masham, North Yorkshire. The countryside within a twelve mile radius provides him with all the inspiration he needs for his detailed paintings. Simon's watercolours meticulously record a medley of familiar features – ancient angled bridges over canals, high stone walls bordering ploughed fields and tumbledown farm buildings scarring the crimson moorland. Modern villagers break the sentimentality of his scenes – "clustered like churchmen, dressed in layers of floppy clothes and doing something completely pointless" – looking themselves, like scarecrows. . .

These startling characters reminiscent of Bosch or Breughel give Simon's narrative paintings their enigmatic titles. Many of the scenes are based on biblical events although all his paintings have an uplifting spiritual quality. 'Ruth Returning with Naomi' (1997) is a perfect example. The bustling figure of Ruth, struggling with two suitcases, as though she has just alighted at a country railway station, marches with her elderly relative through an avenue of trees shaped by the wind into a cathedral arch. The Old Testament story telling the loyalty of Ruth for her mother-in-law, Naomi, is catapulted into the present while the receding images of the two women are parodied by the figures of scarecrows standing sentinel in the adjacent field.

"I find scarecrows sinister," confesses Simon. "Their presence helps to desentimentalise a beautiful landscape. I don't like quaint and pretty in my pictures because the countryside is not like that. Nature is harsh. They also lend an interest to the texture of a field. You are totally free to select the colour and style of their clothing to enhance the composition. Also, scarecrows are futile as they are never very effective. They are something created out of discarded objects – an old broom handle, a tin bucket, discarded old clothes. They are forlorn, left out in all weathers. An anthropomorphised object."

GARDEN SCULPTURE

Glasgow Garden Festival was a temporary exhibition that took place in a vast redevelopment of abandoned docklands on Clydeside in 1988. Its aim was to bring an exciting collection of works by contemporary artists to integrate with a variety of gardens and landscapes specially created to enhance the riverbank. Alongside exhibits by distinguished sculptors – Henry Moore, Eduardo Paolozzi and Benno Schotz – appeared a motley collection of scarecrows made by Theatrecraft Workshops, a charitable organisation for mentally handicapped adults and people with physical disabilities. Their witty fabrications included a Johnny Onion Man with striped shirt and beret, pushing his bicycle, and an African woman with colourful headscarf and gold earrings, carrying a waterpot. Highlight of this "festive urban scene" was Jo Lewington's gigantic 'Three Corbies', contructed of cement on steel armature, which appeared threatening with the crows' cruel beaks and talons.

A friendly giant scarecrow formed from flowerpots towers over the exotic gardens of Groombridge Place, near Tunbridge Wells, in Kent. This historic moated manor can be reached by steam train which

opposite: 'Terrycotta' at Groombridge Place.

Judith Holmes Drewry's bronze 'Dancing Scarecrow'.

runs through woodland along the Spa Valley Railway. The grounds boast a number of attractions including an Enchanted Forest with an authentic Romany caravan, a barge which transports visitors along a miniature canal and a recreation of Sir Arthur Conan Doyle's study where he wrote a Sherlock Holmes' detective story, *The Valley of Fear*, featuring the remarkable drunken yew topiary at Groombridge Place. The flowerpot sculpture was created by Head Gardener, Ivan Hicks, who was a frequent guest on BBC2's 'Gardeners' World.' It's a lady scarecrow named Terrycotta and several plastic crows are permanently perched on her long, outstretched arms.

Scarecrows cast in bronze employing the complicated lost wax casting process are occasionally the subject of husband and wife team of sculptors, Lloyd le Blanc (born 1940) and Judith Holmes Drewry (born 1950) Generally, Lloyd prefers to model garden sculptures of animals and birds while Judith is foremost a figurative sculptor who specialises in graceful dancers, particularly ballerinas. Their three magnificent bronze scarecrows were created purely upon a whim. "It was a chance remark by a close friends that inspired us to create them," explains Judith. "We had so much fun making them. People adored our efforts and commissions followed."

Lloyd le Blanc, an American of French-Canadian parentage, trained at Yale University where he was appointed assistant lecturer during his final year. He opened his first studio in New England before building his own foundry in California but when he married Judith, the couple transferred both studio and foundry to England. They now live in a 17th-century farmhouse in Saxby, near Melton Mowbray, on the border of Leicestershire. Judith grew up there, one of six girls born to a farmer, and she has watched the hamlet shrink over the years to a few cottages and a baroque church, although even that is scheduled for closure since the congregation has dwindled to just one devout member.

Rugged paths meander through their extensive wild country garden surrounding the solid sandstone farmhouse. It is planted with a profusion of trees and shrubs appreciated by songthrushes, finches, barn owls and tree creepers. A squadron of damselflies dart over the stream inhabited by great crested newts while koi carp laze in the deep water of the lily pond. Bats skate over the surface at night and red kites circle the adjacent fields at sunset. This idyllic garden is a showcase for the sculptors' graceful bronzes: a wicket keeper stoops to catch a stray ball, a group of children link arms to play ring-o'-roses, a girl tilts a watering can over the lush lawn while a reposeful lady reads in a Lloyd loom chair. Along one side are farm buildings converted into a studio. "We open the garden to the public by appointment," says Judith. "Art students are particularly welcome to inspect our unique foundry."

Judith has just completed a dancing scarecrow which, she says, was a natural subject for her to undertake. He is the first of a limited edition of twelve, the same as all her other sculptures. His stance

opposite: Lloyd le Blanc's bronze 'Straw Man'.

unintentionally imitates Ray Bolger's in the MGM film, *The Wizard of Oz*. Judith's scarecrow strikes a gangling pose with one leg extended and an arm raised on which a fearless crow perches with a twig in its beak ready to fly away and build a nest. "Our statues will last a thousand years," assures Judith, "although we cannot guarantee their success in scaring birds."

Nearby, Lloyd's Straw Man towers over the ripening artichokes and espalliered apples in the trim allotment. His genial face peers out from underneath a superbly modelled straw hat. He postures with both arms extended providing a convenient perch for wrens. He wears green Wellington boots, a green shirt, a tattered jacket and gardening gloves. The detail is charming. A plump rabbit raises his head between the Straw Man's legs and a family of mice pop their inquisitive whiskers out of a side pocket. This model had the distinction of featuring on a stand at Chelsea Flower Show in 2003.

Lloyd's previous bronze scarecrow was commissioned by Chef Patron, Raymond le Blanc, to stand in the vegetable garden of his restaurant, 'Le Manoir aux Quatre Saisons', at Great Milton, near Oxford. Once again there is tremendous attention to detail. Lloyd's 'Scarecrow' wears a dress shirt complete with bow tie, trousers belted with string and a smart trilby tilted at a rakish angle. A songthrush preens himself on his shoulder, a water rat peers out of a side pocket and a family of harvest mice peep above the rim of his green Wellingtons. His expression is decidedly roguish and completely winning. "And he does have Raymond's nose," whispers Judith mischievously. "Our little joke which has not yet been spotted."

Ballymaloe Cookery School Gardens are located at Kinoith, near Shanagarry, County Cork, Southern Ireland. Originally, they were created in the early 1800s by the Strangmans, a Quaker family who maintained them impeccably for decades until shortly after the Second World War when they deteriorated into a wilderness. Now the gardens have been restored to perfection by Tim and Darina Allen who came to Kinoith in 1970 and established their prestigious cookery school, housed in a converted apple barn, which attracts culinary and horticulture students worldwide.

The Allen's cookery school is ideally located. Fishermen from Ballycotton, a nearby coastal village, supply seafood from the Atlantic Ocean including crabs, clams, lobsters, sea urchins, scallops, summer plaice, lemon sole, winkles and roghans (blue octopus). Neighbouring farms provide dairy produce such as organic sheep's milk ricotta cheese, goat's milk yoghurt and unsalted butter churned from morning milk supplied by herds of Kerry cows. Foraging expeditions in autumn among the hedgerows towards the sheltered bay yield sloes, damsons, blackberries, blueberries, samphire, sorrel, seaweeds and wild mushrooms. Animals roam freely about the extensive gardens including rare breeds of chickens that provide plentiful eggs and two saddleback sows whose litters, practically, are destined for the pot.

Darina Allen has shared her expertise in a number of sumptuous cookery books and she is lauded as the food ambassador of Ireland. Her latest bestseller, *A Year At Ballymaloe Cookery School*, presents a tempting array of seasonal delicacies – sorrel soup, seakale with melted butter, lemongrass lemonade and lavender ice cream – all tried and tested by her talented students.

Her famous gardens are freely open to visitors. They cover one hundred acres and are divided into manageable plots by deep beech hedges planted in Victorian times. These include a herb garden, a kitchen garden and an ornamental fruit garden. All the fruit and vegetables for the school are either picked or dug up minutes before they are required for cooking. Latest development is a yew tree maze based on an ancient Celtic pattern and an octagonal underground shell grotto. This has high gothic windows, a pebble floor and delicate shells decorating every surface.

The organic gardens are further enlivened with intricate wickerwork sculptures by Norbert Platz. Norbert, who originates from Germany, was inspired by the tradition of basket making in the West of Ireland where he moved twenty years ago to found the Irish Basketmakers Association. His robust creations handwoven at his workshop in County Cork include giant wicker domes, wigwams to support sweet peas and a multitude of fruit and vegetable containers. He grows several varieties of willow which are cut every year during winter before the sap rises to produce a rod with little pith which is more flexible to handle. Willows are left to season and then soaked prior to use for shaping into different styles of baskets that have become his speciality. At Ballymaloe, Norbert also created marvellous wicker male and female scarecrows (and one friendly dragon) whose hollow frames in winter resemble shivering skeletons in the snow.

Annually, Ballymaloe Cookery School holds its own scarecrow making competition for surrounding village schools. These have become such a popular event that the children's efforts are displayed in marquees. Ambitious tableaux have numbered a wedding party with the bride dressed in a country smock and flowing veil and the groom wearing a grey top hat and tail coat holding hands beneath a decorated bower and a boating party with the rowers resting on the riverbank eating a hamper lavishly stocked with cookery school delicacies. Another novelty is a series of scarecrows made from household objects such as tin cans, buttons and cutlery that encourage visitors to pop waste materials into their mouths which conceal bins for recycling materials.

When French radio chef, Jean-Pierre Coffe, found that wild birds were raiding the fruit and vegetables in his potager at Châteaudun, south of Chartres, he had a brainwave for solving the problem. He commissioned seventeen young French artists to design novelty scarecrows. M. Coffe had only recently turned to gardening, determined to serve only the best produce in his own restaurant.

He purchased a wildly overgrown and derelict plot from an adjacent château and restored it to its heyday 'between the wars.' Now he is almost completely self-sufficient with this two-acre kitchen garden enclosed by a high laurel hedge where he grows cabbages, courgettes, chards, spinach, onions, herbs in rectangular beds and espalliered pears and apples. The trouble was that Jean-Pierre soon discovered that birds were benefitting more from his carefully cultivated patch then his customers.

M. Coffe, a former actor, has always been interested in scarecrows. He once wrote a play about them, *L'Orielle Verte* ('The Green Ear') which toured extensively in France. "It is their ephemeral nature that fascinates me," he explained. "They are designed to be ugly and scary while at the same time to decay slowly as the changing weather takes it toll. Just as everything in nature – including us – dies and decays, eventually." His brief to the students was explicit. They must incorporate noise and movement into the design of their scarecrows which should only be built from degradable materials.

The art students vied with each other to make innovative figures. Ideas ranged from a chicken wire monster containing trolls which it had supposedly devoured, to an Indian Chief totem pole formed from fabric daubed with alarming images including a spider and a ghoul. One of the simplest designs was the most effective. One artist had painted, then stacked, wooden fruit crates into the shape of a man. The only traditional scarecrow was a deceptively gentle figure of a village spinster holding an umbrella. On closer inspection, she was found to be wielding a vicious claw formed from a cultivating fork.

German artist, Peter Klasen, presented a startling scarecrow from an assortment of oddments. He used a 'No Entry' road sign for a face, a plunger for a nose, a rake for a moustache and a feather duster for hair. William Wilson produced a brightly painted bark figure of a masked African native surrounded by helium filled balloons while Pierre Zanzucchi topped his papier mâché scarecrow with a chimney cowl which emitted a mournful wail as it spun in the wind. Yet more eerie sounds emanated from the kitchen garden. A male figure exposed his insides consisting of a gory wind chime made from bells and bones while his female companion wore a skirt comprised of rattling casino chips. A corrugated cardboard rock star was mercifully silent since he collapsed in a heap with his guitar snapped in half.

Fred Peri formed his scarecrow out of an alluring mannequin borrowed from a department store. She was clad in a corset made from corn kernels, a mini skirt decorated with sunflower seeds and a straw hat adorned with plastic fruit. (The birds found this tantalising since they were all coated with lacquer.) Jean-Paul Chambas modelled an extraordinary scarecrow by mounting a stuffed bull's head on a stainless steel plinth. Then he added nostrils breathing fire and horns shaped from mirrors. His theory, in which there may be some truth, is that birds are frightened of their own reflection.

These sentinal scarecrows were duly installed on Midsummer's Day 2002. During the first weekend almost one thousand people passed through the potager's ornate iron gates to view them. All the figures weathered the extremely wet and windy summer in Northern France before being dismantled and transported to the 'Fraîch Attitude Gallery' in Paris. They have since been exhibited at the Palace of Versailles before being staked out in a public garden near Lyons. Happily, M. Coffe reported that the only major damage that season had been to the grapevines spanning his orangery and they were out of the jurisdiction of the students' scarecrows.

Miriam Macgregor's 'Scarecrow'.

6. SCARECROWS IN THE FIELD

TODAY scarecrows are thriving in the gardens, allotments and fields of Britain. More ornamental than ominous, they nevertheless perform a real job of work in keeping wild birds away from crops and vegetables. While they are less effective on large farms where they are unable to sustain their reign of terror they certainly earn their keep on smaller organic plots and self-sufficient small-holdings.

WORKING SCARECROWS

Mike Armstrong, a retired civil servant, freely admits to growing fond of his working scarecrow which has seen duty over several seasons on the allotment which he rents from the council in Newcastle upon Tyne. The allotments are on the outskirts of the city next to Walkergate Hospital and were established in the 1920s as therapy for patients who were mainly soldiers incapacitated during the First World War. "The diminutive scarecrow was bought for me by my wife, Joan, from a garden centre," he explains. "We call him Nelson because he keeps a close eye on our plot whenever we are away." Nelson gained notoriety when Mike won an award for the best organic allotment in Newcastle in 2001. His cheery scarecrow with its hessian smock and straw hat was photographed as part of the publicity following the competition. He was also adopted by the allotment organisation to feature extensively on their leaflets promoting health and safety and advertising their annual shows. "Nelson is beginning to show signs of wear and tear apart from over exposure to the elements," concedes Mike, "but he is still a highly regarded member of our team."

"We have about twenty-five scarecrows on our farm where we grow conventional crops such as wheat and oil seed rape," explains William Pitts, a farmer from Northamptonshire. "Scarecrows that we make are always put on a wooden frame. We dress them in a pair of trousers, a jacket or a shirt, loosely tied, with a bag for the head, a pair of gloves and a hat if we're feeling extravagant." Farmer Pitts shares a feeling in common with other agricultural workers when he regards his scarecrows as personal friends

opposite: Tony Cruse's family of scarecrows, Wiltshire

Romney Marsh scarecrow.

opposite: Scarecrow guarding cabbages in Kent.

overleaf: Working scarecrow in the fields of Kent.

doing a real job of work. "Yes, you have to smile at it when you knock it in the ground and leave it there with perhaps a word to it before you walk away. Maybe our chaps don't look like good old Worzel Gummidge because we don't have much time to make them. If you made a scarecrow with a turnip head, for example, it would probably fall off about three weeks later or an animal would eat it. And, of course, they need moving from time to time because the birds soon get used to a static display. But the man who invents a scarecrow that is reliable and doesn't need any maintenance yet frightens everything around him will probably make a fortune."

Farmer Pitts is most economical with his creations and ensures they last a lifetime. "The worst end for a scarecrow would be for him to meet his maker going up the front of a combine harvester. He would be smashed to bits, I suppose, because we're not going to pick up any bits that come out of the rear! That would be the end of the scarecrow for us. They're never burned. We must have some that are ten or fifteen years old. If he's lost a particular piece of clothing, we'll try and put something else back on more suitable. And then they're stacked up in a barn or put up in a loft, somewhere dry and out of the way, until they are brought out again next season."

Scarecrows favour the flat fields of the Eastern Counties. Charles and Molly Elmy manage their modest farm, 'Golden Acres', at Middleton, near Aldeburgh, which, they think, must straddle "the only hill in Suffolk." They insist the title of their farm does not indicate their accumulated wealth but is named, mundanely, after a variety of cabbage. Their farm is devoted mainly to sheep but the couple are proud to be self-sufficient providing their own meat, eggs and vegetables. "Everything has to earn its keep," says Charles. Even Timmy, the farm cat, a sprightly tabby who lives in the barn, catches his own supper – rabbits, moles, mice and even snakes.

The Elmy's scarecrow, Percy, who stands waist high above the purple sprouting broccoli, has certainly done good service for as many years as they can remember. Every year he is brought out to protect their allotment planted with salad vegetables and summer flowers. This season he wears a bright yellow Laing waterproof hooded jacket and although he is in a truly dilapidated state he still acts as a deterrent to hungry birds. Sadly, straw now pokes through his polythene bag face and both hands have disintegrated.

Their original scarecrow was a lady dressed in a frilly dress and sunhat found at the back of the wardrobe. She had a pair of tights stuffed with straw for a head and a stiff petticoat which made her dress stand out proud. "Once, a short sighted neighbour stood talking to her for a full ten minutes from the road," confides Molly. "Next time we met she gave me a real dressing down for not answering her. I had a hard job convincing her she had been talking to our scarecrow."

"We always made our own scarecrows as children," recalls Charles. "I reckon I've been making them for nigh forty years." Recently, he and his wife entered a fancy dress competition held in the village hall. Predictably, they dressed themselves as Worzel Gummidge and Aunt Sally and were over the moon when they won first prize.

Along a nearby leafy lane that twists and turns through bluebell woods stands a hand carved sign of a bull announcing the presence of Peak Hill Farm at Kelsale. This eighteenth-century moated farmhouse, whose bowed walls are bound with iron ties, is approached via a little hooped bridge. A colourful garden is planted with daffodils, tulips and hyancinths while bullfinches dart among the magnificent magnolias. The River Hundred trickles here as a stream and fills the garden pond which occasionally floods within an inch of the kitchen steps.

The farmhouse kitchen abounds with low beams, the walls are adorned with intricate carved panels and threadbare carpets cover the flagstone floor. A pendulum clock marks the passing of time, a copper kettle mirrors the interior while a flourishing hibiscus obscures the sunlight from the low windowsill. Farmer Richard White sits on an antique Windsor chair at the head of his pine kitchen table covered with a hand embroidered cloth while his two rescue dogs – Charley, a mongrel, and Wizz, a cocker spaniel – settle down by the Aga.

Guardian of the cabbage fields.

Raggedy scarecrow and Kentish oasts.

Richard White and his son, Robert, manage the four hundred acres – part owned, part rented – of this organic beef and arable farm. A London lad, he was determined to be a farmer and so he started his career by walking behind a combine harvester. "The bailiff invited me to ride and before long I was tying up bales of hay which was the beginning of my long farm life." Previously, he owned a small farm in Surrey, then a dairy farm in Cornwall before moving to Suffolk with his family over thirty years ago. He is a David Brown tractor enthusiast and regularly hosts an event, 'Harvest Past', featuring classic tractors, steam threshing and heavy horse ploughing in aid of East Anglia Air Ambulance.

"I've used scarecrows all my life," he confides. "It has become something of a tradition on this farm. They are invaluable for frightening pigeons away from newly-sown peas and beans. Our first one was dressed in my mother's unwanted clothes when she moved into an old folk's home. The one we have at present has been on the farm for at least fifteen years, maybe longer. Every so often I send my wife down to the charity shop to buy fresh items so the scarecrow can have a face-lift. We tend to have an affection for them and treat them as old friends."

He swears to the effectiveness of his creations. "The trick is to move the scarecrow every once in a while so that the birds are fooled into thinking it is a real person. Once I was taking down one of my figures when a rat jumped out of the top pocket. It gave me quite a start. Now I always lay them down on the ground and let the dogs have a good sniff round before I move them."

Rooks present Farmer White with a quandary. "They eat the leatherjackets harmful to crops so we don't want to discourage their presence entirely," he remarks. "Rooks are notoriously crafty. They go up and down the rows and when they see a young shoot they start to dig deep until they find the sprouted grain."

The White's current scarecrow, which guards their spring wheat, has a head made from a plastic container painted with a rusty round car mirror on top intended to reflect the sunrays. He is dressed in a chequered Burberry coat over dungarees with a woollen scarf thrown, nonchalently, over one shoulder. He leans alarmingly on his iron stake as though he has seen better days and is weary of life. Perhaps, he, too, is ready for that retirement home?

Ipswich, the county town of Suffolk, has sixteen allotments but these are constantly under threat since the council discusses selling them off for building land. One sizeable allotment known as 'Maidenhall Field' can be seen adjacent to the railway line near Ipswich Station. Jane Flatt manages them voluntarily on behalf of Ipswich Borough Council. "People come from all walks of life to tend our allotments and everyone is proud that they can grow their own fresh vegetables," she says. "We are also encouraging wildlife so that now the birds, butterflies and bees are plentiful." Indeed, a friendly blackbird pops into her house adjoining the allotments for a quick snack in the kitchen followed almost immediately by a fearless robin.

Maytime, generally, is when scarecrows appear on these allotments but some figures remain on site almost all year round. Plot 215 has borders planted with marigolds, wallflowers, forget-me-nots and a sweet honeysuckle that climbs a makeshift arbour. Upturned plastic bread baskets make improvised gates leading to paving stone paths that crisscross the busy plot. There are so many scarecrows here that it has the appearance of a garden party. Hostess, 'Mabel', is a fashion-conscious society lady dressed in a gaily patterned blouse and a cerise pleated skirt. She has a knitted striped scarf and a hat fashioned from a raffia shopping basket worn at a provocative angle. Incongrously, she carries a child's plastic beach trowel presumably to enable her to weed among the rhubarb.

There is a variety of bird scaring devices on this particular plot such as containers painted with jolly faces stuck on poles that resemble oversize hand puppets and strings of flower pots looking like garlands. A companion scarecrow wears a pink nightgown and a sombrero while several large colourful paper fish hover like kites which all adds to the carnival atmosphere.

Entertainment is provided by a black scarecrow on neighbouring Plot 196. Known as 'Bob Marley', he is a portly character who gyrates among the rows of onions, carrots and ripening peas. He wears soiled dungarees but a smart new padded cream jerkin over a navy blue sweater. He has a black nylon stocking padded with straw for a face with features made from painted cardboard. Additions are surgical gloves, a summer hat and stout brogues.

One trendy scarecrow sways to his tuneless guitar on Plot 186. This surrealistic character has a head formed from an empty paint container with features marked in black felt tip. He is dressed in paint-stained dungarees with a high-visibility tabard borrowed from a railway maintenance worker. The slightest breeze animates him so that he pirouettes like a ballet dancer. All this must be a strange sight

'Bob Marley' at Ipswich.

overleaf: Dancing scarecrow and 'Mabel' working on Ipswich allotments.

for passengers to witness, fleetingly, from the windows of their high-speed trains en route for the Metropolis.

Another scarecrow to be found near a railway line is a modern miss who permanently resides at 'Evegate Farm' beside Ashford International Railway Station in Kent. She stands in the centre of an island protecting fish ponds near Mersham next to a sprawling electricity converter station. Eurostar trains whiz by to the south while to the north is the M20. These fish ponds had been closed for over a year while the high speed rail link was built between Folkestone Central and King's Cross. They now provide a welcome oasis amid such noise and chaos.

This female scarecrow is brand new and replaces one that rotted away after seven summers. Actually, she is a shop mannequin complete with black curly nylon wig. At present she models a cream dress with almost matching marigold rubber gloves and poses elegantly with a striped umbrella for an outsize parasol and a handbag carried in the crook of her arm in imitation of the Queen. Her main task is to keep cormorants away from the ponds but she also keeps a wary eye on the licensed fishermen who have named her 'Millie.'

Gordon Smithers, a retired health and safety consultant, is up at five o'clock most mornings to secure the best wooden peg or landing stage of the embankment around the main pond. He enjoys the tranquility of this early start when he can observe the abundant birdlife that includes moorhens, coots, wrens and kingfishers.

The ponds are stocked with roach, tench and bream but he is always hoping to ensnare that elusive 13lb carp. "Fish here are crafty," he says, "so I have to offer them a choice of bait – bread, maggots and even luncheon meat." Both the ponds and the farm are strictly environmentally friendly. All fish are returned to the water after recording and no barbed hooks are permitted.

"The cormorants, too, are crafty", assures leasee of the ponds, Gordon Sylvester. "They are a real pest and eat a lot of fish. My bailiffs, Roger and Taffy, gave me quite a surprise when they secretly rowed across to place 'Millie' on our island. But they will have to replace her frock shortly because it has become faded by the sunlight and the birds have become accustomed to it. The beauty of her is that she does a real job and her flapping skirt certainly keeps the cormorants at bay." Last glimpsed, though, Millie was down to her bra and pants causing consternation not only to cormorants but commuters on the London Express. The scarecrow she replaced now lies, incongruously, ditched among the dead nettles besides the banks of the fish pond.

The Bean Farm at Worth-next-Sandwich, also in Kent, has recently celebrated its centenary. Begun by John Bean in 1901, the farm is a true family business which today is run by his four sons and four

daughters. Their 650 acre sprawling estate straddles a busy main road on the outskirts of this pretty village and marshland beside the coastal railway running from Deal to Sandwich. Eventually the farm will pass into the capable hands of a third generation of dedicated young farmers.

Surprisingly, this arable farm has only recently introduced scarecrows. Jean Bean was responsible for the twenty comical characters protecting transplanted cabbages, cauliflowers and calabreses. "Initially it was to save time," she explained. "My husband, John, used to go out early every morning in spring to fire his shotgun over the fields but the artful birds always flew off whenever his white landrover appeared. "Naturally, they returned the minute he drove off," she despaired.

Jean insisted that her scarecrows have been a far better deterrent. "The secret is that they are arranged in groups," she revealed. "The birds are fooled into thinking they are farmhands and they stay away in droves."

Every evening for a fortnight Jean returned to her modern bungalow, 'El Surprise', armed with a couple of stout poles. After tea, she disappeared into the garden shed and started hammering away, much to her family's amusement. She rummaged through bags of clothes collected from various boot sales to dress her creations which she propped against the front door waiting for distribution.

The villagers so much admired her handiwork that they soon arrived with donations of castoff clothing. Jean's parents gave rainmacs, school children called with hand-me-downs and one elderly neighbour knocked on the door with her woolly cap and nightgown!

Haute couture included a pink polka dot dressing gown, a pretty patterned dress and a weatherbeaten anorak in which someone had left their shopping list in the top pocket! Encouraged by the enthusiasm of the villagers Jean began to experiment with fantasy characters and soon the original residents of the field were joined by Goldilocks wearing a dainty floral frock and beribboned rope plaits; a monkey with a realistic mask; a Saracen with turban and flaming sword and, to keep the peace, a policeman wearing a hat from a fancy dress shop!

Jean created heads from plastic flowerpots covered with pillow cases and bed sheets. Her daughter, Debbie, lent a hand drawing cheeky faces with felt tips. Crowning glory was the collection of knitted

"Allo, 'allo, what's goin' on 'ere?"

Opposite: Jean Bean's polka dot scarecrow, Kent.

bobble hats which give Jean's scarecrows their distinctive style. "Farmhands remove their woolly hats and hide them whenever I appear with flasks of tea at breaktimes," laughs Jean. "They think I'm going to steal them which I would never dream of," she winked, "although there's one bright red one I have my eye on. . ."

Lanky George stood alone one season guarding the experimental plants growing in the 'Larch Nursery' at the neighbouring village of Woodnesborough. He was made by Jonathan Vickers and his young daughter, Megan, from orange waterproofs discarded by the nurseryman. His hooded face was formed from a polythene bag and his lively features inked in with black felt tip pen. Although he lacked both hands and feet, twine strung from his thin arms held dozens of silver foil baking cups which clattered and sparkled in the breeze.

Long after he had completed his task George was left in the field even though the hollyhocks had reached the top of their stalks and the cabbages had gone to seed. He swayed in the breeze in time to the fresh washing on the line of the neighbouring house.

And although his only friends were earwigs and ladybirds, he managed to keep a cheery smile on his torn and tattered face. Perhaps he could now walk tall knowing that he had completed a job well done scaring off the marauding pigeons?

Later in the year George was joined by two friends, 'Albert' and 'Fred.' They had been waiting in an adjacent barn to be kitted out in fresh waterproofs ready to begin work protecting the new season's cauliflowers. Craftily, the nurseryman kept them in storage because, he knew, if they were put out too soon, the pigeons became accustomed to them and lost their initial fear!

'Bo-Boy,' the rook scarer, stands among irises and columbines in the centre of a vegetable plot in David Parfitt's extensive garden at the rear of his bungalow in East Studdal, near Dover. 'Bo' is dressed as a country gentleman with a straw sunhat, tweed jacket, blue striped shirt and black trousers courtesy of British Rail. His arms are outstretched to shoo away birds from the raspberry bushes. Kentish name for a scarecrow is 'Bo Boy' which, apparently, derives from the startling sound boys made in former times when employed to frighten birds.

'Bo's smiling face was formed from an inverted Sutton Seeds sack and his portly body made from tightly packed bags of hay. He makes an arresting garden feature although David doesn't pretend he is really effective. "He's there to amuse the grandchildren – like the treehouse and the topiary." A steam train pulling carriages shaped from clipped yews circuits the lawn and a seat is thoughtfully provided for children to ride inside the engine. David, himself, was employed by British Rail for forty years and steadily worked his way up from a station cleaner at Dover Priory to a train guard at Dover Marine. For

opposite: 'Lanky George'.

many years he was a shunter on the steam trains serving Tilmanstone Colliery on the defunct East Kent Light Railway.

One scarecrow who became a local celebrity was made by two children, Gemma and Lewis Whitnall, to stand on their grandad's allotment on the hillside between Dover and Folkestone. Their white-faced scarecrow was named 'Charlie Chalk' after a favourite television character. The children made him over one wet weekend with the help of their granny who took them on a tour of the charity shops in search of suitable materials.

Dad surrendered his dirty blue dungarees which were stuffed with straw to form the torso and mum lent her old peg bag which was slung over one shoulder. (This soon proved an ideal nesting box for harvest mice) Charlie's face was formed from an old bed sheet tied at the neck with string and covered with a crimson silk scarf. Padded material shaped his prominent nose, antique glass buttons served for his eyes while a string of bells formed his mouth. His wig was chestnut-coloured wool tucked under a straw sunhat decorated with embroidered flowers. Charlie was spotted by a freelance photographer working on a project on fashion for scarecrows and one spring his impish face graced the front cover of *Country Life*.

Bill Shrubsole's scarecrow, 'Gary', has stood for a couple of years in the centre of his allotment clearly visible from a curve in the railway line near Ashford International Station. In spring he protects newly-planted cabbages; in summer he towers over pungent leeks. At the end of the season he rests against a makeshift shed and bobs among gay sunflowers. His cheeky features are painted in carmine onto a cheap polythene bag with the addition of a champagne cork for a nose. Each year Bill gives him fresh accoutrements to smarten up his faded apparel – an orange knitted scarf, for instance, or a pork pie hat. Passengers travelling to the Continent on Eurostar may catch a rapid glimpse of him as they speed past before entering the Chunnel, patriotically waving his Union Jack donated by a London cabbie.

One striking scarecrow was made by a student of the Horticultural Research Station International on the outskirts of East Malling near Maidstone, in Kent. He was created as a decoration for the Harvest Ball at nearby Bradbourne House by Adrian Harris who hails from Worksop, Nottinghamshire. An assistant entomologist, Adrian is currently researching diseases of blackcurrants, although locally he is noted mainly for his collection of pet exotic spiders, stick insects, centipedes, cockroaches and scorpions. After the ball was over, his scarecrow, called 'Rebus,' was placed in a field behind the student hostel where he serves a practical purpose keeping birds away from the rows of experimental strawberries.

'Rebus' wears a battered felt hat, chequered shirt, gardening gloves and pinstripe jacket in the pocket of which are damp pages torn from a pruning manual. His head is formed from a pillowcase stuffed with

opposite: 'Bo Boy'.

overleaf: 'Rebus'.

straw and his face is meticulously embroidered with coloured silks. "Originally I sketched his features with felt tip," explains Adrian, "but a friend, Kate, from New Zealand, decided to improve them with marvellous cross stitch."

The Henry Doubleday Research Association is the largest organic gardening organisation in Europe. Its purpose is to carry out scientific research to improve organic horticultural methods worldwide and among its laudable schemes are re-afforestation programmes in Africa and India. H.D.R.A. headquarters are at Coventry but for educational purposes there is a sequence of domestic gardens throughout history which are open to the public at Yalding, near Paddock Wood, West Kent. This sequence of authentic period gardens includes a thirteenth-century apothecary's garden, a medieval paradise garden, a Tudor knot garden, a Victorian cottage garden and an Edwardian herbaceous border. Most intriguing is the post-Second World War allotment.

Governments encouraged people to become self sufficient and grow their own vegetables during both world wars. Vast acres of public and private land were converted into over two million allotments which produced one tenth of the nation's produce. They appeared on railway embankments, beside football pitches and across recreation grounds. Even London's Hyde Park was converted into one grand vegetable plot! Soldiers returning home after hostilities found time on their hands and turned to gardening to supplement their family's food while rationing continued. A great deal of land was reclaimed and allotments gradually declined although a sufficient number was retained, primarily as a leisure pursuit, in the 1950s.

Yalding's post-war allotment features a vegetable garden divided into three plots so that rotation can be easily practised. Crops are grown in neat, straight rows at recommended spacings and a limited number of typical vegetables are cultivated such as runner beans, carrots, sprouts, peas, leaks, spinach, parsnips, onions, beetroot and broccoli. Intriguingly, a few vegetables bear wartime names: 'Victory' tomatoes, 'Spitfire' cabbages, 'Home Guard' potatoes and 'Pilot' pea (although this latter variety predates the war) Yalding also grows period sweetpeas including 'Winston Churchill', 'Air Warden' and 'Princess Elizabeth'. A compost heap, manure pile, cold frames and rhubarb patch all have permanent sites. At one corner is a potting shed which still displays faded patriotic posters including 'Dig For Victory.' There are the obligatory hen coop and cages for rabbits, both important sources of food. The garden is grown organically although pesticides such as DDT were commonplace at the time. (Strange to think how chemical warfare was adapted for growing produce!) Presiding over the allotment is 'Desmond Day' – 'D. Day' – a wartime scarecrow complete with tin helmet rescued from an attic leaning nonchalently on his hoe.

'D. Day.'

'Digby.'

Two young French students, confusingly-named Emilie and Amelie, have added scarecrows to liven up another of the period gardens. The nineteenth century Cottager's Garden, which is modelled on the writings of William Cobbett, the radical political campaigner who had a lifelong passion for gardening, has an artistic scarecrow whose body is simply made from hessian. The face beneath a straw hat lacks features but nonetheless presents a quizzical expression. He bobs happily in the wind amongst the pungent lavender investigated by bees and drooping sunflowers invaded by dragonflies. Staring out from a corner cabin is a scarecrow made entirely from wicker which makes visitors to the garden jump with fright. The staring eyes (washers on string) peeping out from the hollow skull are truly scary. Indeed, the whole figure looks like a skeleton.

The South of England Rare Breeds Centre at Woodchurch, near Ashford, in Kent is a commercial enterprise run by the Canterbury Oast Trust, a charity that seeks to provide opportunities for adults with learning difficulties. The centre offers a wide range of training and jobs for these students who live on site in a family-style residential home. Their working farm, which welcomes visitors, preserves old and endangered breeds, once common on British farms.

Members of the public are encouraged to handle a variety of small animals including rabbits, guinea pigs, ferrets and chipmunks. They are introduced to a host of characters in their paddocks – Archie and Alfred, long wool rams; Bonnie and Clyde, pygmy goats; Blubery and Simon, friendly alpacas and Jingle and Bandit, Shetland ponies. Stars of the show are undoubtedly the famous 'Tamworth Two' – Butch and Sundance – who hit the headlines in January 1998 when they escaped from an abbatoir in Wiltshire seconds before they were due for the chop. Their bold dash for freedom captured the hearts and imagination of a nation who joined in their hunt along with the R.S.P.C.A., a helicopter and 150 press cameramen with the aid of a police description – "Height: the size of a big dog; Colour: pink with ginger bristles; Weight: 110 lbs but with a deceptive turn of speed." The *Daily Mail* sponsored their rehoming at Woodchurch after their eventual capture and now fat, spoilt and pampered they luxuriate in a plush sty. The story of their great escape was the subject of a BBC film presented at Easter 2004.

At the rear of the centre is Rainbow Nursery where the students made a portly scarecrow one winter to stand between their polytunnels. Digby's head was made of papier mâché moulded over a balloon which was then painted with garish features. He was dressed in Dave's old working boots, Karolyn's old wax coat, Nick's old jeans and Ian's old gardening gloves. He stood in the vicinity of a battered caravan where he was rumoured to retreat on cold dark nights. One year, it is promised, he will have a wife and family to help him guard the vegetable plots.

CHARACTER SCARECROWS

'Cedric the Scarecrow' pokes his tongue out at visitors to the entrance of Acton Scott Historic Working Farm tucked away among the hills of the Welsh Marches. Billed as 'the tallest scarecrow in Shropshire', he stands roughly ten feet tall on a knoll beside a restored Victorian roadmender's horse-drawn hut. He wears a smock made from sacking, a colourful striped waistcoat and a wicker hat which provides a handy nest for a cheeky crow. Cedric was created by Ian Wall, resident chair bodger, who also designed the challenging willow cartwheel maze.

Acton Scott seeks to recreate life on an upland farm at the end of the nineteenth century. Tractors are absent since the land is worked by a waggoner and his team of heavy horses pulling vintage farm machines. Throughout the farming season visitors are able to watch ploughing, sowing, reaping and harvesting of corn and root crops and there are regular demonstrations by the farrier, blacksmith, wheelwright and woodland craftsmen. Further activities include hand milking, butter churning, lace making, bee keeping, cider making, sheep shearing, rick thatching and steam threshing.

Rare breeds permanently on display number Long and Shorthorn cattle, Shropshire sheep and Saddleback pigs. Acton Scott tries to be completely self-sufficient and in a good year enough food is grown to sustain all these animals with the sale of any surplus going towards the cost of running this twenty-three acres farm.

Probably the world's tallest scarecrow was the one which Bruce Burton placed on his dairy farm at Tedburn St Mary, Devonshire, in 1985. Bruce learned that a giant statue of Venus de Milo, which had graced Gossard Bra Factory at Exeter, was about to be demolished. He hired a crane to lift the half ton plaster figure onto his tractor and transport it to his farm. "I always wanted to rescue a damsel in distress," he quipped, "and this was love at first sight." His wife, Sally, was unsure at first how to cope with this second woman in Bruce's life. Eventually, she capitulated. "I must admit I was jealous at first," she sighed, "but now we get on quite well. And she makes an excellent scarecrow."

A most glamorous scarecrow once graced the fields at Brewood, Staffordshire. She was created from a dressmaker's mannequin borrowed by Norman Crewe who was clearly enamoured by his human 'bird.' Her dressed her in glad rags which included a revealing loincloth made from sacking and a wicker basket for a cloche hat. Trespassers, when challenged, confessed they had been tempted to stray from the footpath by her erotic pose.

A complete family of scarecrows inhabit Tony Cruse's garden in Orchestron, near Salisbury, Wiltshire. Tony, a retired civil servant, lives in a picturesque thatched cottage with a tall brick chimney and a catslide roof. His triangular parcel of land which backs onto stables is enlivened with figures including Bill and Ben made entirely from flowerpots who wave plastic sunflowers in welcome beside the front door.

Tony started modestly twelve years ago by making scarecrows from an old coat draped over a stick but now he must be regarded as an expert maker for his garden is densely populated with figures including a suave black scarecrow who sports a brown jacket and smokes a cigar!

He has created a whole family of scarecrows headed by a proud father, with straw hair and a stubble beard, dressed formally in a tailcoat, waistcoat and cravat. He is accompanied by his wife, incongruously wearing a geometrically patterned skirt and poke bonnet. Their son has tousled ginger hair and wears a white shirt and short trousers held up by braces while their daughter is dressed in a red paisley patterned blouse, grey pleated skirt, gold boots and straw bonnet. They make such a handsome group strolling among the ripening onions and rotting cabbages.

The birds, however, have long since ceased to be frightened by these figures. "They don't take much notice now," admits Tony, "though I move them around and change their clothes – but that's mainly to keep the villagers amused. Folk play tricks with them and once they took them for a stroll round the village. But the best time was when some French tourists stopped to ask them for directions!"

Catherine Ellwood, a cashier in a bank, has a unique 'Alice in Wonderland' scarecrow that takes the form of a rabbit! She made it in memory of her adored chinchilla rabbit which had a floppy ear. 'Mr. Floppy' stands among sweet peas in an allotment opposite her house in Stanhope, near Bishop Auckland, County Durham. His torso is made from a bin liner stuffed with grass and clothes with a shirt and trousers borrowed from her brother. Her young neice, Tanja, from Sweden, modelled the face from hessian but the ears are made from white socks pulled over a bent wire coathanger.

On one occasion Mr Floppy was stolen but returned by a neighbour who found him abandoned along the street with both ears ripped off. Catherine carefully restored him and treated him to a new shirt. Now he is admired by children walking to their nearby primary school. When Catherine recently visited her aunt in Canada, she was surprised to find that she, too, had a scarecrow in her garden. "It must be a family trait," she concludes.

Uniquely, a scarecrow afloat can be found aboard a redundant M.O.D. assault craft permanently moored alongside The Hard in Portsmouth Harbour. Members of the Net Fishermen's Association use this converted barge to store pots and floats and for landing crabs and lobsters. Their nautical scarecrow was created to keep the deck clear of wheeling seagulls and to discourage starlings that roost in the

Carved timber face scarecrow from
an allotment in Chiswick.

opposite: Scarecrow afloat
in Portsmouth Harbour.

rigging of the adjacent Victorian iron clad battleship, *H.M.S. Warrior*. Members regularly change their scarecrow's clothes, usually after a few beers, to fool the seabirds and, they say, this also guarantees night time security. Their jaunty scarecrow wears a white sports jacket, blue shirt, bow tie and straw boater. At times he even reclines in a deckchair, sipping a gin and tonic with a cane balanced across his knees. Yachtsmen call him 'Horatio.'

London has its fair share of scarecrows and examples can often be spotted in the tangle of allotments beside the railway loop of prosperous West London. At Chiswick there is a dapper carved timber figure sporting a cravat and sunhat, obviously a weekend gardener, while at North Sheen appears a more harassed City gent wearing a pinstripe suit, collar and tie, resembling a true 'Hooray Henry.' Victor Osborne, a freelance journalist, writes a regular column about Ascot Allotments at Ealing in the *Daily Telegraph*. He has developed a variety of bird scaring devices which are fairly effective on his own organic plot. These include cutting panels into plastic bottles and affixing them to iron rods so that they swivel in the wind and sticking feathers into potatoes to make novel 'spud hawks' suspended from bamboo poles. Such ruses tend to keep the majority of birds from newly-planted vegetables but to keep ravenous starlings from his prized currants Victor resorted to making a traditional scarecrow.

Victor describes making a strange bisexual scarecrow in his book, *Digger's Diary* (2000) He found a plaster head of a female shop mannequin abandoned in a skip and nailed it to a wooden cross. Then he dressed it with an old jacket and shirt stuffed with straw, suspended a pair of shoes on wires below the trousers and added a cowboy hat bought as a souvenir from a wildwest show at Disneyland, Paris. Final touches were an empty champagne bottle, a red handkerhief in the top pocket and one of his wife's long scarves to flutter in the breeze to alarm the birds. While thinking of a suitable name for his alluring creation, ('Mona Lisa', 'Baby Jo' and 'Poppy' came to mind), Victor was daunted by his wife's comment that his scarecrow greatly resembled George Melly.

'Old Jem' was a heroic character who lorded it over the hallowed cricket ground at Lord's each September. "London pigeons are very partial to grass seed and we have enormous problems protecting our pitches on the cricket square," revealed Head Groundsman, Michael Hunt. "Every autumn we overseed and then cover with a light topping of soil ready for the next season. We used to knock up a scarecrow from old pieces of timber and dress him in bright clothing – a raincoat, a sou'wester and Wellington boots. After a while he looked a bit pathetic so it was little wonder the birds weren't scared of him. They're no fools, pigeons. Nowadays we tend to use gas bangers or fireworks which doesn't go down too well with the neighbours."

MACABRE SCARECROWS

Wendy Dare runs an award-winning guest house, 'Mill Dene', at Blockley, near Moreton-in-the-Marsh, Gloucestershire. This was once an industrial area where ten watermills worked along Blockley Brook which flows through the heart of the Cotswolds. They were corn, wool or silk mills but 'Mill Dene', a seventeenth-century stone building with Norman foundations, became an iron factory producing metal frames for cottage pianos during Queen Victoria's reign. Wendy has converted the miller's cottage into a comfortable 'bed and breakfast' voted among the country's ten best by *Which*.

The tower of the neighbouring twelfth-century church of SS. Peter and Paul provides a glorious backdrop to the spectacular gardens which are regarded as being of national importance. Features include a potager, dye plants, tromp l'oeil, a grotto with gleaming shells and a cricket pitch with panoramic views over the Cotswolds Hills. Herons, kingfishers and dippers frequent the millstream whose bright orange water rushes through the scented gardens.

Wendy acquired a striking scarecrow to protect her vegetable plot quite by chance when she noticed him for sale while driving through the nearby village of Evesham. He is made out of metal strips and his moulded features include a top hat. "I call him Mr Voodoo because he resembles the chap who jumps out of the grave in the Bond film, 'Live and Let Die.' He is dressed in an old shirt and waistcoat but no trousers which tends to alarm our guests. Anyhow, the birds like him, so that's all that matters," she quips.

Two malevolent scarecrows have stood for several seasons on the tiny parcel of land beside the trackway leading to Brook Farm, Belleau, near Alford, mid Lincolnshire. They were created by Geoffrey Baldock who has lived all his life in the neighbouring farm cottage and whose pretty garden boasts a weather vane, a dovecote and a working well. This pair of threatening figures has proved most effective in keeping pigeons off his organic garden.

One scarecrow is seated on a high-backed, timber chair pointing a realistic carved wooden shotgun. He wears soiled jeans, stout boots and a scarf, casually slung over his shoulders. His head is ingeniously fashioned from a shaved coconut, with hair taken from the bristles of a chimney sweep's brush. Patiently, he smokes a wooden pipe while waiting to take aim at any intrepid bird. Back-up is created by a second sinister figure, poised at a distance and armed with another deadly rifle. He wears a luminous council workman's jacket while his hood reveals flowing orange locks formed from generous twists of baler twine.

Geoffrey's cottage is in an idyllic location but it is far from lonely. Ramblers regularly stroll down the farm track while horse riders gallop over the Wolds. There is the chatter of bullfinches, the mocking call of a distant cuckoo and the shrill cry of Canada geese flying in formation overhead to disturb the stillness of the hamlet. And the aggressive style of Geoffrey's scarecrows belies his gentle nature. An adjacent cattle shed houses his homemade nesting boxes which he nails to trees on the nearby grass verge to encourage swallows to breed. "They will keep the insects down," he promises. "Swallows are flying low today which is a sure sign of a good summer."

An itinerant scarecrow hit the headlines when he was kidnapped from a country estate at Enville, near Stowbridge, Staffordshire. This ferocious looking scarecrow had been made from a pillow case stuffed with straw and dressed in a boiler suit by gamekeeper, Andrew Crump, to keep crows away from a laying pen for pheasants. After only a few days Andrew was distraught to find his creation had gone missing. In its place was a handwritten note: "Fed up with standing here all day. Gone on holiday. Jack Straw."

Andrew was further baffled over the next few weeks when he received a series of holiday snaps of his scarecrow riding on a steam train, rowing a boat on a lake, enjoying a pint in a pub and propped up against a police car being breathalysed. "I seem to have drawn the short straw by being left at home," he remarked before retiring to his local, 'The Cat.' At the end of a lonely fortnight Andy's scarecrow returned from these jaunts unharmed to the estate, although who the pranksters were remained a mystery.

A pair of scarecrows were recruited to uphold the law in the historic village of Merrymeet, Cornwall. Reckless motorists who tended to roar through the main street without fear of being caught, braked hard when they spotted a policeman aiming a radar gun at their speeding vehicle. Only when they slowed down did they realise they had been fooled by a scarecrow wearing a luminous tabard and a joke helmet. PC Gummidge proved to be such an effective deterrent that he was soon accompanied by a

Malevolent guardian of Brook Farm, Lincolnshire.

fake policewoman to reinforce his warning to keep to the speed limit.

Villagers themselves thought up this audacious ploy after they had campaigned unsuccessfully for a reduction in speed on the main road dividing their village. "My front wall was forever being rebuilt after cars and lorries crashed into it," complained Peter Radcliffe who lives close to a notorious blackspot. "There are a couple of accidents every year at the crossroads as well as countless near-missses. We all got together to build the scarecrow and made his speed gun from a plastic lunchbox and a polythene cup. Traffic instinctively slows when drivers see him and it is getting the message across that this is a dangerous stretch of road.

"It is one of the few places where people can overtake and inconsiderate drivers race through at over 100 mph. People who live on the main road are constantly aware of screeching brakes and blasting horns. Ideally, we would love to see a real policeman here but we are always being told there are not the resources. Not only is PC Gummidge doing a great job but we do not have to give him a day off or pay him overtime." Devon and Cornwall police approved of the initiative and stressed they welcomed any reduction in speeding.

Police gave a different reaction to a similar scarecrow made by Gerald Tucker from the village of Aller in Somerset. His straw-filled dummy was dressed in a fluorescent jacket and rubber boots before being propped against an authentic police speed check sign which he had acquired when he was a parish councillor. This time the police were not amused and despatched a patrol car to investigate. "The policeman confiscated it immediately," complained Gerald, a community regeneration officer. "He told me they were considering prosecuting me for impersonating a police officer. But after reconsidering, they changed that to impersonating the activities of a police officer – even though his head is stuffed with straw."

Occasionally, scarecrows themselves have had a brush with the law. John Liddiard was banned by his local council from putting up a couple of scarecrows which they deemed far too scary! John placed his two dimensional figures on his own 1,400 acre farm which, he said, was "black with rooks," at Great Shefford, Berkshire. These scarecrows were little more than cardboard cutouts painted red and yellow carrying sticks made to look like rifles. All the same he was soon confronted by an officious footpaths inspector who ruled that the gaudy pair in his cornfield "might look intimidating to ramblers." Farmer Liddiard was irate. "Scarecrows are supposed to be scary" he thundered. "How can any townie make such a fuss?"

God-fearing parishioners were deeply offended by a nude scarecrow which appeared in the village of Trunch, near North Walsham, Norfolk. Allan Jones, a motor engineer, was surprised at the adverse response he received after posting an "anatomically correct" scarecrow to stand watch over one of his four allotments. Shocked villagers contacted their parish councillors who tersely wrote to inform Mr Jones that his scarecrow must be removed forthwith under an obscure public order act for causing "harrassment, alarm and distress." Perhaps the offence was exacerbated by the fact that Mr Jones's naturist scarecrow – known as 'Mr Viagra' – stood on church land next to the Vicarage!

This offending two dimensional scarecrow was rudely crafted from an old sheet of plywood. The figure was then mounted on a reclaimed vehicle hub that enabled him to twirl in the wind. He stood over six feet tall and his oversize appendage was cut out with a jig saw. Several villagers admired the saucy scarecrow and sent anonymous letters of admiration to Mr. Jones. Holiday makers posed for photographs beside him and he became the main topic of conversation in the bar room of the local pub. Nonetheless, the law had to be obeyed and faced with a court appearance and possible hefty fine, Mr. Jones sawed off the offensive protrusion, watched by two laughing policemen.

"I thought of him as a piece of abstract art or a fertility symbol," confessed Mr Jones. "He was never really intended as a joke because he did a good job of work. I have tried all types of scarecrows in the past and found that the old boiler suit stuffed with straw had only limited success. Mr. Viagra certainly put the willies up the pigeons which are a real problem. I will be sad to see him go. . ." A censored version of Mr. Jones' naturist scarecrow still spins, although weathered, on his allotment bordered with plantations.

Hamish MacInnes, one of the world's leading mountain rescue authorities, describes a ghoulish scarecrow in his second volume of true life stories, *Sweep Search*. A founder member of the Glencoe Mountain Rescue Association, MacInnes operated in a hostile region running approximately east-west across the glen, eighteen miles from Fort William and midway along the rugged coastline of Western Scotland.

MacInnes's exploits encompass the pioneering days of quartering the mountains with teams of trained dogs to the development of thermal imaging intensifying equipment, instant two-way radio communication and the advent of helicopter rescue at Glencoe. His graphic details of heroic missions across this most famous and most fearful glen are related with such a disarming modesty that they belie his skill and courage while revealing his beguiling sense of 'gallows humour.'

His taste for the bizarre extended to his mountain garden. . .

One summer he nursed a vegetable patch and immediately met with an unwelcome challenge. Hoodie crows are regarded as the most cunning birds and they are vehemently hated by shepherds in the Scottish Highlands. They are known to pluck the eyes from ailing ewes and the tongues from weakling lambs. "They zipped open my pea crop," complained MacInnes, "and devastated my

overleaf: Menacing and threatening figures, Kent.

radishes." In defence he formed a scarecrow which, he confesses, was a truly macabre work of art.

"Having a well-equipped workshop at my disposal, I put together a tall, articulating skeleton of wood and alloy, suitably padded with polystyrene foam and sporting a moulded plastic head and face of corpse-like pallor. Indeed, everything about it was corpse-like because I had used clothing and equipment from bodies which we had taken off the mountains over the previous months of rescues. I usually burn such messy gear, but just then there seemed to be quite a grisly collection lying in a locker of the rescue truck.

The mangled selection made up the wardrobe of his new garden guardian: a gore-encrusted helmet, a scree-tattered anorak, threadbare trousers, a holey pullover and a pair of boots with one sole missing, all colour co-ordinated – red! At six feet tall, astride a row of turnips, the scarecrow presented a daunting and evil-looking apparition. "I felt that I had given birth to a Frankenstein monster," he recalled. "It possessed a frightening realism, its arms and sometimes even its head moved in the wind, and its painted eye-sockets seemed to embrace every corner of the garden with an Argus-like vigilance."

The high visibility scarecrow survived the rigours of winter but MacInnes admitted that it presented an even more unpleasant presence in the garden as time went by. Perhaps this hero of the hostile mountainside finally lost his nerve for, come the spring, he determined to destroy his monster. On a fresh April morning "as the cherry blossom was gay and the sun drenched the hills" he lit a bonfire to burn his blood-red creation. Even as the gory effigy was consumed by the flames it eerily resembled a funerary pyre.

AROUND THE WORLD

Extraordinary methods of scaring birds have been attempted around the world. Italian farmers in the past placed animal skulls on the tops of tall poles to scare away birds and protect their crops from diseases. This distasteful custom has passed down to the present day because one modern farmer in Sri Lanka finds it discourages both birds and humans from trespassing.

Celluloid dolls heads stuck on stakes – a grisly reminder of the guillotine – on the railside allotments at the approach to Paris are momentarily glimpsed from Eurostar trains. Less grotesquely, a cultivator in Belgium puts dummy cats in strategic places on his smallholding to deter wild birds. Most curiously, a carved figurehead of a buxom beauty atop a single pole graces a garden in the nautical town of Annapolis on California's North Coast.

Ancient Methods

Ancient Egyptians, Romans and Greeks forced slaves to patrol their plantations banging gongs, beating drums and shaking rattles in the scorching sun to frighten away wild birds. Egyptian farmers harvested wheat and barley twice a year on the fertile banks of the River Nile. Men cut grain just below the ear using short curved sickles leaving the straw to be reaped later for animal fodder, basketry and brick making. Annually, they made their offerings to the cobra-headed goddess of harvest, Renenutet.

Egyptian farmers set traps for birds not only to reduce the threat to crops but also to provide a rich source of food. They stretched fine nets over wooden frames with hinged flaps held open by strips of papyrus. Flocks of quail or pigeons were either tempted into these traps by bait or driven towards them by beaters and then taken home for a tasty supper. Alternatively, nets were simply closed in on water birds at an appropriate moment by hunters hidden among the reeds of the marshes. One hunter would make a silent gesture by waving a piece of cloth as a signal to his companions who pulled a rope that threw a net over the unsuspecting birds. During the migration season they might net ducks, geese, snipe and teal. Wall paintings in pyramids and tombs show that it was also common for hunters to row light skiffs along the delta, hurl curved sticks at wildfowl and retrieve the stunned birds with the aid of trained cats.

The principle of using distress calls to alarm birds and cause them to take flight may have been known to the Ancient Egyptians. A painting on the wall of a tomb in Thebes dating from the eighteenth dynasty depicts birds hunters in canoes in the papyrus swamps of the River Nile. One man holds a live cormorant and a boomerang while the other throws his club to kill a bird rising from its nest in the colony. The decoy, which is held by its legs, is clearly in distress and this would suggest that its calls of plight were being employed to attract others within short range.

The Israelites of Old Testament times cultivated grapes in stepped terraces on the parched hillsides of Palestine. A most important task in vine cultivation was the annual pruning which was carried out after blossom time when the grapes had formed. Guards were posted to protect the ripening crops from roving foxes and jackals which showed a great fondness for fresh grapes. Watchmen, specially hired for the season in larger vineyards, took their position either in a simple booth or on an elaborate watchtower. A substantial bivouc might be made from interlacing branches and these were inhabited by growers when they were keeping an eye on their vines or vegetables. The Hebrew word for booth is translated variously 'cottage', 'hut', 'pavilion', or 'tent.' The prophet Isaiah mentions both a "booth in a vineyard" and "a lodge in a cucumber field" (Isaiah 1 v 8). Huge boulders were piled high alongside these constructions as an additional precaution. These mounds, which were white washed, took fantastical shapes and acted as primitive scarecrows. Fruit ripened from July onwards but it was not gathered until around September when whole families were recruited to help with the grape picking which was treated as an occasion for a grand holiday. During the Feast of Tabernacles the Jews lived in tents for a week to celebrate the vintage but also to remind themselves they were originally nomads led through the wilderness by God.

Japanese farmers still believe the power of the god of the fields ('Ta No Kami') is manifest through scarecrows fashioned in human form. In its divine presence farmers offer prayers for abundant crops in the spring and of thanksgiving after the harvest. Initially, they hung chunks of rotting meat, fish bones, rags or fur from bamboo poles and set them in the middle of their paddy fields. Farmers believed the disgusting smell would keep wild animals and birds away and therefore call their garish constructions 'kakashis'. (The word means stench.) Thankfully, such hideous creations have generally evolved into more familiar scarecrows resembling people. They are made of straw and dressed in a raincoat formed from reeds with a round straw hat rising to a peak in the middle. Typically, they wield bows and arrows which make them appear more threatening. These true scarecrows are also called kakashis although, fortunately, they lack that revolting smell.

One tradition was that because birds sometimes fly courageously close to the figures they told their secrets to the god of all kakashis. This benevolent deity was called 'Sohodo-no-kami', which means 'Protector of the Fields'. After the harvest in mid October Japanese farmers believed it was high time for the spirit of the god to return to the mountains. The farmers duly brought all their scarecrows in from the paddy fields, put them in a great pile and surrounded them with special rice cakes for the god to consume on his homeward journey. Then they torched the kakashis. This ceremony was called 'the ascent of the scarecrows'.

Today Japan has an autumn 'National Festival of Scarecrows' (known as 'Kakashi Matsuri') held at Tsukioka Park in Kaminoyama City. This is a hot spring town in a rice-producing region around Kaminoyama Castle. Farmers from across Japan honour gigantic scarecrows formerly placed in rice fields as guardians of good harvest and proudly parade them through the streets. Subjects of this colourful masquerade range from sports personalities to cartoon characters although the most popular tend to be those satirising politicians. The contest attracts around two hundred entries and prizes are awarded for the most grotesque.

Man Power

Countries of the Third World where labour is cheap still employ humans as bird scarers. Pokot people use living scarecrows at their farms on the steep, fertile slopes of the Cherangani Hills in the Rift Valley of Kenya, East Africa. This arduous task is usually assigned to children who spend long and tedious hours perched atop precarious platforms made from branches of trees and sheltered by leaves from the intense heat. Native children keep birds from the tribe's precious crops by hurling stones and mud balls which is an unenviable daylong chore.

Zulu children in South Africa are also given the same laborious job of bird scaring. Small boys rise before dawn and take their place in the fields just as the birds become active. They remain there until evening throwing stones and shouting until hoarse to keep granivorous birds from the crops. A later threat also comes from monkeys, baboons and wild pigs which eat the blade or ear of the young crops. Platforms are erected on poles to support conical thatched watch houses which give a vantage over the vast cornfields of the kraal. Sometimes strings of bark are attached to posts dotted over the field and these are connected with the watch huts. When a child on duty notices a flock of finches he gives a tug on the string which sets all the lines in motion, waving the bark and startling the birds.

A witch doctor may be called upon to scare the birds away by magic should they prove particularly troublesome. The birds are allowed to feed freely for several days in order that the witch doctor can gather the chaff. Meanwhile, tribesmen pick green firewood and catch a live frog or toad. The remains of the corn are ground up and fed to the unfortunate creature which is then buried close to the field. Alternatively, a chameleon and a tortoise may be used for the spell. A fire is kindled on top of the buried animal so that medicines and a snake can be consumed by the smoke. The fire is kept burning all night accompanied by sacred chants to drive away the birds. During this time all sexual intercourse is strictly taboo. Then, on the third day the tribesmen wash themselves in the river with a special potion before returning to the fields to continue their chants. If this ritual proves successful in warding off the birds from the crops the witch doctor is presented with a beast as payment for his services. Scarecrows might seem a simpler and surer option. . .

Traditional scarecrows are employed today throughout South Africa. There is one famous tourist site on the main road between Stellenbosch and Somerset West where a strawberry farm, 'Mooiberg', employs 'character' scarecrows to advertise its wares. They are mounted on all manner of vehicles from a penny farthing to a tricycle and ride precariously along the rows of ripening berries. And at the entrance beside the farm stall there is a bevy of beauties – the reformed 'Spice Girls' – dressed in alluring attire in primary colours to tempt customers to buy the farm's summer fruits.

In India, where old men sit patiently in chairs and hurl stones at birds invading crops as their ancestors did long ago, scarecrows are few and far between. Those that do exist are thought to possess supernatural powers and are venerated. In Varcar, South Goa, they are positioned on a plot of land while building is in progress to ward off evil spirits and prevent them taking possession of a new house.

WORZELS WORLDWIDE

Tropical rainforests have been cleared for agriculture around Belize, former capital of British Honduras in Central America. Scarecrows, which may be simply dressed in a striped shirt and straw sunhat, might seem incongrous in this land of jaguars, toucans and venomous fer-de-lance snakes bordering the Caribbean Sea. Nonetheless, they are effective in guarding against a variety of nuisance birds, mainly blackbirds and woodpeckers, as they preside over fields of sorghum in the Mennonite community of Shipyard.

And Chamorrow gardeners spend much time creating fierce effigies on the island of Guam, important for its rich source of crops in addition to being a strategic naval base for the U.S.A. in the North Pacific. A few sticks and some gunny sacks form the outline of the rustic figures while brown paper bags placed over coconut husks, stiffened into shape with varnish, resemble heads. These prove totally effective in discouraging animal visitors, such as deer, as well as birds from their crops of maize, beans, sweet potatoes and bananas.

Scarecrows are popular in Europe. Germans are active environmentalists and compensate for autobahns ripping up their landscape by fiercely protecting the remaining countryside. Farmers make imaginative scarecrows ("die vogelscheuches") wearing frightening masks and having inbuilt sounds and movement such as klaxons or fireworks. Often they are staked out in pairs so that a tubby scarecrow ("bootzamon") may have a chubby spouse ("bootzafrau") although husband and wife are generally placed at the opposite end of one field. Bootzamon wear old overalls, long-sleeved shirts, overcoats, woolly hats and they may also have the distinction of a large red handkerchief tied around their neck. These companionable scarecrows guard cornfields, strawberry patches and cherry orchards.

Country folk remain fiercely superstitious. They have believed since earliest times that their farm tools, particularly the plough, possess magical powers. German farmers sometimes carve wooden witches and place them in their fields towards the end of winter. They think these witches will draw the evil spirits of winter into their bodies so that spring comes speedily. Scarecrows are caught up in this superstition so it is thought bad luck to simply discard them at the end of harvest. Therefore they are made the centrepiece of celebrations such as beer festivals.

One fascinating legend persists in Germany. It tells how, when a small kingdom was threatened by attack from a neighbouring country, all the villagers gathered up their scarecrows for miles around and lined them up in the field of battle. When the enemy saw the figures from a distance, they thought they were outnumbered and retreated.

There is a most attractive tradition among farmers in France. They stack the last bales of straw into giant shapes – tractors, animals, buildings – at the end of harvest. The French word for scarecrows is *épouvantails* which also translates "bogeymen", implying that they are potentially frightening to children. Indeed, French farmers vie with each other in trying to create the most hideous and monstrous creations to ward off, not only predators, but trespassers from their fields.

Portugal, a strongly Catholic country, inexorably links religious rituals with the agricultural cycle. There is a firm belief among the rural population that a divine presence will offer them protection from calamities and pestilence, particularly plagues of wildfowl which may invade cultivated land in the problematic period between the sowing of the seed and the slow maturation of the grain. Figures of

A pair of stray figures from London visit Lincolnshire.

hallowed saints – Martin, Bebiana, John – are formed from straw and rags and paraded through the villages on their appropriate days of veneration. Culmination of these festivities is the remembrance of Judas, betrayer of Christ, whose straw effigy is ridiculed and then publicly burned on Holy Saturday or Easter Sunday – which coincides with the time when the grain must be fiercely protected.

Joaquin Pais de Brito produced an erudite commentary to accompany a photographic exhibition of the Portuguese countryside by Fundão Serralves at Oporto in 1997. There, he compares the procession of the straw figures of these saints with scarecrows which, coincidentally, appear in the fields at the same key points of the Christian calendar. He also finds close links between figures of straw (palha) and the ambivalent character of the clown (palhaço) both of which are intended to make us laugh. "What does the scarecrow scare away if its arms serve as a perch for the birds?", he asks, rhetorically. "Perhaps most of our fears and one of the most frequent means of exorcising them: laughter."

Slovakia maintains several traditions that involve a scarecrow ("strašiak") which take place in the pretty villages of this mountainous country. Folklorists gather to celebrate the end of winter in the snowclad village of Liptovská Teplička. They create a female figure from straw which they dress in their regional costume of a white blouse and pleated skirt with an embroidered bodice. This is supposed to represent Morena, goddess of death. Girls sing songs and recite proverbs while carrying her through the valley. They then undress her and set her alight before throwing her into a brook. This pagan custom signifies the end of winter.

Villagers in Batizvovce join in a grand procession through the streets at Shrovetide (or carnival time) Masked characters follow a blacksmith whose hands and face are smeared with axle grease. Cheekily, he blackens the faces of girls when he makes a surprise visit to their home. Among the company is a wickerman whose body is covered head to toe with straw. There is also a choir accompanied by an accordianist. Egg collectors visit each henhouse and take all the freshly laid eggs. Members of the company are rewarded at a mountainside inn by a breakfast of bacon, sausage and cake washed down by a glass of spirits.

The Museum of Cerveny Klástor, which lies under the Tetra Mountains at Poprad in north-eastern Slovakia on the Polish border, regularly presents exhibitions of folk art in the adjacent courtyard of a ruined monastery. One year there was an exhibition of beehives; another time there was a display of scarecrows. Some figures were wonderfully carved from timber with moveable joints; a few were beautifully dressed in national costume while others held windchimes or mobiles that rotated in the breeze.

Brazil's prison system is plagued with riots and breakouts linked to overcrowding, poor pay for

opposite: A suave black scarecrow in Wiltshire.

prison officers and lack of funds for maintenance. In the summer of 2002, a judge on an inspection tour of a jail near Sao Paolo was horrified to discover how the governor had attempted to overcome his problems of staffing. A scarecrow dressed in a police uniform was positioned in a watchtower to guard more than seven hundred jailbirds. The judge removed the scarecrow, which had apparently been there for days, and took it to court as evidence of "a grave breach of security."

Crows are warned to stay away from the annual Grampians Gourmet Weekend in central-west Victoria, Australia. Visitors who attend the celebrations in May are encouraged not only to sample local fare and premium wines (particularly reds) but vote for their favourite scarecrow. The Montana Winery at Ararat revived the rural skill of making scarecrows ten years ago purely as a tourist attraction and their efforts are displayed against the dramatic landscape of the Grampians.

Mike McRae, the manager who organises the event, became enthralled by scarecrows when visiting the U.S.A. "I thought it would be really great to see a bit of colour in our countryside," he explained, "because it was the wonderful colour associated with scarecrows that struck me more than anything else while in America." Mike realised it needed more than wine to entice tourists to travel the long distance from Melbourne to visit his vineyard. When he started to include scarecrows in the itinerary of his tour he found the number of visitors to this remote vineyard escalated. "People who are often intimidated by the whole wine scene now walk away with a big smile on their face."

Final judging of the most favourite scarecrow by a wine industry personality takes place on the last day of the weekend when the neighbouring towns of Ararat, Great Western and Halls Gap are buzzing with tourists. Each year the criteria changes – they might be asked to vote for something quirky or the one with the best movement – and entries may draw on politics, sport and mythology. They also pay homage to traditional scarecrow construction and some adult themes. One year the winner was the Balancing Handstand Artist although the people's choice was the Bionic Butler. All the characters join past winners as part of Montana's growing scarecrow collection that includes the Lady in the Blue Dress, the Witch, the Iron Crows, the Cricketer and Morticia to keep crows away from the vineyard.

"Apart from being a hugely successful tourist draw card," explains Mike, "the scarecrows entered in the competition actually earn their keep. They keep hungry birds away from Montana's grapes in the crucial weeks leading up to the vintage. Anything that is colourful or moves a little tends to keep the crows on the wing for a long time. And it's a nice passive way of keeping the birds at bay because being close to Ararat we have to be very careful of any noise we create."

Riverside Wines at Puketapu Napier, North Island, New Zealand, holds an annual scarecrow competition. This award-winning company is proud of its wine portfolio (particularly whites) which is headed by superior Chardonnay, Sauvignon, Cabernet, Merlot and Pinotage. Primary school children from the coastal region are invited to make a scarecrow to display at the vineyard. The special day is enlivened with novelty races, face painting, sausage sizzle and pony rides with wine tasting for adults. After judging, rosettes are awarded and the scarecrows are auctioned to raise funds for the children's charity, 'Riding for the Disabled.'

Riverside Wines always take the opportunity to purchase winning scarecrows to protect the grapes on their vineyard. This means the entries must be both scary and durable to be eligible for the competition. "Scarecrows normally live a very isolated life in the middle of a field," said Rachel Cardwallader, one of the owners of Riverside Wines. "Our Scarecrow Days are a great opportunity for them to get together and party or to discuss their finery." Amongst the competitors in recent years have been the ubiquitous Harry Potter Scarecrow and a belligerent Osama Bin Gardening.

Native American tribes throughout North America all employed both bird scarers and scarecrows in times past to protect their corn. Indian farmers who lived in the areas which became Virginia and North Carolina employed adult males to squat on raised platforms and cry aloud if birds came too near the crops. Creek Indians in Georgia moved into temporary huts in their cornfields all summer to protect their crops from birds and animals. Seneca Indians, who inhabited the area that has become New York, soaked corn seeds in a poisonous mixture of herbs that made birds fly crazily around the fields and scare away members of their flock.

Generations of native farmers were at work on this continent long before Europeans arrived in their tiny ships across the Atlantic. When Captain John Smith and his crew berthed along the James River in what is now Virginia, the settlers noticed, scattered around the crop fields, small, rounded huts woven of vines and bark, perched atop wooden posts. They soon discovered that one of the children's main summer and fall chores was to hide in those small basket homes until crows and deer came into the fields to eat. The children would then run after the hungry animals and birds making loud noises and beating drums to chase them away from the crops.

Native American tribes living in primitive Mexico experimented with placing carved wooden hawks on posts in their fields. The birds and animals such as deer kept coming so boys wearing wolf skins over their heads waited to drive them away with slingshots. Sometimes women stayed up all night beating on small drums to keep the animals away from the ripening crops. British colonists took their cue from the Indians and hung strips of cloth, animal skins and bones from rawhide thongs. By the late 1600s they started building scarecrows resembling human figures dressed in cast-off clothes with gourds or pumpkins for luminous heads.

Fashion in the fields of Kent.

In the American South West, Zuni children held contests to see who could make the most unusual scarecrow in the late 1800s. The Zunis also used 'yucca lines' to protect their cornfields from pests. They placed cedar poles about six to nine feet apart across the whole field. Then they strung cords made from the fibre of the yucca plant from pole to pole like clothes lines. Strips of dog or cayote skins and the shoulder blades of animals were hung from these lines. The waving skins and clacking blades frightened away the majority of birds. The Navajos also used scarecrows although one was reported in the 1930s to be merely a teddy bear affixed to the top of a pole!

When Europeans began to settle in North America during the seventeenth century they stood guard in their fields to protect the crops essential for survival. In Plymouth, Massachusetts, every member of the family of the Pilgrim Fathers was expected to take turns at being bird scarers. They had not only to contend with crows but also wolves who were attracted to the fish which these early immigrants had buried with their corn seed as fertiliser.

By the 1700s, the developing American colonies were requiring an increasing amount of grain and they decided that neither the farmers nor the birdscarers were protecting their crops effectively. Towns all along the Atlantic coast offered bounties for dead crows. A century later it was realised so many crows had been destroyed that a new problem had been created. Corn borers and other worms and insects which were once devoured by the crows were now destroying more corn and wheat than the birds had done! Bounties immediately ceased and the townsfolk returned to the less risky business of making scarecrows.

Immigrants who moved to the United States during the 1800s brought with them a variety of novel ideas for making scarecrows. In Pennsylvania, German farmers built human looking scarecrows whose body was a wooden cross and whose head was a broom, mop top or cloth bundle stuffed with straw. As in Germany, the figures were placed in pairs – husband and wife. In Pennsylvania, German and Dutch colonists used a variation on the 'Vogelscheuchen' (bird shooers – often with metal arms that clanked in the wind) by setting up paired men and women to guard their fields. Stories soon circulated that they cavorted in the night!

By the 1800s American scarecrows began to be used as much for decoration as practical reasons. They were beginning to express their creator's artisitic ability and resourcefulness. Whimsical elements crept in and "fencecrows", placed at boundaries to define the owner's territory, sometimes showcased elegant dolls dressed in finery and noted for their beauty.

During the Great Depression of the 1930s scarecrows became enormously popular and could be found all over America. After World War II, however, agriculture became such a big business that farmers decided they were ineffective. They then started spraying or dusting their crops with poisonous chemicals such as DDT until the 1960s when scientists discovered that this method endangered people who ate the sprayed crops. Farmers began to experiment with contraptions such as whirligigs that spun in the air like windmills to scare away birds. One British company exported an automatic crop protector which consisted of a metal box with three arms that was placed on top of a tall pole. The box contained caps that exploded every forty-five minutes while the three metal arms flapped up and down simultaneously. Inevitably, the noise and the clashing metal arms infuriated neighbours who campaigned for their removal in much the same manner as their counterparts had done in Britain.

Scarecrows in modern America are generally associated with the period between Thanksgiving and Hallowe'en. They are perceived as harvest figures because this is the time of year when their tradition and culture is celebrated within the community. Obviously, they still retain a practical purpose in scaring birds but now their image is erected as the centrepiece of annual harvest festivals. They have achieved the level of art and craft because farmers there have become proficient in the art of making character scarecrows. It is also true that as America becomes more urbanised, nostalgic townsfolk tend to embrace the scarecrow as an emblem of their country's agricultural past.

Today there are a number of small towns in America that have annual scarecrow shows which are basically harvest festivals. There are games and competitions for the children; suppers and dances for the adults. Farmers are no longer dependent on getting the harvest in before the first frost but their grand scarecrow festivals serve as a focus on former times when country values were different. Everyone felt a strong family and community link when people, whatever their status, felt safe, secure and valued. Scarecrows serve as a reminder of that lost rural society and they have therefore become a treasured part of American folklore.

The realism that scarecrows have achieved in modern America is reflected by the skills of three different artists interviewed by Felder Rushing in his excellent manual, *Scarecrows*.

Scarecrows take on an almost human form in the mountainside garden of artist and sculptor, Michael Melle, who lives in a log cabin deep in the Berkshire Hills of Western Massachusetts. His minimalistic figures are captured in motion or caught midstride to express the rippling strength of athletes. They play a game of basketball, take a dog for a walk or simply leap for joy on his immaculate lawn bordered by a paintbox of trees every Fall.

Michael twists and shapes branches of cedar, pine, ash or apple wood into realistic limbs which are padded out with wads of hay wound with cotton string to make the skeletons of his strawmen. He finds inspiration for his sensual, muscular figures from the the artistic world and his references range from the

Russian ballet dancer, Mikhail Baryshnikov, to the French painter, Jean François Millet. Yet his knowledge of the anatomy of movement may come from a far simpler source – the miles he walks daily as a postman for the United States Postal Service.

A magical scarecrow garden has been created by Rosalind Creasy at her home in Los Altos, California. Rosalind, who is among America's favourite garden writers and photographers, believes that "a scarecrow can really humanise a garden and give it an emotional dimension." Certainly, her lifelike figures create a charming mood and provide a focal point for her front garden which she constantly redecorates to reflect her own need for "challenge and change."

Rosalind has devised an exquisite tableau of characters from *The Wizard of Oz* who stand alongside a spiralling yellow brick path. All the faces are cleverly constructed from fresh fruit and vegetables which naturally have a short lifespan so constantly need to be replaced. Dorothy has a beautiful painted face having a red wool wig crowned with a garland of garden flowers; the Cowardly Lion has a head made from a pumpkin with straw whiskers and a flaxen mane while the Scarecrow reflects Ray Bolger's own features concocted with red pepper lips and orange chilli nose. Pièce-de-résistance is the Tin Man whose gleaming body is formed from nursery pots and flexible drainpipes sprayed with chrome paint. "He was once borrowed for a school play," smiles Rosalind, "and now a family of wrens are nesting in his plastic oil can."

Julia Allen, a retired nurse, creates imaginative "airy" figures from scrap metal to grace her garden in Jackson, Mississippi. After completing a part time metalwork course where she studied welding, Julia started her own garden sculpture business whose logo is a dancing scarecrow. At first her long-suffering husband was bewildered by her antics but he eventually presented Julia with her own welding helmet. She admits, though, welding wasn't an easy skill to learn and even now she does not pretend to be an expert. "I have to keep a bucket of water handy because, under my heavy coat, leather gloves and helmet, by the time I smell something burning it's usually me!"

Upon leaving college, Julia invested in a pickup truck so she could scour the junkyards and garages for scrap metal. She spends blissful hours shaping her finds into striking metal flowers and figures for her garden. Julia is passionate about the environment. She firmly believes her metal sculptures are a way of recycling waste in a way that will bring pleasure to future generations. "Today's world is moving too fast," she thinks. "Everything is becoming disposable and we mindlessly throw it away. I find the discarded scraps of our lives, recognise their inner beauty and recover them for others to enjoy, maybe, forever."

An extraordinary event in America, which in some measure relates to scarecrows, takes place annually in the Nevada Desert and focuses on the strange cult of the 'Burning Man.' The tradition had humble origins on the beach at San Francisco in 1986 but now attracts over 25,000 Americans who create a temporary city with the threefold aim of self reliance, self sufficiency and self expression. Chief attraction is experimental art and bizarre exhibitions ranging from human body painting to decorating mini cars with Barbie dolls. Culmination of the communal gathering is the ritual burning of a giant effigy of a man which one year was created entirely from secondhand books.

Curiously, a fleet of friendly scarecrows is actually employed to protect wild birds threatened with extinction in the immense tar sands of the River Athabasca in Alberta, Canada. Engineers have recently experimented with synthetic oil in their attempts to find alternatives to the world's diminishing fuel resources by drilling into the shale deposits of these vast, remote sandbanks. Ancient lakes and inland seas in the vicinity left deposits of organic materials encased in the beds of sands which have already yielded trillions of barrels of 'synfuel.' Environmentalists, concerned at the plight of wildfowl, have placed hundreds of luminous scarecrows on buoyant rigs floating on the contaminated ponds caused by this bonanza. At their feet ride propane cannons booming twice a minute to further discourage protected species of birds from alighting on the treacherous sands and becoming polluted by oil and tar. This use of such alarming figures for humane purposes demonstrates an extraordinary evolution for our humble scarecrow.

Dancing in the fields
of Kent.

7. SCARECROW MAKERS AND FESTIVALS

MAKING SCARECROWS for farms, allotments or small holdings is now a thriving cottage industry while scarecrow festivals held in villages and hamlets across Britain have become a novel way of raising funds for charities.

ARTISTIC SCARECROWS

Award-winning children's author and former school teacher, Michael Morpurgo, formed an educational charity, 'Farms for City Children' in 1976. Funding for this scheme came initially from his wife, Clare, with an inheritance from her father, Allen Lane, founder of Penguin Books. Two of Michael's most popular titles, *War Horse* and *Farm Boy*, are true stories set on his own grandfather's farm during the First World War. The couple decided to provide urban primary school children with an opportunity to gain experience of life on a working farm and thousands of deprived youngsters have enjoyed a week's residency at one of their three farms in Devon, Wales and Gloucestershire.

The trio of farms are 'Wick Court', an Elizabethan moated manor house nestling in a loop of the River Severn; 'Lower Treginnis', a restored farmhouse set on a peninsula overlooking the sea close to the cathedral city of St David's, and 'Nethercott', a Victorian mansion whose land runs down to the River Torridge, famously frequented by Henry Williamson's *Tarka the Otter*. Visiting children are expected to participate fully in the daily running of these organic farms and the physically demanding tasks will certainly include collecting eggs, feeding pigs, rearing lambs, digging potatoes, picking apples, cider making and cheese pressing. "Most popular jobs," jokes Michael, who personally manages 'Nethercott', "are hosing down the stables and mucking out the cowsheds."

Everyday is packed with absorbing activities which range from milking the cows before breakfast to

opposite: Apples for sale, Faversham.

storytelling round a camp fire at supper. The benefits children gain from their week of fun and fresh air are incalculable. "More than one child has experienced the rich joy of sitting down to a proper breakfast for the first time," says Michael. "At night the stillness of the countryside and the brightness of the stars, undimmed by light pollution, is sensational. The absence of television goes unremarked." And Michael will never forget the time he encountered a shy boy, "hampered by a fearful stutter, leaning over the stable door talking fluently and confidently to our resident donkey."

Scarecrows, of course, form part of the farm experience. "The children make them up and have lots of fun doing it," laughs Michael. "They really look the part but, to be honest, I'm not sure how effective they are in keeping the crows away!"

Michael was commissioned by Birmingham Junior Schools Music Festival to write the libretto for a short comic opera, *Scarecrow*, with music composed by Phyllis Tate. The operetta was premiered at Birmingham Town Hall in June 1981 with Peter Davies conducting a massive choir of five hundred schoolchildren. A giant scarecrow presided over the stage which was dressed to resemble a field in open countryside although the opera was cleverly conceived to be adapted to any stage or classroom with minimum costume, props or scenery.

The ingenious plot has a mildly pagan theme. Once upon a time on 'Nethercott Farm', all the crops failed, the hens refused to lay and the cows were reluctant to give milk. Morris, a lonely scarecrow, became redundant and bewailed his uncertain fate in this plaintive song:

> My home in the winter is dusty and damp.
> I'm thrown in the corner just like an old tramp.
> Come March when I'm needed, they patch me up fast,
> Tie me up all in string to make sure I'll last.

Morris, the "underemployed scarecrow", is blamed for the crop failure by the bullying Farmer Benbow who threatens to throw him on the bonfire. His inquisitive daughter, Rosalind, befriends the scarecrow and imparts his secret. She reveals that it is only by singing and dancing that the dormant crops will awaken from their winter repose and be enticed to grow. The operetta is drawn to its joyful conclusion by the appearance on stage of a massed choir wearing harvest colours representing the ripening wheat and barley.

Charlie Smissen became so attached to his family of scarecrows that he, too, has written a series of booklets about their imaginary adventures long after he – and they – retired from duty at Naboth's Nursery, Faversham, Kent. For over a decade these half-size scarecrows – 'Percy', 'Gorgeous Gerty' and

their offspring – lined the busy Canterbury-Faversham Road drawing attention to the nursery and attracting passing trade. Charlie's customers were mainly local people who walked up from the town to make their choice of garden plants. "Everyone knew the scarecrows," smiles Charlie. "Children used to bring them nosegays."

Charlie worked on the land for most of his life. He started at the age of ten on a farm in North Kent. Through hard work and industry, he rose to become Waggoner's Mate and he is still proud of this title. He was put in charge of two Shire horses – 'Rodney' and 'Strawberry' – who pulled the wagons. His day started at 5 o'clock every morning when he had to feed the horses in the stable and prepare them for ploughing. "I worked one 'yoke', which meant the first stretch from 6. 30 a.m. until 2 p.m., after which time the horses were fed, watered and groomed, before I ate my own dinner at 5. 30." Did a twelve hour day exhaust a lad of fifteen? "Not a bit! It toughened me up. Made a man o' me."

There were always scarecrows on the farm, Charlie remembers. "They watched over oats, tares and grey peas for cattle feed. Their heads were made from worzels, four times as big as a turnip, which have an orange skin much like a pumpkin. We cut out holes for eyes and stuck the head on a stake with a straw hat." It was Charlie's affection for these Kentish 'bo-boys' that made him decide to use them to advertise his nursery when he took it over ten years ago. Now he cannot bear to part with them so they squat in his garden shed – stuffing out at hands and knees with noses held together by giant safety pins – where he writes his stories and reminisces about farming days.

Installation artist, Moss Fuller, once filled an entire field with moving scarecrows in the village of Laxfield, near Woodbridge, in Suffolk. She had noticed scarecrows dressed in overalls with crude square heads made from plastic containers on a nearby farm. Moss was inspired to make her own similar scarecrows wearing white paper suits but with carefully modelled straw faces. She pegged them out in a friend's meadow and attached strings to their arms and feet which made them appear to dance across the grass and over the hill. "I kept adding to them," said Moss, "so that in the end there were almost fifty dancing scarecrows. They were spotted by a passing member of the Gulbenkian Foundation who turned them into a short educational video to record their unique sense of place."

Another artist, Judith Alder, who has a studio in Bournemouth, made a decorative straw man while studying life drawing at Brighton University. A friend asked her to make a scarecrow as a favour to feature in her country garden. At the time Judith was fascinated by Leonardo Da Vinci's medical drawings and was determined her scarecrow should be anatomically correct. She moulded a precise bodywork of poles and chicken wire before covering the figure entirely with straw. He has sat patiently beside a goldfish pond for several years and only occasionally needs patching up. "Although he is solidly built he is not too effective as a scarecrow," Judith admits. "He tends to attract the birds who perch on his shoulders and peck at his head."

When Margaret Marangon inherited a field from her parents at North Green near Pulham St Mary in Norfolk, she was dismayed to find that plans had already been approved for an estate of one thousand houses with a bypass less than a mile away from it. Margaret, a mature student in visual studies at Norwich School of Art and Design, decided to make a line of scarecrows wearing placards as a silent protest which could be seen from the nearby crossroads.

Her row of 'Ten Little Scarecrows' was made from second-hand timber with heads formed from pillow cases stuffed with paper, straw, old socks and holey vests. Their features represent hours of work sewing on buttons, beads and felt pieces. They were then dressed in non-synthetic clothes bought from jumble sales and charity shops with woollen scarves, artfully wired so that they appeared to wave in the wind, and hats acquired on holidays from all parts of the world.

One special scarecrow named 'George' is dressed in grey cords, a bow tie and a checkered shirt which accidentally got scorched when he was leant against the hob of the Aga. Actually, he is a shop dummy representing a delivery newspaper boy which won first prize in a competition when Margaret worked as a window dresser for Debenhams. "I keep him at home and sit him in an armchair by the window when we go away, to discourage burglars," she jokes.

All the scarecrows have names and characters. There is 'Jock', identified by his tartan scarf and beret, 'Giovanni', wearing a stylish raincoat over a pullover and cords, and 'Doris', the only female, dressed in a floral print frock and straw hat with silk flowers. Their telling handwritten placards include the legends: "Say no to concrete"; "How loud is quiet?" and "Where are the butterflies and bees?" From even a short distance the scarecrows appear formidable and look as though they are on a protest march.

Margaret's static straw demonstrators were made with the help of her close friend, Mary Brister, who works in advertising for the *North Norfolk News*. They turned up one spring morning and worked away in the raw March wind staking the scarecrows into the hard ground. Their efforts were greatly admired by the villagers who turned up with plates of biscuits and mugs of coffee. They appreciated the fact that Margaret planted the sparse hedgerows with trees at her own expense to attract wildlife and provide nesting sites for birds.

Margaret has yet to decide what to do with her field which was originally common land. "There have been lots of suggestions so far ranging from kite flying to bonfire parties. Last winter we lit thousands of tea lights to extend the shortest day and this year I plan a ghost story telling evening with friends. At the end of my course I invited all of my fellow students over to my field for a ploughman's lunch.

Overleaf: Margaret Marangon's 'Ten Little Scarecrows', Pulham St Mary, Norfolk

I brought along a box of old clothes and let them dress up as living scarecrows for a video."

Margaret's scarecrows express her own passion for care of the countryside. "Although I live in the city of Norwich," she says, "my parents owned a dairy and arable farm, so I am a country girl at heart." Her college studies and design projects were mainly centred upon environmental issues. Margaret firmly believes in protecting trees, reducing pollution and encouraging recycling which are all vital elements in ensuring the survival of our planet. "You cannot bring the countryside back once you have lost it – that's the bottom line."

Scarecrows were also employed in a protest march when 'Friends of the Earth' paraded them through Folkestone and Hythe in November, 2004. This influential group from Shepway voiced its concern that regular crops might be contaminated by genetically modified varieties. Members held aloft their scarecrows while collecting signatures to pass on to Michael Howard M.P., for representation during a debate in the Commons.

SCARECROW MAKERS

Making scarecrows has become big business in Britain. Regular courses showing how to make them take place at 'Hope End', Ledbury, Herefordshire. This imposing Georgian house was the childhood home of the Victorian poet, Elizabeth Barrett Browning. Inspired by the beauty of the verdant countryside, Elizabeth first began to write poetry in a room atop the Clock House. Scarecrow making takes place in the magnificent eighteenth-century walled garden which is part of the wooded parkland laid out by the Regency landscape archtect, Loudon. Course tutor is art teacher and portrait painter, Louise Pilditch, who leads her students of all ages and walks of life through the basic technique of constructing a scarecrow – "traditional or funky." They are then treated to an organic lunch on the terrace before being given the opportunity to explore the garden features including an orangery, a fernery and a Victorian plunge pool.

Scarecrows by post is the idea of husband and wife business team, Neil and Kate Cooper from Bishop's Stortford. Coopers of Stortford, which specialises in novel kitchen and garden gadgets, advertises its wares in national newspapers and colourful brochures. Their imported scarecrows are dressed in bright hessian clothes and arrive by post in slim polythene bags. They come in two sizes. 'Sally' stands approximately two feet tall and is ideal for small flowerbeds, herb gardens, planters and window boxes. 'Sidney' towers over her at six feet and is supported by a bamboo pole. The pair are marketed as a useful garden ornament but there is a disclaimer: "All scarecrows deteriorate from weathering over time."

"Our scarecrows may look friendly," warns Kate, "but with hands and feet made from corn that rustles in the wind they will stop the bravest of birds from invading your vegetable patch. We took the idea from a farm worker nearby who has an immaculate cottage garden kept free from birds by a watchful scarecrow. My husband is only keen on light gardening which means we have no real need for a scarecrow on our front lawn. But I gave one to my mother-in-law as a birthday present and he stands in pride of place in her seaside garden at Sidmouth."

Lynn Hooke-Overy, who trained as an artist but has now taken up hairdressing, makes scarecrows professionally with her friend, Silvia, a market researcher. Lynn lives in a converted railway carriage on a guinea plot of land won in a game of cards in the nineteenth century. This unusual home adjoins the busy Whitstable-Canterbury Road on the north coast of Kent. It has a long timber verandah decorated with hanging baskets and tubs of flowers. Striking features of 'Pumpkin Cottage' include a large iron kettle standing on a restored Victorian cast iron kitchen range, painted milk churns, candle lanterns, witches' broomsticks, bamboo windchimes and a pottery pumpkin on which perches a plump crow.

An indolent pair of scarecrows nonchalantly lean over the fence in the adjoining paddock to advertise Lynn's thriving new business, known as 'Posh Crows.' They are both fishermen and have lead weights, glass floats and carved wooden fish in a wicker basket. The stockier figure wears a floppy sun hat, a thick woollen jumper and a teddy bear tie. He holds a nobbly walking stick. His companion has cord trousers and an anorak. In his top pocket is a mobile phone. Their faces are carefully defined with straw beards, moustaches and eyebrows. A spider has spun her web linking these static figures. The pair were without a name until a neighbour's children christened them 'Jim' and 'Old Bill'.

Lynn and Silvia thought of their profitable idea for making scarecrows professionally when driving past a field near Canterbury. They spotted a scarecrow poorly made from sheeting with a felt tip face and an upturned bucket for a hat. "We could do better than that!" they both thought, and so the idea of making scarecrows on a commercial basis was formed. They have sold their creations to herb farms, garden centres and private estates. Their speciality is a 'dolly' scarecrow made from hessian draped over crossed sticks but with gingham trim on collars, hats and top pockets. The material is often stencilled with a pattern of fruit and flowers which looks particularly effective if it stands in an orchard.

"For a friend's wedding, which took place in a converted barn, we made a straw replica of the bridegroom, purely for fun," laughed Lynn. "We kitted him out with top hat and tails. Even the buttonhole matched!" This comical figure brought immediate orders from guests but for Lynn it is simply a matter of finding the time to make such detailed character scarecrows with her house full of pets – four cats and two dogs.

Steve Haywood lives in a 1930's semi-detached house in the centre of Birmingham. He shares this house with over sixty scarecrows. They occupy every nook and cranny. An inquisitive old lady peeps from behind the net curtains of the front bay window; an elderly couple, 'Herb' and 'Gladdie', celebrate their golden wedding in the lounge while 'Miss Moneybags', dressed in a floral print frock with an enormous raffia handbag on her lap, sits contentedly listening to a battered wireless on the garden seat. There is even a straw-filled dog chained to the loggia.

Steve is happy to show visitors around his fantasy world of scarecrows which he calls 'Stonesthrow', in the village of 'Notfar.' Indeed, his amusing creations and their unusual environment were the subject of a documentary, *Our House*, for Carlton Television. Steve dresses eccentrically to match his scarecrows when he does interviews and conducts tours. He dons large-framed spectacles, a bowler hat and a black suit decorated with stripes, medals and a watchchain with a red spotted kerchief in the top pocket. Friends and neighbours refer to him as 'The Crowman.'

An imaginative garden, which boasts a wooden bridge over a stream and a miniature cottage instead of a Wendy House, was conceived by Steve to amuse his daughter, Joanna. On a whim, Steve began to turn it into an adventure playground and populate it with scarecrows. He now spends most of his spare time pottering around this crowded garden pretending it is his country estate. "It's a place where time stands still," he explains, "so in the real world I'm not even missed."

His long suffering wife, Bea, has another version of its origin. "It all started when Steve designed the garden. He had a look around and felt that there was something missing, so I suggested making a scarecrow." She soon regretted her idea since they took over not just the garden but the house as well. Now every corner of their semi is taken up with stuffed figures. "It was a bit strange at first," Bea shivers with the memory. "You feel as if you are being watched all the time. When I come downstairs in the morning the sight of a scarecrow reclining in an armchair in our sitting room is pretty alarming. It does make you jump just for that split second."

Steve disappears for hours making scarecrows in his workshop at the bottom of the garden. Bea often needed to contact him but he didn't like her calling out in her Brummie accent. He said it wasn't "ladylike." He has now installed an old fashioned bicycle hooter to alert him if he is needed in the house. The pair have worked out a simple code – one toot for a telephone call, two toots for a cup of tea, three toots when dinner is ready – which is a fairly efficient system. "Problem is, when a car hurls past our house and sounds its horn I tend to answer the phone," laughs Steve.

opposite: Character scarecrows at 'Pumpkin Cottage' near Whitstable.

Their favourite scarecrow is 'Miss Bootiful.' This glamorous model wears a half hat with veil, plastic spectacles and a billowing Princess line dress in the manner of a 1950s Beauty Queen. She has bright button eyes, rouged cheeks, baby doll lips and a pine cone for a nose! "She digs her heels in when it comes to fashion," says Steve. "Miss Bootiful enters all the beauty competitions. She still worries about winning. . . even when she's the only entrant. And when she comes first, she is modestly surprised."

Once Steve was invited to exhibit his scarecrows in an art gallery at Sulgrave Manor near Stratford upon Avon. Miss Prim was inspired by one of Steve's teachers; a drunk he saw in a doorway gave him the idea for another while a teenage companion was brought to life in Crow's Angel (a biker complete with leather gear and a crash helmet). Steve weaves a story around every one of his scarecrows and he is currently writing their adventures in a series of children's storybooks.

Polly Kettle, a former scenic designer for television, runs her own modest business making scarecrows in the Cotswolds village of Charleston Kingston near Cheltenham Spa, Gloucestershire. Fabric, hessian, scraps of felt and bundles of straw lie covering every surface of her pretty stone cottage. Ceilings are decked with garlands of hops, dried flowers hang from a rustic gate on the wall, trugs overspill with ripe fruit while seed boxes make intriguing shelves stocked with object trouvés. Outside, designer scarecrows are propped up against staddle stones or leant against wooden beehives on the lawn strewn with windfall apples to await their finishing touches before being despatched to customers. They are investigated by members of Polly's mini menagerie – guinea pigs, moulting hens, Cobweb the cat and a friendly robin who nests among the late climbing roses.

"The idea for making scarecrows started when I gave a harvest party in the village hall for my young daughter, Sarah, whose birthday falls in October," reveals Polly. "Her friends came dressed as farmyard animals, they played traditional games and ate country food. There was even an allotment cake decorated with a marzipan scarecrow standing among rows of sugar vegetables. I made a lifesize scarecrow with prezzies tucked inside every pocket for the children to choose. He was so admired by the parents who started asking me to make them, so my business, like Topsy, just grew and grew.

"At first I made each scarecrow look quite different and dressed them uniquely in second hand clothes. Now my business has expanded I market a uniform figure so customers know exactly what they are buying. They are six feet tall and stand on sturdy wooden poles painted a hazy blue. There are two styles for their workmanlike costume but there are alternative colourways. One has a jade-coloured jacket with a wooden button over heavily patched tan trousers while the other has a tan T shirt with green dungarees. They each come with a floppy hat, polka dot scarf, a stuffed crow and a corpulent mouse running up one trouser leg."

Polly Kettle's designer scarecrows.

Originally, the hessian for Polly's scarecrows was hand dyed but now it is printed by a local firm. Their cheerful facial features are deftly stencilled and a rosy blush added to each cheek. The figures are stuffed with wheat straw from the Cotswolds but dressed with thatching straw from Somerset. "I insist on a richer, deeper golden straw for their hair and hands," she says. "This caused a problem when I exported to China because there are strict regulations about importing organic material into that country. A pity, really, because the Chinese particularly admire my scarecrow's short, straight fringe."

Polly declines to name her scarecrows because she feels it is the duty of the scarecrow's owner to personalise it. A delightful touch is that she pops a handwritten note into the roomy seedbag slung over one shoulder of each of her creations. "It probably says that the scarecrow would appreciate an occasional chat and every so often new straw. I prefer to remain anomymous so I simply sign the letter 'Maker of Scarecrows' but I do leave my address for people to correspond. They often report on their scarecrow's progress and say where they have put him and how he is faring."

Polly's scarecrows have been exported to countries far and wide including America, Germany and Holland. An interior designer from Sweden suspends one from his kitchen ceiling while another won an award at a scarecrow festival in Illinois, U.S.A. Nearer to home, she sells everywhere from London stores to garden centres and her clients range from pop stars to the aristocracy. Cliff Richard and Roddy Llewellyn are just two celebrities who are proud owners of Polly's creations. Garden writer, the late Rosemary Verey OBE, acquired one to grace her potager at Barnsley House near Cirencester and yet another has been glimpsed propped up behind the editor's desk at *Country Life*. They have appeared one season at Chelsea Flower Show but one permanently resides in the Museum of Garden History at Lambeth Palace.

Polly calls her company 'Scarcity of Scarecrows' since she deeply regrets their absence in Gloucestershire. There isn't even a regional name for them so she has invented one – 'grimwolds.' "Their rarity throughout this county is a pity," she thinks, "because they do brighten up a dull corner of a garden or vegetable patch. I realise, of course, that people don't have any spare time to make scarecrows – which is why I supply a ready market – but it has to be admitted that you cannot beat a hand-me -down."

Joyce Warren, known as 'The Queen of Scarecrows', is the only full-time professional scarecrow maker in Britain. Originally, she was a ceramic potter working in Mill Hill, London, but she eventually moved with her two young sons, to the coast of Dorset. For a time she rented a tiny, pink washed cottage at the top of a steep garden in the Marshwood Vale, near Charmouth. But the countryside seemed incredibly lonely to this merry Cockney widow. Then the thought struck her: "What this landscape lacks is scarecrows!

"I made my first scarecrows using bits of old clothes and when I stuck them in the fields I started getting commissions from farmers," revealed Joyce. "When I exhibited several characters at an agricultural college they were photographed for the national newspapers which brought me welcome publicity. I realised that I could make a living from making scarecrows and applied for a small business grant." Her income is erratic, she admits, which is why she makes it a rule never to talk about money. The orders, though, came in fast and furious. Soon scarecrows overtook her home – they lurked under the table, occupied all the chairs, stared out of the windows and even grimaced from trapdoors in the ceiling – so that she was forced to move house several times. She is now practically a nomad.

Joyce has a warm, friendly, cheeky personality which is akin to the idealised character of scarecrows in children's fiction. She dresses in a practical fashion with blouse and slacks and perhaps a string of cheap beads from her workshops. She also wears pretty floral summer bonnets which she weaves herself from spare raffia.

Joyce's lucky mascot is 'Fred' who just happens to be one of the first scarecrows she made. This typical country gentleman is dressed in a tweed jacket with a bright handkerchief in his top pocket, a mustard waistcoat, blue cravat and a flower in his button hole. He has bright orange hair fashioned from farmer's twine and a monocle made from a curtain ring. An essential requisite for this affluent scarecrow was a mobile phone. For a long time Fred occupied the best armchair in Joyce's sitting room and he often accompanied her when driving the family car. Eventually he found a home on a family farm in West Staffordshire. "It was Fred," remembers Joyce," who pursuaded me to become a professional scarecrow maker."

She has created hundreds of novelty scarecrows in all shapes and guises including a Scottish Highlander, morris dancers, a punk rocker and a Pearly King. "She made a Father Christmas scarecrow for a shop window display and a circus clown for Comic Relief. An oddity was a Thomas Hardy scarecrow which was displayed for two years at the Dorchester Museum. "I spend a long time researching my characters and finding the right clothes most of which come from charity shops or jumble sales," elaborated Joyce. "They become real people and not just things with their arms and legs stuck out from stuffed clothing."

Joyce makes a skeleton for her scarecrows from chicken wire, which allows for moveable joints, and this flexible frame is then stuffed with straw. The scarecrows all wear underwear which gives them a realistic shape. Faces are given a three dimensional effect by the clever use of household objects such as buttons, buckles, thimbles, toggles and cotton reels. Joyce insists on using natural materials and spurns synthetics, preferring woollen clothing. Thoughtful neighbours leave bags of secondhand

opposite: Polly Kettle's scarecrow and friendly crow.

clothes on her doorstep and one elderly lady turned up with her late husband's wardrobe.

Joyce continually organises scarecrow projects for children and recently arranged a 'Scarecrows on the Loose' festival on the Isle of Wight. All the scarecrows were dressed from natural materials found while beachcombing. She regards her workshops as an excellent opportunity to involve children in conservation of the countryside. She demonstrates how to make miniature scarecrows from sticks, rags and raffia. They are sometimes used as puppets for speech and drama. Joyce is kept busy lecturing to schools, colleges, societies and W.I.'s but she takes time out each year to lead workshops in America and Canada where, she says, "they take scarecrows most seriously."

Students who attend Joyce's scarecrow making masterclasses find they often relate to their own creations better than real people. "Straw is therapeutic," she insisted. "When children make scarecrows at school and position them on the playing field they often end up talking to them. Quite unconsciously! Scarecrows are indeed very magical."

Joyce tours several of her favourite scarecrows whenever she leads workshops as examples of her expertise. They take a novel and surprising form. For instance there is a Parisian lady outrageously attired in striped stockings with orange garter beneath billowing lace petticoats, a cape, bodice and half hat with veil and feathers; a photographer dressed in smart brogues, cord trousers, checked shirt, knotted tie, tweed jacket with a kerchief spilling from top pocket, Fair Isle sweater and Ilford Sportsman camera slung around his neck. And there is a touching tableaux of three generations of one family with the widowed grandmother dressed in weeds, plaid shawl, buttoned boots, leaning against a bamboo-handled brolly sitting, contemplatively, next to her daughter and grand granddaughter on a rustic garden seat.

Joyce has made a host of celebrity scarecrows which has brought her fame, if not fortune, nationwide. These are primarily works of art because they take something like twenty hours to complete and can cost several hundred pounds. Among her diverse subjects are Anne Widdicombe, David Hockney, Jimi Hendrix, Lenny Henry and Dr Who. She has made Charlie Chaplin, complete with trademark bowler hat and walking stick; David Beckham, sporting his former Manchester United football kit and Mr Bean, who seemed an obvious choice for a smallholding specialising in runner beans. Perhaps her most impressive scarecrows were James Bond, complete with dinner jacket, bow tie and pistol, and the former Beatles drummer, Ringo Starr, wearing a psychedelic patchwork jacket, kipper tie, mirror sunglasses and cowboy boots. She feels he would certainly have been at home standing in an Octopus's Garden.

She also made replicas of disc jockey, Steve Wright, for his radio programme and presenter, John Craven, for an edition of 'Countryfile.' Another time she made Freddie Mercury, outrageously flaunting

opposite: Joyce Warren and some of her colourful creations.

a crown and a cloak, for television's 'Big Breakfast.' When a primary school engaged her for a workshop during their art week she spiced up the timetable by organising the young pupils to recreate the pop band, 'Spice Girls.'

Occasionally, Joyce has attempted scarecrows of royalty. The figures that caused the greatest stir were Charles and Camilla. This, she insists, was the first time they had been seen together in public which resulted in photographs of their straw effigies appearing in the press worldwide. Most popular was a scarecrow of the Queen Mother, "respectfully made" for Her Majesty's 90th birthday celebrations. The nation's favourite grandmother was typically dressed in a pale blue outfit with a double row of pearls, floral hat and veil, handbag and gloves. In addition, she carried a paper bouquet and football pools token.

Joyce's scarecrows have been exported to Japan. This started when a Japanese businessman from Tokyo ordered miniature scarecrows to decorate dolls' houses and bonsai trees. A lady from Essex saw them and commissioned Joyce to make a lifesize figure which would protect her koi carp from herons. Joyce obliged by creating a beautiful Geisha girl wearing a white kimono, carrying a fan and holding a parasol. "Originally, my idea was for a sumo wrestler which at the time seemed impossible as I was not so experienced," admitted Joyce.

Joyce specialises in Lookalike Scarecrows. The "rich and famous" commission her to make a scarecrow of a living person in secret. The effigy is always larger-than-life and dressed in a replica of the subject's clothes. Alternatively, it may be dressed to represent that person's profession, everything from a barrister to a ballerina. It is then unveiled at a celebration such as a birthday or retirement as a complete surprise. Often, it is the cause of great hilarity and simply makes a party.

'The Enjoy Organic Company', a subsidiary of Sainsbury's, commissioned her to make a trio of naked scarecrows as a novel way of publicising healthy eating options. The company, based at Lambourn, Berkshire, thought this a brilliant idea to publicise the benefits of buying their organic food products which included pastas and sauces. The company insisted Joyce used only biodegradable or recyclable materials and definitely no plastic which was strict company policy. The scarecrows who had gone back to nature were positioned on several sites holding banners over country roads.

Joyce recently produced her own video and set up her own website (www.scarecrowland.co.uk) In the near future she plans to open her own theme park, 'Scarecrowland', at Brogdale National Fruit Farm, near Faversham, in Kent. And she still has an ambition to assemble the biggest number of scarecrows in one place so she can be entered in the *Guinness Book of Records*. "Business has never been brisker," Joyce claims. "This is probably because there is so much magic in scarecrows."

opposite: Joyce Warren's countryman.

SCARECROW FESTIVALS

Wray

The charming village of Wray in Lancashire holds an annual scarecrow festival when all the inhabitants make scarecrows and place them in their front gardens to attract tourists and raise funds for local charities. This novel event was first mooted as a publicity stunt by David Hartnup, a portrait and landscape painter, who lives in a stone built cottage near the old salt road with a date stone: 1704.

David conceived the idea during a disastrous holiday in France. "I had broken my leg while climbing which put paid to a planned camping holiday in the Pyrenees. Instead, my wife drove me around the French countryside where we came across a place which held a scarecrow festival as a tourist attraction. The village of Campin was fairly dotted with scarecrows – peering from windows, peeping out from doorways and even swinging from a tree above a strawberry patch, which gave us quite a turn – but the strange thing was there were few visitors to appreciate them.

"When I came home, I mentioned the idea to our village committee as a way of promoting our fair which has been held here since 1838. Naturally, they were cautious yet unanimously agreed to offer our entire savings as prizes for the best dressed scarecrows. It was quite a risk. By pure chance, a producer from Granada Television motorcycled through the village on the first day of the fair and she arranged for our scarecrows to be shown that evening on the news programme. Next day, we were inundated with tourists and by the end of the week we had raised a small fortune to be shared equally among the village school, the church, the chapel and the Women's Institute," chuckles David. "I was the hero of the hour."

That was in 1996 when the theme for Wray Fair was the Olympics. Children's television programme, 'Blue Peter', also heard about the fun event and asked to feature twenty of the best scarecrows. David took along a sprinter, a pole vaulter, a shot putter and a horse rider and arranged them in the famous 'Blue Peter' garden. "We transported them by open lorry, which must have looked quite a sight! After the programme the scarecrows were bought wholesale by a farmer from the Isle of Wight."

Wray Scarecrow Festival has been held every year since (apart from the outbreak of foot and mouth disease) and themes have included V.E. Day, World Cup and Country Matters. "One time we decided upon a French theme with characters from the t.v. sit-com, 'Allo', 'Allo', which was very colourful. We are twinned with Grez Neuville, a village in the Loire Valley, and so invited villagers to attend with their own Continental scarecrows. When they saw our Johnny Onion man dressed in a black beret and striped jumper, with a string of onions around his neck, riding a bicycle, they were completely baffled.

opposite: Desperate Dan, Wray Festival.

Apparently, they had never seen anything remotely like that in France – apart from the bicycle!"

Each year around two hundred scarecrows are made by the people of Wray. "It is all a closely guarded secret," laughs David. "Noone will reveal what their character is going to be until it suddenly appears, as if by magic. Of course, I can tell straight away who has made which scarecrow. If you think, they will all be made to fit the cast-off clothes of their owner. Consequently, the height and build of the figure will correspond exactly to their maker. One day I will photograph scarecrow and maker side by side and it will be a revelation."

Giant comical scarecrows made from straw bales standing in open fields on the road from Lancaster point the way to the spring festivities at Wray. The village, which nestles in the Lune Valley, is rich in character. There are rows of neat, sandstone cottages with cobbled forecourts, a stone built church with exposed bells and a timber porch, a post office-cum-general stores and two pubs which serve 'Scarecrow bitter', specially brewed for the occasion. Stone bridges straddle the River Roeburn, which has a tendency to flood, and high on the hill above the village, hidden amongst bluebell woods, are the remnants of a silk mill which formerly provided industry for the inhabitants who made top hats.

Early morning on the first day of the Scarecrow Festival villagers are staking out their scarecrows. The event takes a whole year in planning and the week culminates on May Bank Holiday Monday with a traditional fair held in a nearby show field. There will be maypole dancing, rare breeds, dog handling, birds of prey, Punch and Judy, a farmers' market and a traditional fairground. All week there are stalls in the main street selling plants, bric-a-brac and miniature scarecrows handmade by pupils of the local primary school. First event is a challenging 10 kilometre race where competitors brave the steep inclines of the surrounding Fells to win

a prized trophy. The race is filmed by a BBC television outdoor film unit whose crew just happen to be straw-stuffed figures with a camera made out of a cardboard box with protruding lens formed from Pringles tubes.

Theme for 2004 was 'Characters from Books and Television.' Bob the Builder, Mickey Mouse, Mary Poppins and the Pink Panther all made their appearance in straw effigy. Children at the village school made characters from 'A Bug's Life' while a figure of the Sheriff from Dodge City, who appears in countless Westerns, was voice activated, which was guaranteed to surprise passers-by. Desperate Dan from the comic, *Dandy*, with his familiar bow legs and stubble chin, struggled to devour his gigantic cow pie standing next to Rocky the Rooster, (Chicken Run) making his escape from Mrs Tweedy's farm on a trade bicycle, with Ginger and Babs, furiously knitting, in the wicker carrier.

An entire cul-de-sac was taken over for makebelieve filming of *The Wizard of Oz* with the familiar characters – Dorothy, the Tin Man, the Cowardly Lion and the Scarecrow – dancing merrily along a hastily constructed Yellow Brick Road. *Alice In Wonderland* also inspired village youngsters to make a lifelike Alice tempted by an array of plaster cakes, a White Rabbit consulting his large pocket watch, the Caterpillar smoking his hookah lazing on a giant mushroom, the Red Queen playing 'Crow-quet' and the Mad Hatter pouring from an outsize pot of Yorkshire tea. These together made a beautiful riverside tableau.

A magnificent scene from *Pirates of the Caribbean* was conceived by Anna Fellows, a teaching assistant, and her two children, Harry and Rosie. Captain Jack Sparrow stood in a hedgerow making his triumphant entrance into harbour riding atop the mast of his sinking ship. His body was built around the pole of a washing line and his realistic face mask was moulded in papier mâché. Anna, a fan of the star of the film, Johnny Depp, raked around her children's dressing up box to find suitable attire but the boots came from a jumble sale and the wig from a joke shop. "We all had great fun making him," she said. Even the family cat, Queenie, couldn't resist getting in on the act, posing for photographers as the ship's mascot.

Clearly, making scarecrows for the festival brings out the artistic talents of the entire village. Novelty scarecrows, unrelated to the current theme, included a magician sawing a lady in half, a bobby arresting a criminal caught holding his swag bag and a teddy boy with quiff, sideburns, tapering jeans and blue suede shoes, energetically rocking around the clock. In addition there appeared a squadron of pilots, wearing bomber jackets, flying helmets and goggles, steering wooden wheelbarrows converted into biplanes with the caption, 'Red Barrows', and a musician, dressed in a tuxedo, lying under a steam roller with the caption, 'Roll Over Beethoven.' One comical idea was a scarecrow attached to the back of a

opposite: Shaggy and Scooby Doo, Wray Festival.

tandem which the maker took for a ride at intervals. "We always try to include a couple of traditional scarecrows," reveals David. "It keeps the event in perspective and reminds us that our own artistic versions evolved from working scarecrows placed in the fields."

Inevitably, Scarecrow Festivals offer the chance for satire and social comment. Hence, George Bush (whose body was made from a holly bush) was dressed for combat at the time of the Iraq conflict while Victoria Beckham (her body was made from a shop mannequin) seemed ready for combat with David's mistress, Rebecca Loos. One skinny model had obviously been on the Atkins diet! There were several straw figures tangled in shrubbery with the placard, 'I'm a Scarecrow Get Me Out of Here' and a David Blaine effigy looked forlorn suspended from his sealed box above the roadway.

On a personal level, a fisherman dressed in jerkin, baseball cap and waders lazed in a folding chair having just netted a fish. Beside him were the obligatory pack of sandwiches, flask and wicker fishing basket. He was made by a member of the 'George and Dragon Fishing Club' who, according to his wife, regularly went fishing all day and came back with nothing. Placards in the flower beds expressed sparring between the spouses: "My wife says, If I go fishing one more time, she's goin' to leave me – I'm sure gonna miss her", and "I live with fear and danger every day but sometimes she lets me go fishing".

After ten days the whole event is drawn to a close by a torchlight procession through the village with children dressed as scarecrows led by the Mayor of Lancaster. This twilight parade is headed by giant scarecrows carried on the shoulders of strong adults. They are dressed as St George, Worzel Gummidge, Aunt Sally, a Green Man and a Belle of the Ball. Prizes are awarded for the best dressed scarecrows that season. Invariably these consist of either pottery scarecrows or statuettes made by local artists and they will be proudly displayed in cottage windows for weeks to come.

Kettlewell

The picturesque village of Kettlewell, at the heart of the Yorkshire Dales, annually hosts a scarecrow festival. The River Wharfe races through the village which nestles snugly in a valley surrounded by the mysterious, misty Fells. Kettlewell boasts three good pubs, a few shops, a post office, a primary school with just thirty pupils and four bridges that straddle a stream known as the Beck. The backdrop of robust stone cottages was the location for the controversial film *Calendar Girls* which told the story of the daring W.I. ladies who posed nude for a calendar and raised a quarter of a million pounds for charity.

Once a year Kettlewell holds its famous summer festival which attracts tourists from North Yorkshire. Scarecrows appear in every shape and form to enliven each enticing nook and cranny. Visitors might be

Taking tea at 'Chestnut Cottage',
Kettlewell Festival.

overleaf: Eliza Doolittle, Kettlewell
Madonna, Kettlewell

pleasantly surprised to find the entire cast of *The Vicar of Dibley* attending an outdoor committee meeting waiting for the Rev. Geraldine, still stuffing bars of chocolate into the pocket of her cardigan, and a beautiful bride with her attendant maid and page posing for a wedding photographer beside the lychgate of St Mary's Church. Humorous touches might include a pickpocket locked in the stocks by the war memorial and the striped tail of a cat burglar disappearing with his swag bag through an upstairs window.

Main theme one year was 'Musicals.' An outrageous Madonna flaunting her conical bra and waspie corset was strapped around a telegraph pole while an elegant Michael Crawford wearing a half mask and purple-lined cloak clung to the creeper of a stone wall surrounded by musical notes. Mary Poppins danced on a lawn under her umbrella, Carmen Miranda balanced an outsize bowl of fruit on her head, Joseph pranced in his coat of many colours inside the church porch and a perky Eliza Dolittle sold baskets of flowers from her Covent Garden stall. And there was a wicked depiction of Michael Jackson, surrounded by children, precariously feeding Baby Blanket from a bottle hidden under a veil. A slight hitch occurred when the papier mâché effigy of Elvis was stolen and one hundred pounds reward was offered for his return. Eventually, a motorist raised the alarm when he thought he found a dead body lying face down on the main road and dialed 999.

"We were one of the earliest villages in this country to hold a scarecrow festival," remarked Jennie Howarth who lives at Bridge House. "We spend almost the whole year planning for the next event and my two boys have grown up with scarecrows being made inside the house." Jennie impressed everyone with her clown theme adapted from the musical, 'Barnum.' There were jugglers, plate spinners, clowns and even a snake charmer outside her cottage. Pièce de résistance was the trapeze artiste swinging high above the river surrounded by bunting. "Her costume was one I wore for a murder mystery weekend and I forgot about it until it fell out of the wardrobe."

"This is our tenth year," explained one of the organisers, Geoffrey Queen, "although it is only our ninth festival because one year we were closed due to foot and mouth disease. We raise funds for the church, school and village hall, so everyone benefits. The beauty of the event is that it attracts folk from miles around who stay in guest houses, rented accommodation or caravan sites. Whereas a jumble sale might raise a hundred pounds, our scarecrow trail brings in thousands of pounds and all of it from outside visitors."

The imposing straw figure of Admiral Nelson lorded it over the village perched atop a column of oil drums next to Kettlewell Garage. He cut quite a dash in his naval uniform complete with plum sash, tricorn hat and silver sword. His face was moulded in papier mâché with striking, if not accurate, features of twirling moustache and beauty spot. The garage was originally a wooden building when it was opened in the 1930s but it is now owned by two brothers, Bill and Mick Wilkinson. "We employed a tractor with a bucket to hoist His Lordship to the top of his plinth," said Mike triumphantly.

Topical touches were a smartly-suited Tony Blair peering over a garden wall, searching for weapons of mass destruction, and Saddam Hussein, wearing a hallmark beret, thick spectacles and a moustache, lurking in a dark corner against a scrawled notice: "This is the last place to think of looking for me." Sir Edmund Hillary climbed a paper mountain to plant a Union Jack as a tribute to his momentous climb, fifty years previously. He was the inspiration of David Greaves, owner of an outdoor clothing store, who happens to be an amateur mountaineer. "The ice axe, crampons, windsmock and backpack are authentic," he explained, "but I added welding goggles, thermal gloves, a medical mask with washing machine tubing and fire extinguisher canisters for oxygen cylinders."

A children's corner centred around the tea rooms. Humpty Dumpty sat on a high wall surrounded by uniformed king's men and horses. Above the entrance sat Bill and Ben made from flowerpots and an endearing Andy Pandy with Looby Loo. Bob the Builder and Postman Pat also made an appearance around the village. One delicate tableau showed Mary, Quite Contrary, dressed in a floral crinoline and poke bonnet watering her arbour of country flowers. Alas, another Mary from the world of nursery rhyme had exchanged her traditional lamb for Dolly the cloned sheep.

There were some novel ideas for additional fund raising. A gipsy sat permanently at her table with a crystal ball and a tub of handwritten fortunes which could be read upon crossing her palm with silver. Alternatively, visitors could place their head over the body of a lifesize scarecrow wearing a choice of hats to have a photograph taken. Prince William, too, posed patiently on a roadside bench waiting for a suitor to have her picture taken beside our handsome heir to the throne.

A really clever touch was to introduce scarecrows dressed as ordinary people and scatter them around the village. There was, for instance, a mechanic under the bonnet of a car, a workman poking his head out of a hole in the middle of the road, a sweep forcing his brush through the top of a chimney; a single mum pushing a buggy outside the village store and a hiker wrapped up in her plastic mac with knitted gloves and stout walking shoes consulting her ordnance survey map with her pack of sandwiches and flask of coffee. Quite charming were the mother and child – hard to believe they were straw figures – watching the children dance round the Victorian maypole on the village green. The boys all had bow ties, straw hats and bright sashes while the girls wore printed floral summer frocks with matching hair bands. And as the wind moved their hands, it gave the illusion of them tugging at the coloured ribbons to make the criss-cross pattern round the ancient maypole.

A delightful pair of scarecrows were to be found taking tea on the lawn of Chestnut Cottage, a guest house run by Sheila and Conrad Lofthouse. The man with his cloth cap and carrot nose was pouring tea from a silver pot for his lady who was seated wearing a straw hat, woollen shawl and pleated skirt. They were the focal point of a pretty terraced garden, also inhabited by Fred, the forty-year-old tortoise, which sloped down to the River Beck. Nearby, appeared the only working scarecrow to be found in the village. Humbly formed from crossed sticks and dressed in plastic bags with a flower pot head, he stood in the hen coop where he prevented crows from eating the chicken feed. Previously, he was employed keeping pigeons off turnips but he still does a grand job, according to Con, although the crows nowadays "tend to be a bit cheeky".

Tetford

Another annual scarecrow festival is held at Tetford which nestles in the South Wolds of Eastern Lincolnshire. A gentle stream, whose banks are bordered with lilac trees, runs through this picturesque village that still boasts a post office, a pub, a primary school and a medieval church. (St Mary's contains memorials to the Dymoke family who, from the 14th century until 1821, were required to be present at every coronation to challenge any opponent of the monarch to mortal combat as Champions of the English Crown). The whole area, which is in the heart of Tennyson country, is designated one of outstanding natural beauty. A one mile circular road runs through the heart of the village. This makes it ideal for visitors to tootle around in their cars and peer out of the windows to admire the scarecrows while listening to the melodious church bells. The event is advertised in the parish magazine, *Tennyson Chronicle*, and it raises considerable funds for the parish church.

Theme for Tetford's third scarecrow festival was Royalty, considered appropriate to mark Queen Elizabeth II's Golden Jubilee. Her Majesty herself deigned to appear and the gardens were all spruced up for the occasion. The Queen's effigy stood graciously for three days on the front lawn of a row of council houses in the centre of the village. The Queen looked perfectly regal in a pale blue floral gown with a blue shawl, long white gloves and the obligatory handbag carried in the crook of her arm. She wore a double row of pearls, a butterfly brooch and a gold crown decorated with gummed paper shapes representing jewels. Queen Elizabeth's face was moulded from papier mâché and the artist had perfectly

overleaf: H.M. The Queen and Prince Philip visit Tetford Festival.

A fox eludes Prince Charles at Tetford.

Philip
Elizabeth
And
Windsor

CHARLES

HE HUNTS

HE SHOOTS

HE FISHES

WHERE ARE
YOU
CAMILLA?

Queen Victoria is not amused by visitors to Tetford.

captured her solemn expression. Her Majesty was escorted by Prince Philip wearing a double breasted suit with a row of medals hanging from red, white and blue ribbons. The royal couple were circled with miniature union jacks while at their feet was a stuffed toy corgi wearing a giant identity tag, 'Windsor.'

Prince Charles strolled through the grounds of a neighbouring bungalow. He was dressed for the country in a tweed jacket with a cloth cap, spotted kerchief, smart brogues and a hazel walking stick. His face was painted on an upturned pheasant feeder but his ears were mischievously formed from plastic flower pots. The Prince was cobbled up the night before by retired gamekeeper, Mr. Ivor Bee, who had difficulty stuffing the torso with six old shirts and five worn jumpers. A toy fox, unseen by the prince, scampered across the top of an austere clipped hedge.

The whole village took on the nature of a royal pageant with lifelike effigies of historical Kings and Queens. William the Conqueror sat on a kitchen chair at the entrance to the village clearly exhausted having just shot an arrow into the eye of Harold who fell a long time dying on the triangular green at the entrance to Tetford. Boadicea appeared riding her chariot pulled by a pair of rearing black horses; Elizabeth I wandered around a delightful box parterre; Charles I underwent the humiliation of a second public execution on the roadside while Charles II once more secreted himself among the branches of an oak tree. The Widow of Windsor scowled at passers by from her vantage point just inside the garden gate of an attractive cottage. Her sculptured features clearly revealed that she was definitely "not amused" by the intrusion of so many visitors. Even Britannia made an appearance with her shield and trident resting against the family saloon in the gravel drive. . .

Imaginative interpretations on the theme of royalty abounded. The Queen of Hearts proffered her tarts outside the parish hall; King Neptune held aloft his trident as he rose from a fish pond; a Queen Bee buzzed behind a low hedge; Elvis Presley, King of rock 'n' roll, thumped out melodies from a marquee while King Kong rocked astride the chimney pots. There was even a self-styled King Crow with a purple cloak, cardboard crown and row of medals awarded 'for scaring crows.'

There were interesting modern touches. Straw figures of the children from Edward Richardson Primary School scampered over a fence dressed in their uniform of yellow baseball caps and green sweaters bearing the emblem of a cornstook while toddlers tumbled down the grassy banks of St Mary's Church. One scarecrow made a breathtaking dive from a high crane inside the yard of a tree specialist while another straw mechanic lay underneath a gleaming vintage Austin Seven to fiddle with the engine. Oddities were the Loch Ness Monster ascending from a well, Spiderman scaling a wall, Enid Blyton's Big Ears, a Dalek and a Spaceman!

Albert, the chimney sweep, looked remarkably elegant dressed in a pinstriped suit with a gold chain dangling from his waistcoat pocket. He sported a handsome brush moustache but there were sooty smears across his sculptured face. He was expertly made from a jointed wooden frame but was so heavily stuffed with straw that his maker found immense diffculty in fitting his trousers. All the same he seemed inordinately proud of the royal crest painted on the gate bearing the legend: "By appointment to the Queen." Opposite, one traditional scarecrow with button eyes and carrot nose lent over the wooden fence to survey visitors along the cul-de-sac, oblivious to the fact that harvest mice were nibbling at his lunch. One couple, fancy dress enthusiasts, turned up from London with their own scarecrows and stuck them in adjacent fields where they seemed perfectly at home.

One of the organisers of Tetford's festival is Joyce Bennett. "Everybody in the village is involved in the event although nothing is overplanned which means I have to sit biting my nails until the day to discover how many scarecrows will appear," she confesses. "Some people knock them up the night before; others take endless trouble over them." Her worries always prove groundless, however, since there are never less than sixty exhibits. "For older people, there is a romantic appeal about scarecrows that is closely linked with memories of childhood when they were commonplace in the fields of Britain."

Brampton Bryan

A scarecrow festival with a sporting theme took place one summer in the hamlet of Brampton Bryan which borders on three counties: Herefordshire, Shropshire and Radnorshire (now swallowed up in Powys). This charming hamlet in the Welsh Marches boasts a working forge, a wheelwright, tea rooms and a post office with a Ludlow letter box. In the centre stands a thirteenth-century castle and grand hall owned by the influential Harley family. Houses on their estate are painted with the distinctive livery: "Harley blue."

Unusually, the Harleys held their castle for the Parliamentarians during the Civil War. The heroic Lady Brilliana Harley, with one hundred garrison, resisted a month's siege by the invading Royalists. Her castle did not capitulate even when it was pounded by fire from a cannon mounted on the nearby church roof. Cromwell rewarded the courage of the inhabitants of Brampton Bryan by allowing their

church to be rebuilt – square and spacious – which was a rare occurrence during the Commonwealth.

A more peaceful battle took place when an entire football team of stuffed straw figures was staked out on the triangular village green. A cloth-capped goalie dived to make a dramatic save while a stern-faced referee flashed a red card at a player who had delivered a foul. England's captain, David Beckham, was poised for kick off. He was made by two University students, Jessica Cremer and James Yeoward. They moulded his face out of papier mâché, drew convincing features in felt tip and added a straw mohican hairstyle. Beckham still wore his Manchester United football shirt, presumably because news travels slowly in country districts. Indeed, rather then being transferred to Real Madrid, Becks ended up in Jessica's grandfather's field where he became a soggy figure after a heavy downpour.

About twenty sports were represented at Brampton Bryan including golf, badminton, cricket, lacrosse, tennis, swimming and snooker. A skier was shown with his bobble hat, sunshades and scarf flying in the wind while a fisherman dextrously cast his line across an entire front lawn. A rugby scrum fought for the ball against the stone wall of the hall which claims the longest yew hedge in the country, while an archer fired at the weathervane of the parish church which must possess the slowest chiming clock in the county.

Barton Mills

Barton Mills, a quiet village near Mildenhall, Suffolk, has been put firmly on the map since it began its scarecrow festival in 1998. The carved village sign shows the original post mill but a corn mill is being reconstructed as a dwelling on the banks of the River Lark. An annual scarecrow event is organised by members of St Mary's Church Preservation Trust. People now come from all over East Anglia, alerted to the summer festival by the local radio network. Thousands of pounds have been raised over a very short period which is shared equally among the ancient church and local charities.

"Fund raising often consists of a summer fete organised by a few dedicated people but with a scarecrow festival the whole village is involved," enthuses Colin Brotherton, a consultant civil engineeer, who is a founder trustee. "People are surprised by their own inventiveness", adds his wife, Elisabeth, another trustee and professional photographer. "Everyone can make a scarecrow. It's such fun. People find themselves chattering and laughing about their efforts for months afterwards."

"The great thing is to chose a theme with a lot of scope," confides Colin. "The Jubilee provided an obvious subject and the Olympics will be just perfect. We turn our festival into a miniature county show with buskers, jazz bands and barbecues. People open up their gardens to visitors who are often surprised

opposite: Albert the Chimney Sweep, Tetford Festival.

to find models of The Royle Family or The Mad Hatter's Tea party on the lawn. My dream is to organise a National Scarecrow Day."

Barton Mills achieved a certain distinction when the village was awarded a certificate by, although not an entry in, the *Guinness Book of Records 2000* for the most human scarecrows erected in a single place. "Our total score was seven hundred and sixty which was at that time a world record," announced Elisabeth. "This discounted 101 dalmatians and over three hundred stuffed sheep in the churchyard. We took over the record from Tunbridge Wells, in Kent, but lost it ourselves to a town in Portugal."

One year the villagers held a Pedal Car Grand Prix which added to the carnival atmosphere. Teams of racers built cars from scrap and were sponsored by charities to make several laps round Church Meadows, a modern housing estate. There were photographers in press boxes, mechanics at pit stops, marshals waving checkered flags and champagne shaking for the winning team. One pedal car achieved 18 m.p.h. on the straight which was verified by a policeman with a radar gun.

"Another time we had enormous fun making authentic likenesses of parishioners to display in the church," revealed Colin. "We took great care making plaster casts of each other's face to turn into papier mâché masks and then dressed lifesize scarecrows in our own clothes. We made over one hundred replicas – everyone from the organist in the loft to the Vicar in the pulpit – so that we rivalled Madame Tussaud's."

St. Mary's Church invariably becomes a focal point for the festivities. "One year we built a gigantic Noah's Ark complete with pairs of animals walking up its slope in the churchyard," said Elisabeth. "All the animals were made from cardboard and sacking on a wire frame stuffed with straw and looked terrific apart from the camels whose humps went soggy after it rained. We held a 'Songs of Praise' in the open air and the Vicar took a scarecrow apart to show that at the centre is a cross."

There is always sadness at the end of each festival when the straw figures are taken down. Once a kindly farmer gave a donation to charity to acquire several scarecrows to work on his land. As he towed the lifelike figures away in his trailer he was watched suspiciously by a policeman. Most, though, are stored throughout the winter in attics, barns or lofts. "Mine keeps a permanent look-out from a top floor window," said Frances Lewis, a retired schoolmistress. "I find him not only comforting but a deterrent to burglars."

Faversham

Scarecrows provided the theme for a novel fund raising event one autumn when residents of Painter's Forstal, near Faversham, in Kent, created around forty straw figures and displayed them in their front gardens. The Scarecrow Trail was organised by Joan Tovey, a lively inhabitant of this rambling hilly

opposite: Joan Tovey and her village characters near Faversham.

above: Pirate and crew at Faversham.

below: Headgirl and pupil at Faversham school.

hamlet, to raise money for the restoration of the Victorian church clock. Visitors purchased a map and walked, cycled or drove through the leafy lanes to locate the amusing creations which stood beside buckets to collect coins.

Parishioners showed imagination and flair when constructing their novelty scarecrows. There was a witch, a mermaid, acrobats and a chef wearing the obligatory check trousers, frilled hat and striped apron. Television personalities numbered Bart Simpson, Postman Pat and Mr Blobby. Sheer inspiration was Marilyn Monroe wearing her windy dress that featured in 'The Seven Year Itch.'

Local characters were also depicted. Journalist, Jan Thom, modelled her effigy on a neighbour, Ruby Sutton, who had been a landgirl during the Second World War. 'Ruby' stood beside sacks of freshly dug potatoes and Jan's caged pet speckled Sussex hen, 'Georgina', while an air raid siren sounded at intervals. A caricature of the local vicar was not particularly flattering. He appeared, leaning against the lych gate of the Church of SS. Peter and Paul, Ospringe. Members of the Sunday School who had constructed him had pinned tracts to his vestments: "God loves wahts inside" and "Appearance dose not matter' (Scarecrows are notoriously bad spellers)

Cutest figure was a baby scarecrow dressed in rompers with a bib and feeding bottle beside a handwritten notice: 'Small crows only please'

Star attraction was the talking pirate who stood beside a horse chestnut tree in his colourful attire of striped shirt, spotted kerchief, crimson pantaloons and tricorn hat displaying the skull and crossbones. Further refinements were his twirly moustache, eye patch, gold earring, silver pistol, cutlass and arm hook. Passers by were startled to be greeted personally by this jovial pirate in between bouts of his singing sea shanties: "Yo, ho, ho and a bottle of rum." The audacious device of rigging up a concealed microphone and loudspeakers was the idea of practical joker, Andrew Keel, Chairman of Brogdale Parish Council. His children, Eleanor and Joseph, made the pirate one afternoon assisted by their grandmother who scoured charity shops for nautical clothing.

Organiser, Joan Tovey, displayed beautifully crafted scarecrows on the banks outside her Georgian farmhouse adjacent to the extensive orchards of Brogdale National Fruit Trust. Pride of place was awarded to a genial, bearded farmer with a wooden pitchfork, a pipe in his top pocket and a knitted lamb cossetted in the crook of his arm. . . and 'Agnes', the village spinster, dressed in tweed suit with her straw bonnet, golfing umbrella and Wellington boots. "Apart from raising considerable funds for the church," asserted Joan, "our project brought the whole community together in a marvellous way. We plan to make this an annual event."

Television Treats

A fascinating six-part documentary, 'A Country Parish', was broadcast on BBC2 in Spring 2003. It traced the life of a young priest, Rev. Jamie Allen, as he moved from the former mining town of Nuneaton to a tranquil village, Semington, near Trowbridge, in Wiltshire. This rural backwater boasts a store-cum-post office, several picture postcard pubs and three ancient parish churches within a radius of three miles which all came under his pastoral care. After moving into the vast, daunting Rectory with his wife and three daughters the new Rector was soon introduced to his congregation which comprised of retired army officers, farming families and landed gentry. His menagerie of pets also took time to acclimatise themselves to the upheaval and their amusing antics captured on camera included chickens escaping from their coop, a ginger tom swinging on a hammock and even the Rector riding to evensong on horseback.

Mr Allen's new parish was the epitome of Middle England. Community life followed a predictable pattern with cricket on the green, narrow boats on the canal and fox hunting across Salisbury Plain. First grand event of the summer was a Scarecrow Hunt in Bulkington, near Seend, which attracted welcome publicity. Villagers placed groups of nursery rhyme characters on their front lawns for visitors to guess their identity and win prizes. The competition took eighteen months to plan and involved parishioners making thirty-five scarecrows representing every conceivable character from Little Bo Peep to Humpty Dumpty. Mary, Quite Contrary was busy watering her garden flowers; Rock A Bye Baby slept in her tiny hammock which swung from a pine tree; a maid hung out washing as a blackbird pecked at her nose although the showpiece was a circle of children on the village green dancing 'Ring A Ring O' Roses.' Even the trendy vicar was roped in to help assemble the amusing tableau of Little Johnny Stout helping to pull out pussy from the well.

Over one thousand visitors converged on the village (normal population 268) from as far afield as Bristol, Devizes, Swindon and Salisbury. Additional activities included a steam fair, rides on a model railway, a church flower show and a beer festival at the local pub, 'The Tipsy Toad.' Money raised was divided equally between local hospice care and the church restoration fund. Organiser, Susan Noad, recalled, "There was this wonderful image of grandmas and grandpas chanting nursery rhymes in the street and trying to jog their childhood memories of all the characters. Reference books were handed over garden walls and mobile phones were commandeered to answer questions. Our only mishap was when an excitable puppy chewed all the Queen of Hearts' woollen fingers and ate her woven tarts."

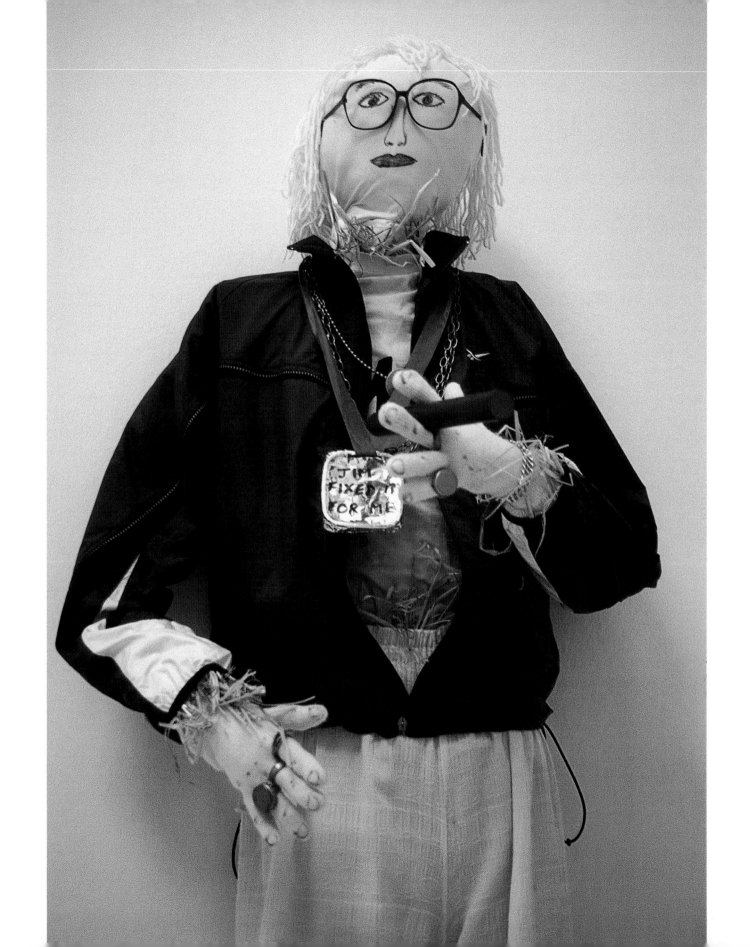

New British Art 2000

One artistic scarecrow from a village festival was rewarded by being displayed at London's Tate Britain. Artists, Jeremy Deller and Alan Kane, collaborated to present a temporary exhibition of traditional folk art that included such diverse items as photographs of bikers' tattoos, videos of morris dancing and homemade crafts sold at Womens' Institute bazaars. These two enterprising artists toured Britain for a whole year hunting for prize artefacts that would not normally be classified as 'Art.' The result of their nationwide search appeared in the bold exhibition: 'Intelligence – New British Art 2000.'

The straw figure that caught their attention appeared at the original Scarecrow Festival at Wray. It was an effigy of Sir Jimmy Saville OBE, the vivacious disc jockey knighted for his charity work and fund raising for hospitals. Sir Jimmy Scarecrow wore a track suit, T shirt and trainers. He clutched a trademark cigar, his gloved hands were weighted with gold sovereign rings fashioned from beer bottle tops and round his neck was a medal attached to a red ribbon: 'Jim Fixed It For Me.' This audacious figure was made by Julie and Graham Whitely to stand outside their house beside a placard: 'Now then, Guys and Gals, welcome to Top of the Pops.'

Eventually, Sir Jimmy was pursuaded to make a flying visit to the Millbank Gallery to inspect firsthand his lifesize double. The veteran entertainer confessed to rarely being interested in art but was flattered by his straw counterpart. "I've been scaring birds away for years," he quipped. "I hope my namesake has better luck!" And he added with immense admiration: "For a scarecrow to finish up in the Tate is amazing in every sense of the word!"

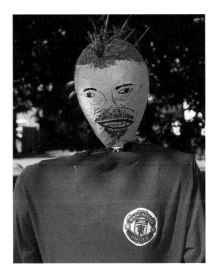

opposite: Sir Jimmy Saville OBE at the Tate.

left: Beckham at Brampton Bryan.

Acknowledgements

The following friends, colleagues, librarians and institutions have offered invaluable help by supplying information. They have patiently answered my often obscure questions when I was simply clutching at straws. My apologies if I have left anyone out:

Alex of Comicana
Stephen Alexander
Darina Allen
Margery Allingham Society
Sheila Anderson, Railton Hyde Library, Staffordshire
Artbank, Canada Council for the Arts
Rev. Joan Ashton, Vicar of All Saints Church, Arksey
The Rt. Hon. Lord Baker of Dorking, C.H.
Ruth Beadle, Senior Librarian, Romsey Library, Hampshire
Jean Bean
Chris Beetles
Betty Bennett
Rev. Sonia Berry
Archie Bevan
Terry Bishop
Simon Brett
British Film Institute
British Library, Department of Manuscripts
Mary Burgess
Debbie Cesvette, House of Commons Information Office
Gillian Chiverton
City Art Gallery, Leeds
Peter Collins, Arts Librarian, Westminster Reference Library
Denise Coe, Team Assistant, Reference Information and Local Studies, Deal Library and Staff of Dover Group Libraries
Dave of Forbidden Planet
George Eastman House International Museum of Film and Photography
Embassy of Japan
The English Film and Dance Society
The Followers of Rupert
House of Fraser
Stanley Gibbons
The Golden Hind Bookshop, Deal
Rev. Christopher Hardwick, Rector of St Mary's Church, Ripple, Hereford and Worcester
Maria A. Hellman, Information Officer, The National Gallery
Dr. Nicholas Hiley, Head of the Centre for Cartoons and Caricature, University of Kent at Canterbury
Simon Howes
Michael Hunt, Head Groundsman, Lord's Cricket Ground
Richard Hurley, Chairman, Stanley Spencer Gallery, Cookham

John Lawrence Jones and Fluck and Law of 'Private Eye'
Tim Jones
The Just William Society
Joy Leonard
Peter Lloyd
Gregor MacGregor
Stuart McKay
Mary McKenna
Alan Major
Marcel Marée, Curator of Ancient Egypt and Sudan, British Museum
Deborah Metcalf
The Mitchell Library, Glasgow
Amicia de Moubray
The National Archives, Public Record Office, Kew
The National Museum of American History, Smithsonian Institute
Nick Robinson, Head Gardener, Yalding Organic Gardens
Nestlé Rowntree
Fiona Pearson, Senior Curator, Scottish National Gallery of Modern Art
Norbert Platz
Portuguese Embassy
M and C Saatchi
David Schutte
Sue Scott
The Scottish Poetry Society
Mark Seddon, Editor, 'Tribune'
The Shakespeare Centre, Stratford-upon-Avon
South African High Commission
Ms. Jackie Spzera, Scottish Department, Central Library, Edinburgh
Jamie and Jill Stenhouse
Ken Stephens
John Sunley
Karen Swindlehurst
Ashley Taylor
Amanda Tempest-Radford
Barbara Thompson, Witt Librarian, Courtauld Institute of Art
Pip Threlfall, Chairman, Portsmouth Net Fishermen's Association
Jill Todd, Events Manager, Groombridge Place
Joan Tovey
Emmanuelle Toulet, Conservateur en Chef, Musée Condé, Château de Chantilly, France
John Vince
Helen Wallder, Librarian, Central Library, Doncaster
Jane Walsh, Reference Librarian, Salem Public Library, Massachusetts
Tim Warmoth

Judy Wilson
The P.G Wodehouse Society (UK)
Neil Wright
Wychwood Brewery

Thanks are also due to my publisher, Hugh Tempest-Radford, for his patience and encouragement throughout this project and to the designer, Mick Keates, who has brought my photographs of scarecrows to life.

The publisher's own scarecrow 'Strudwick' getting ready to watch over the vegetable seeds in Norfolk.
Photograph © Unicorn Press

Newspaper and Magazine Sources

American Cinematographer February 1979
American Art Vol 8 Summer/Fall 1994
Artforum Vol 19 Summer 1981
Artists and Illustrators November 1995
Art and Artists Vol 12 May November 1977
Artmagazine November/December 1979
The Bioscope 21 Oct 1209 29 Oct 1909 14 Sept 1911
    1 Aug 1912 10 April 1913
Birmingham Post 3 December 1962 11 April 1998
Country Life 15 April 1999 6 July 2000 17 October 2002
The Countryman Summer 1955 Autumn 1962
    Spring 1995 High Summer 1995

Country Talk No 11 May 1995
The Independent 24 August 2002 Weekend Magazine
    4 May 1996
Design Issues Vol 12 Autumn 1996
Daily Express 29 May 1985 26 July 2003 6 August 2003
Films and Filming July 1985
Kent On Sunday 15 September 2002
Daily Mail 22 May 1995 9 August 2002
Mail on Sunday 2 June 1985
Sunday Mail 23 April 2000
Morning Post 3 December 1962
National Geographical July 1938 September 1977

February 1981 January 1982 September 1993
    December 1995
Oriental Art Vol 40 Summer 1994
Daily Record 10 September 1994
Stafford Express and Star 20 April 1998
Daily Telegraph 29 September 1967 20 April 2002
Telegraph Magazine 7 March 1998
The Times 29 April 2005
Times Educational Supplement 19 April 20
American Cinematographer February 1979

Bibliography

The pioneering book on scarecrows is the fascinating but long out of print 'The Scarecrow: Fact and Fable' by Peter Haining (Robert Hale 1988). There are several photographic books on the subject including 'Scarecrows' by Colin Garratt, while 'Scarecrows' by Felder Rushing is mainly an arts and crafts manual but does include intriguing interviews by makers in America.

Les Trés Riches Heures du duc de Berry introduced
    by Jean Longnon and translated by Victoria Benedict
    Thames and Hudson 1969
Books of Hours John Harthan Thames and Hudson
    1977
Art and the Garden Glasgow Garden Festival
    Graeme Murray 1988
Complete Catalogue of the Works of Stanley Spencer
    Keith Bell Phaidon 1992
John Sell Cotman editor Miklos Rajnai Herbert Press
    1982
American Genre Painting Elizabeth Johns
    Yale University Press 1975
Thomas Bewick, A Memoir Oxford University Press 1975
An Engraver's Globe edited by Simon Brett
    Primrose Hill Press 2002
Unknown Terrain: The Landscapes of Andrew Wyeth
    Whitney Museum of American Art, New York 1998
Bronze in my Blood Benno Schotz Gordon Wright 1981
Allotments R.P. Lister Silent Books 1991
Digger's Diary, Tales from the Allotment Victor Osborne
    Aurum Press 2000
A Year At Ballymaloe Cookery School Darina Allen
    Kyle Cathie 1998

Penguin Dictionary of Art and Artists Peter and Linda
    Murray Penguin 1959
World Encyclopedia of Naive Art Chartwell Books 1984
Catalogue of Political and Personal Satires Vols. 8 and 10
    Mary Dorothy George British Museum 1947
Every Day Life in Old Testament Times E.W. Heaton
    Batsford 1956
Roman Sex John R. Clarke Harry N Abrams, Inc 2003
The Garden of Priapus Amy Richlin OUP 1992
Gods with Thunderbolts Guy de la Bédoyère Tempus
    2002
Ritual Sacrifice, A Concise History Brenda Ralph Lewis
    Sutton 2001
The Golden Bough, A Study in Magic and Religion
    Sir James George Fraser Penguin 1996
The Druids Nora K Chadwick University of Wales Press
    1997
A Brief History of the Druids Peter Berresford Ellis
    Robinson 2002
Jubes' Dictionary of Mythology, Folklore and Symbols
    Scarecrow Press 3 Vols 1994
The Woman's Dictionary of Symbols and Sacred Objects
    Barbara G Walker Harper / Collins 1988
Man and Birds R.K. Murton Collins' New Naturalist Series
    1971
All The Birds of the Air Francesca Greenoak André Deutsch
    1979
Creatures of Celtic Myth Bob Curran Cassell 2001
Country Seasons Philip Clucas Windward 1978
Thomas Bewick's Vignettes edited by Iain Bain
    Scolar Press 1979
Thomas Bewick, an Illustrated Record of his Life and Work

Iain Bain Tyne and Wear County Council Museums
    1979
Thomas Bewick, A Memoir edited by Iain Bain OUP
    1975
A History of British Birds (2 Volumes) Thomas Bewick
    Longmans (6th edition) 1826
1800 Woodcuts by Thomas Bewick and his School edited
    by Blanche Cirker introduced by Robert
    Hutchinson Dover Publications, New York 1962
Natural History of Selbourne Gilbert White 1789
Charleston Kedding, A History of Cottage Gardening
    Susan Campbell Ebury Press 1996
The Luttrell Psalter (facsimile) British Museum 1932
The Luttrell Psalter Janet Backhouse British Library 1989
Arte of Rhetorique Thomas Wilson edited by G H Mair
    Clarendon Press 1909
The Farmer's Boy Robert Bloomfield edited
    by Donald H Reiman Garland, New York 1977
Life in Rural England William Coles Finch
    C.W. Daniel 1928
Five Hundred Points of Good Husbandry Thomas Tusser
    Allen 1812
The Book of Days Robert Chambers W and R Chambers
    1866
Allotment Folk Chris Opperman New Holland 2004
A New Dictionary of Kent Dialect Alan Major
    Meresborough Books 1981
Ask the Fellows who Cut the Hay George Ewart Evans
    Faber and Faber 1956
Old Farms John Vince Shire Publications 1982
The Victorian Country Child Pamela Horn Alan Sutton
    1990

Rural Rides William Cobbett Vols I, II and III
 Everyman Library 1912

The Progress of a Ploughboy to a Seat in Parliament
 William Cobbett Faber and Faber 1933

Weekly Political Register (14 August 1819)
 William Cobbett

A Tour Round England Vol I Walter Thornbury
 Hurst and Blackett 1870

Directions for the Gardener at Sayes-Court John Evelyn
 edited by Geoffrey Keynes Nonsuch Press 1932

Cherries in the Rise Alan Major S.B. Publications 1997

A Kentish Childhood Alan Major S.B. Publications 2003

A Yeoman Farmer's Son, A Leicestershire Childhood
 Harold St. G Cramp John Murray 1985

The Journal of a Country Parish Robin Page Davis-Poynter
 1980

A Farmer's Year Sir Henry Rider Haggard introduced by
 Ronald Blythe Cresset Library/Century Hutchinson 1987

A Nature Journal Richard Mabey Chatto and Windus
 1991

The Country Child, An Illustrated Reminiscence
 edited by Piers Dudgeon Headline 1992

The Story of a Norfolk Farm Henry Williamson
 Faber and Faber 1941

From Crow Scaring to Westminster George Edwards
 Labour Publishing Company 1922

Tiger Moth Stuart McKay Midland Counties Publications
 1999

So Few David Masters Eyre and Spottiswoode 1941

Sweep Search Hamish MacInnes Hodder and Stoughton
 1985

Queen Victoria Christopher Hibbert Harper Collins
 2000

The Giant Book of Superstitions Claudia de Lys Citadel
 1979

Dictionary of Slang and Unconventional English Eric Partridge
 Routledge and Kegan Paul 1937

Concise Scots Dictionary edited by Mairi Robinson
 Aberdeen University Press 1985

Oxford Classical Dictionary Clarendon Press 1970

Oxford English Dictionary Clarendon Press 1933

The English Dialect Dictionary Joseph Wright
 Henry Frowde 1903

Seeds in the Wind (Poems in Scots for Children)
 William Soutar Andrew Dakers 1932

Poems Scots and English W D Cocker Brown and Sons
 and Ferguson 1932

The Wizard of Oz (Official 50th Anniversary Pictorial
 History) introduced by Jack Haley jnr.
 Hodder and Stoughton 1989

The MGM Story John Douglas Eames Octopus Books
 1975

The Wizard of Oz Salman Rushdie British Film Institute
 1992

Rainbow – The Stormy Life of Judy Garland
 Christopher Finch Michael Joseph 1975

The Making of the Wizard of Oz Aljean Harmetz
 Pavilion Books 1989

100 Years of Oz John Fricke Stewart, Tabori and Chang
 1999

History of Film David Parkinson Thames and Hudson
 1995

To Please A Child, the Life of L. Frank Baum Frank Joslyn
 Baum and Russell P. MacFall Reilly and Lee Co.,
 Chicago 1961

Stan and Ollie, the Roots of Comedy Simon Louvish
 Faber and Faber 2001

Fight, Kick and Bite: The Life and Works of Dennis Potter
 W. Stephen Gilbert Hodder and Stoughton 1995

Cinema Year by Year (1894–2002) edited by Robyn Karney
 Dorling Kindersley 2002

Halliwell's Film and Video Guide 2003 edited by John Walker
 Harper/Collins

Halliwell's Filmgoers' Companion 1993 Leslie Halliwell
 edited by John Walker Harper/Collins

*An Illustrated History of Horror and Science Fiction Films,
 The Classic Era 1895–1967* Carlos Clarens Da Capo,
 New York 1997

Hammer Films, The Bray Studio Years Wayne Kinsey
 Reynolds and Hearn 2002

Scarecrows Valerie Littlewood Julia Macrae Books 1992

The Scarecrow Book James Giblin and Dale Ferguson
 Crown Publishers, New York 1980

Scarecrows Felder Rushing Storey Books 1998

Scarecrow's Legion: Smuggling in Kent and Sussex
 Geoffrey Hufton and Elaine Baird Rochester Press
 1983

Come the Dawn Cecil M. Hepworth Phoenix Press 1951

Buster Keaton Rudi Blesh Secker and Warburg 1967

Buster Keaton David Robinson Thames and Hudson
 1970

My Wonderful World of Slapstick Buster Keaton
 Allen and Unwin 1967

Tim Burton's Nightmare Before Christmas Frank Thompson
 Roundtable Press 1993

The Faerie Queene Edmund Spencer 1590 introduced
 by Douglas Brooks-Davies Everyman 1976

Jude the Obscure Thomas Hardy 1896

The Return of the Scarecrow Alfred Noyes Cassell 1929

The Scarecrow and other Stories Walter de la Mare
 Faber and Faber 1945

Beyond the Wild Wood, the World of Kenneth Graham
 Peter Green Webb and Bower 1982

The Story of the Scarecrow Edith King Hall Blackie and Son
 1907

The Scarecrow and other Stories G. Ranger Wormser Dutton
 1918

Famous Short Stories compiled by Frank C. Platt Signet
 1966

Hawthorne, A Life Brenda Wineapple Alfred A Knopf 2003

Tomato Cain and other Stories Nigel Kneale Alfred A Knopf
 1950

Slowly, Slowly in the Wind Patrica Highsmith Heinemann
 1979

The Harlequin Tea Set and Other Stories Agatha Christie
 Berkley 1998

The Life and Crimes of Agatha Christie Charles Osbourne
 Collins 1982

The Fifth Ghost Book edited by Rosemary Timperly
 Barrie and Rockliff 1969

Night Shift Stephen King New English Library
 Hodder and Stoughton 1978

The Golden Scarecrow Hugh Walpole Macmillan 1915

The Arrogant History of White Ben Clemence Dane
 Cedric Chivers 1971

Further Fables for Our Time James Thurber
 Hamish Hamilton 1956

Twentieth Century Children's Writers Tracy Chevalier
 St. James Press 1989

Rupert, A Bear's Life George Perry Pavilion/Michael Joseph
 1985

The Story of Puffin Books Sally Gritten Penguin 1991

Richmal Crompton, The Woman Behind 'Just William'
 Mary Cadogan Sutton 2003

The Scarecrows Robert Westall Chatto and Windus 1981

Waltz of the Scarecrows Constance W. McGeorge and
 Mary Whyte Chronicle Books, San Franscisco 1998

The Sherlock Holmes Encyclopedia Matthew E. Bunson
 Pavilion 1995

Everyman Dictionary of Literary Biography
 D.C. Browning M.A., B. Litt. Dent 1958

Peake's Commentary on the Bible edited by Matthew Black
 Thomas Nelson and Sons 1962

Penguin Dictionary of Quotations J.M. and M.J. Cohen
 Penguin 1971

An Illustrated Encyclopedia of Japan Kodansha International
 1993

Zulu-Land Lewis Grout African Publication Society 1861
 (reprinted 1970)

The Bantu-Speaking Peoples of Southern Africa
 W.D. Hammond-Tooke Routledge and Kegan Paul
 1974

The Social System of the Zulus Eileen Jensen Krige
 Pietermaritzburg Shuter and Shuter 1950

British Toy Figures Norman Joplin Arms and Armour Press
 1987

Index

Traveller on Romney Marsh.